FOREVER A FARMER

WRITTEN BY: DONNA GENE STANKEY
CO-AUTHORED BY: RAMONA HAMMEL

ISBN (Paperback):   978-1-958920-11-4
ISBN (eBook):   978-1-958920-10-7

Contents

INTRODUCTION

Forever a Farmer is the last manuscript I have written depicting my Dad's life. The last year is 1922, which is only four years before I was born. This was the most difficult to write because there were so many details I didn't know.

I sure thought my Dad had an interesting life. I'm glad I could write these three manuscripts so others can know about our family, both Setteringtons and Brewbakers. I have endeavored to depict farm life as it was before such large scale operations, with all the present day equipment and computer technology, insecticides, and weed killers. Since I was such a tomboy, I always wanted to relate events in great detail. I wonder what Millie and my Dad would think of farming as it is done today.

In the Epilogue, I have included some facts about my relationship with Aunt Balance and Uncle George. They were a large part in my getting to know my grandparents and great-grandparents. They were a very important part of my life growing up.

ACKNOWLEDGEMENT

A very big thank you to Mary Williams, Senior Author Advisor, who stuck with me through tears and laughter and many hours of phone conversations and emails. I couldn't have done it without her.

Also thanks to Mark De Villar for the amazing cover designs.

DEDICATION

This is dedicated to my friends and family who grew up on a farm. And to all those who love American History, especially those who love life on the farm.

CHAPTER 1

The sun shone brightly drying the results of last night's heavy dew which had sparkled from every tree branch, each bush, and the grass along the roadside and fields. Ralph gave Pearl her head and she trotted along at a good clip. The fluid movements of the horse filled him with pride. Pearl was not only good-looking. Her bay coat was sleek and shiny. She was fast and this was a distinct advantage for a boy just past sixteen.

Ralph was on his way to Elsie to school. Thus far, he hadn't minded having to drive the three and one-half miles each morning and afternoon. They had moved back to the farm in March and Ralph was glad they had made the move. It wasn't that he'd been unhappy living in the town but it was simply that he liked the farm best. Pa had bought more cows and had said he figured they should raise a few more hogs. They already had a suitable flock of sheep. If they increased their herd of cattle some more, they would quite likely need someplace to pasture the sheep come summer. Sheep eat the grass extremely close to the ground and they leave nothing for cows or horses in a pasture of normal size.

Ralph crossed the iron bridge over Maple River where the gristmill stood. As he started up the gristmill hill, he saw Miss Kate Finch turn east from River Road to head toward Elsie. Kate was the seventh and eighth-grade teacher. Ralph had to repeat the seventh grade, because he missed too much school, due to a severe leg injury. So he ended up having Miss Finch as his teacher for three years. She was by far his favorite teacher.

When Kate recognized what rig was coming up the hill, she touched her buckskin with her whip and the horse broke into a run.

Kate chuckled to herself. Pearl hated having any horse ahead of her, so she tried to increase her speed. Ralph held her back until they were a few lengths beyond where the River Road met the main road. Ralph then released the pressure on the lines. Pearl responded instantly. She rapidly closed the gap between Kate's buggy and theirs.

Kate looked back and saw that Ralph was gaining on her. She stood up in the buggy. She then used her whip on her poor buckskin, and in a most undignified manner, yelled encouragement for him to move faster. Wisps of hair loosened and flew around her face but she paid no attention. Her main focus was on her horse hoping she'd reach the village limits before that young rapscallion overtook her.

Ralph and Pearl continued to gain. Then, Pearl turned out to pass. Ralph held her in check to keep abreast of Kate for a few moments.

"Gosh, Kate, is that all the faster that nag of yours can move? Guess you didn't have enough of a head start." He flashed her an irritating grin but missed her reply because they were almost to the village limits. He let Pearl pass then slowed her to a fast walk. Kate had done the same thing.

About once or twice each week, these two went through this same process. Kate realized she could never win but she didn't readily admit the fact even to herself. Ralph respected her all the more because she always tried. When he was away from school, he always called her Kate but in and around school he respectfully referred to her as Miss Finch.

He didn't know how old she was (she was born in 1864), but it seemed as though she'd been teaching forever. She'd had Blanche in class and Blanche said there were those much older than she who'd been in Kate's room. Golly, maybe she was near the age of his parents. Anyway, he figured she was getting on in years--of course, anyone past thirty was getting on in years in his estimation.

For her age she sure had a lot of gumption. Ma never wanted a horse to trot for more than a short distance let alone run. Ralph laughed to himself as he thought of the vast difference between his mother and Kate. No way would his mother stand up in a moving buggy to urge her horse to go faster. He could not envision his mother using a whip on an animal either. He was just glad he drove a horse that was fast enough to beat Kate's buckskin. He thought Pearl had the advantage of being younger than Kate's horse, but neither he nor Kate had ever spoken of this. At least that poor buckskin had a lot of spunk because he sure gave everything, he had to try to beat Pearl. Guess that horse and Kate made a good pair.

Ralph considered Kate the best teacher he'd ever had. He'd never got away with much in her classroom but she'd never held it against him because he tried.

He had given thought to letting her win a race just once but he knew Kate would see through such a ploy, and she'd not appreciate it. She'd like to beat him that much was certain but she wanted the race to be on the up and up. She had once said her head start was his handicap which had made him laugh.

Fleetingly, Rate wondered why Kate had never married. He didn't recollect hearing her name connected with any men, so he sort of thought she had never even had a beau. Guess maybe she was too independent and didn't need some man to take care of her. She lived on the farm her parents had settled on. He thought he'd heard they had come from Ohio. Maybe she had felt duty-bound to take care of aging parents. Anyway, even though she was an old maid, he'd never heard anyone make fun of her like they did some others. People often chuckled about Mildred Chamberlin since she and Elzie Call had split up. They often made unkind comments regarding Miriam Downey who they said never dated anyone and just seemed to enjoy working for Mr. Ferguson that also took care of her folks.

* * * * * * * * *

Since her father's death, Miney's niece, Hattie Sickels had written to Miney quite regularly. It seemed that her sister, Mary, wrote less often. Reading between the lines of Hattie's letters, Miney feared that Mary's health was deteriorating. Miney and Lorin had spoken of this and Lorin had the same feeling. Yet, Mary's letters gave no hint that anything might be amiss but that was to be expected. Mary was like their mother and was not one to complain. Miney could not help being concerned. She wished Mary still lived in Elsie where she could see her often. Certainly, was a shame that families had to be separated. She wondered if Mary ever missed her and Lorin.

Since they had moved back to the farm, Ralph no longer went to Sunday School. Most of the time he even missed church. Miney had tried to assert her authority but Millie had intervened. He had said, "Since Rate's sixteen, he's old enough to make up his own mind 'bout goin' to church." Miney knew there was no use to argue. When Millie had that tone to his voice nothing, she said would make him change his mind. She had certainly learned that much over the years.

Sometimes, Ralph drove his mother to church. Although he seldom dressed up to attend services with her. He was perfectly willing to do the driving. Blanche sometimes spent a Saturday night with a girl friend but if she was home, she accompanied her mother. At least Miney derived pleasure from this. She thought that if Millie had attended church regularly like her father and Father Setterington, Ralph would never have rebelled. She often asked Ralph to drive her because she

3

always hoped Ralph would relent and attend services. She wondered if she had somehow done something wrong with his upbringing. She had always attended church regularly and had taken them as children. Ralph and Blanche both had attended Sunday School as well. While they lived in town, they both attended meetings which were held for the young people and had usually participated in the activities for this group. What could she have done differently? She had certainly tried her best.

It had rained Friday night and most of the day Saturday. However, on Sunday morning the sun broke through the few remaining clouds and the world was bright and cheery even though waterlogged in places. Water stood in the fields.

Rate had said he would drive Miney to church. Blanche had stayed over to Fern's and would meet her mother at church. Rate sat in the buggy, rather impatiently waiting for his mother. As usual, she was running behind. Rate often wondered why it was that his mother was never ahead of time, seldom on time, always a few minutes late. He'd never delivered her late for church only because Pearl was fast and she could make up the time. He suspected that if Ma drove herself, she quite likely would have been late on more than one occasion since she always drove the safest, slowest horse.

Miney came out of the house in a rush, climbed into the carriage, and settled back in her seat. "I know I'm a trifle late but I think we can still be there in time for the beginning of services, don't you?"

"I guess so", Rate answered since his mother seemed to expect a reply.

Rate had long ago trained Pearl to respond when he scuffed his foot on the floorboard by surging forward to run. He did this now and Pearl leaped forward. Rate had momentarily forgotten that there was a large puddle just where the driveway turned into the road. The buggy had only recently been newly painted, and Ralph did not want to get it splattered with mud.

He yelled, "Whoa!" Pearl stopped dead still.

Miney, who was not expecting such a sudden stop, had not been hanging on or even bracing herself. Rate watched in dismay as with a little scream, his mother sailed out of the buggy onto the front wheel then slid on down into the mudhole. Pearl stood patiently waiting for another command. Rate quickly fastened the lines and moved to help his mother.

"Gosh, Ma, I'm sorry. I never thought this would happen. Are you hurt? Here, let me help you."

Miney was soaked with the muddy water. Her hands were covered with mud. Rate took her hand and helped her to her feet and propelled her off to the drier ground. Her good shoes squished with each step and mud clung to the sides of them.

"Why did you stop Pearl? And why did she start off on a run? Must you always do something wrong?"

"I said I was sorry. I never intended this to happen. I just didn't want to get the buggy splattered with mud."

"You just never *intend* anything. In your opinion keep the buggy clean but it doesn't matter about your mother. I guess I had better get changed. You certainly made it impossible for me to go to church today. It's a good thing Cap and Flo, Richard and I aren't scheduled to provide special music until next Sunday.

Miney had a very nice soprano voice, but she also had been blessed with what was termed "perfect pitch." She could look at a music note on a song page and sound that particular note which would coincide exactly with that note if struck on the piano. Not many people had this ability. Cap and Flo Rummel and Richard Fizzell had formed a quartet with Miney and they often provided special music for a Sunday church service.

Miney had gone a few steps further when she partially turned and said, "I suppose you know that you still have to pick up Blanche after service?"

"Reckon so." Rate sounded somewhat resigned.

Miney flounced off to the house. She did look kinda funny and Ralph was tempted to laugh. However, his face looked completely innocent when his mother gave him one more disgruntled look just before she went up the steps to the porch.

Miney wasn't angry she was just upset. Would the time ever come when Ralph didn't cause some sort of trouble? She had thought by now he would be more responsible. Well, perhaps responsible wasn't the proper word. Ralph did his work well and in that respect, he accepted responsibility well. It was just that all these unforeseen problems seemed to arise with a degree of regularity. She had thought that as he grew older incidents such as this would cease. My, it had certainly been a blessing that she had had Blanche. She felt she never could have coped with two like Ralph.

Millie looked up from the newspaper when Miney came into the dining room, banging the screen door behind her. She had already removed her shoes on the porch and carried them in her hand.

"What happened? You look like something the cat drug in."

Miney explained. Was that a glimmer of laughter in Millie's eyes? While he spoke placatingly, Miney had a suspicion that Millie thought the whole episode was funny. Men! The Setterington men certainly had a strange sense of humor.

Miney's day was ruined. She'd have a time soaking the mud out of her dress and on Sunday too. She couldn't leave it until wash day tomorrow or the mud would stain the dress. Of course, her petticoat, bloomers, and stockings were wet too. Later, she'd try to impress Millie that he should haul some gravel from the pit up on the Ridge Road so there could never be a recurrence of this disaster--for disaster was how Miney viewed the situation. She was just lucky she hadn't broken some bone as she thought bitterly. She did have a tender spot on her side and she wondered if the spot would be black and blue come tomorrow, not that she expected anyone to care except perhaps her daughter.

Millie bought a couple more cows that were due to freshen in June. That brought their total to eight. They had room for a couple more but Millie decided he'd buy more hogs instead. He figured he and Rate could go out separately looking for feeder pigs. If they each bought eight or ten that would quite likely be as many as they could comfortably handle.

Millie and Rate left right after dinner. One headed north and the other headed south. However, Rate arrived back at the farm before his father.

He had six sleek white pigs. He felt quite satisfied with his purchase, and he wondered what kind of luck his father was having. He put the pigs in a pen and gave them feed and water.

It was much later when Millie returned. He had a total of fourteen pigs. When he asked Rate how much he'd paid for the six he bought, Rate told him and he burst out laughing. "Boy, I think you got taken. I got these fourteen for the same amount. Thought you had more sense than that."

Rate said nothing. It smarted to have his father make fun of him but he'd be damned if he'd let Pa know. Besides, he thought his pigs were heavier and looked better. As he carefully scrutinized them, he thought Pa's pigs looked more than a little scruffy--all fourteen of them. He was certain that he wouldn't have purchased them even if they had been dirt cheap. So much for he and Pa thinking alike. Guess when it came time to take the pigs to market, they'd see who had made the best purchase. Course, even then, he'd not expect Pa to admit those fourteen had not been a sound buy.

Since Horatio had raised objections, Millie never played cards of any kind. He and Miney no longer went regularly to Grange meetings since the men played cards and even some of the women were learning to play. However, Millie thoroughly enjoyed a good game of checkers. Most often he played with Cash Waldron but since Rate was older they often played in the evening. Millie had to admit that Rate's game was improving. Millie always won but it was getting much more difficult to beat the lad.

Rate and Millie sat hunched over the checkerboard held on their knees. Their chairs were drawn up by the north door of the dining room to get the fading evening light. Both had been quiet, intent on the game. Each had taken his time to make a carefully thought-out move. Millie moved a checker. Ralph coked up at his father, eyes alight, as he reached to make his next move. Millie realized he had made a blunder and Ralph was going to win. He knew from the glint in Rate's eyes that the lad knew he had the game won. Millie spread his legs and let the checkerboard and checkers fall to the floor. Rate burst out laughing.

"What's the matter, Pa? Couldn't stand the thought of losing?"

"Who said I was gonna lose?"

"I did. You know I had you beat all fair and square."

"Can't prove it one way or the other."

"Only because you intentionally upset the board."

"Why Rate you don't think it was accidental?"

"No, and neither do you." Ralph laughed again while he started picking up checkers. Darn Pa anyway. Like Pa always said, a bird in the hand is worth two in the bush. He should have known Pa would squirm out of losing somehow. At least Pa knew he was beaten even if he wouldn't admit it. This thought gave Rate a certain degree of satisfaction.

The summer was passing quickly for Rate. He helped Millie with a lot of the farm work but he still had time for his friends and time to enjoy himself. He sometimes took Pearl swimming below the dam. In the shallow water, she'd lie down and roll. He often kicked off his shoes and went in the water with her. In the deeper water, if he hung onto her tail she'd pull him while she swam. That horse seemed to enjoy these moments as much as Rate did. During the summer, Rate wore no underclothes and he went in the water overalls and all. It was too near the road to swim in the raw. Besides, when the weather was hot, the cool water felt really good and he knew the overalls would be nearly dry by the time he reached home.

Rate and Curly Sherman had made plans for the Fourth of July. They decided they'd begin celebrating early by tossing dynamite, beginning one minute after midnight. They'd been able to get hold of two sticks of the explosive, some caps, and a length of fuse. Since each stick was about a foot long they could cut them in pieces one inch in length and have about twelve pieces each to throw. They had plenty of fuses and both had a pocketful of matches so they were well prepared. They figured this project could occupy them for a couple of hours if they waited for a little between each explosion.

The eve of the Fourth found both boys down on the river flats ready to begin. They kept track of the time, and Don threw the first piece as soon as his watch showed it was past midnight. They laughed at the resulting explosion.

"Makes a dang good firecracker, don't it Rate?"

"Sure does" agreed Rate as he tossed one of his pieces.

"Bet no one else has begun celebrating yet."

"Curly, I think you are without a doubt right about that. Don't know if anyone else would have thought of using dynamite either."

"Guess that just shows we're smarter than most," said Curly with a laugh. He then tossed another piece of dynamite. "Course I don't suppose a lot of the fellows could have got their hands on a stick of dynamite. Where'd you get it?"

"Pa usually has some around. He won't miss the dynamite but he might miss the caps. But he's not likely to be using any dynamite until next spring."

When they had used all their pieces of dynamite they went to their respective homes. Ralph was to pick Don up by midmorning to go into Elsie for the festivities.

When Rate arrived at Sherman's the next day, Don was not waiting for him as he expected. His friend was never one to keep him waiting; therefore he went to the house to ask Mrs. Sherman where his friend was.

"Ralph, I'm not sure what is wrong but Don is sick. He couldn't keep his breakfast down. I'm afraid he won't be going anywhere with you today. You can go up to see him if you like."

Rate went upstairs to see his friend. Don was pale and his freckles stood out more prominently than usual. He looked miserable.

"How daya feel?"

"Rotten. Ma says I gotta stay in bed. Don't really feel like being up, so I didn't argue. Gosh, Rate, I felt fine last night."

"Curly, I've heard old-timers tell that some people get sick from handling dynamite. Maybe that is what's wrong. You handled a dozen pieces."

"If that's it, why aren't you sick? You look fit as a fiddle," he complained.

"It just didn't affect me. Not everyone has the problem. Pa has handled plenty of dynamite and it never bothers him."

"Don't seem fair. We both threw the stuff, so it's not fair that I'm sick an' you're not." Curly looked at his friend like it was Rate's fault he wasn't sick too.

"Guess that's life," suggested Ralph philosophically.

The boys talked for a short time then Rate left to go to Elsie for the day's celebration. He was pretty much on his own now that he was sixteen but he'd meet the family for dinner. Ma always packed a basket with plenty of good food. He thought his folks enjoyed the holiday as much as anyone. Farmers worked hard all year, seven days a week; therefore, they needed a break now and then. A time when they could enjoy being with friends to watch some sort of entertainment.

Rate wasn't sure if Blanche would be with them or not. Blanche and Elzie Call had gone together for only a short time and a few weeks ago she had begun going out with Ollie Bensinger. Rate didn't know if she was going to be with Ollie today or not. Seemed kind of odd that Elzie Call had quit going with Mildred Chamberlin and had started keeping company with Blanche for such a short time. Ralph knew that Elzie and Mildred had not got back together and that fact had given the old busybodies around town something to talk about. Now, there was Ollie, who had been keeping rather steady company with Mildred Barrett but now he was squiring Blanche around. Oh well, Ralph figured it was none of his business. He thought Ollie was an odd duck and wondered why his sister wanted to keep company with the likes of him.

Blanche's birthday was the 5th and she turned twenty-one. Miney hated to admit that her daughter was an adult, capable of making her own decisions without consulting her mother. It seemed such a short time ago that she had been young and dependent on Miney in so many ways. At least she and Blanche got on well. She'd heard other women complain that when their daughters got older they became estranged and they no longer seemed to confide in their mothers. She could be thankful that Blanche was not like that. Blanche still shared her thoughts and Miney tried not to be judgmental even if she didn't always agree with Blanche's line of thought. Times were changing and her daughter reflected a more modern way of thinking.

It was July 6 and Miney had a phone call from her niece, Hattie Sickels. She informed Miney that her mother, Mary, had gone into the hospital yesterday, scheduled for surgery today. Mary had died on the operating table. Miney wasn't sure what the surgery was for. She only knew that Hattie said that when they cut Mary open the blood just ran and there was nothing the doctors could do. Hattie understandably was distraught so Miney, quite unlike her usual self had refrained from asking questions.

Goodness, Mary had not lived quite a year longer than Jap. Now, Miney and Lorin were the only ones left. The thought made Miney feel very much alone. One just never knew how much time on this earth was one's total allotment. Some never made it past childhood like Millie's sisters and brother. Mary was fifty-seven which was not all that old. Of course, her father had died very young but Ma had lived to be seventy six. Lorin was almost six years older than Mary yet her health seemed good.

Mary would be brought back to Elsie on the weekend. Hattie and Frank had not had time to make all the arrangements before Hattie called. Miney dreaded the thought of another funeral for one of her family. Still, she was glad Mary would rest in the Village cemetery instead of some faraway place like her sister, Ettie. There was some small comfort in that. At least she would be able to go to the cemetery any time she wished and flowers could be placed there on Decoration Day.

Ralph had come into the house rather quietly for him. Even now, he often closed the screen door with a bang. Miney sat in her rocker, her crocheting in her lap but she was staring out the window and her hands were idle. Ralph knew this was unusual. When she turned her head at his approach, he noticed her reddened eyes and knew she had been crying.

"Ma, what's wrong?"

"Oh, nothing. I was just thinking about your Grandma Smith. Two of her daughters died a lot younger than she did. You know, Ralph, Ma was the most mild-mannered person I ever knew. She never lost her temper. I recollect that one time Pa's boys were all home sitting together on the edge of the porch. They were joshin' each other as boys will. I can't remember which one made an unkind remark about Jim. Ma had come onto the porch and had heard what he said. She walked over and nudged him slightly with the toe of her shoe and chided him for being unkind. She never even raised her voice. I'm afraid I'm not much like my mother. Would you believe I still miss her?"

"Guess so. I know Blanche and I often speak of her. We miss her too, partly, I guess because she was so different from Grandmother Setterington. Sometimes, I have a hard time remembering much about her. What I remember best is seeing her sitting in her chair drawn up by the window so she could see to knit or patch. She was always taking off her glasses when I came in. She never yelled at me for anything," he added with a note of nostalgia creeping into his voice.

"Your Grandma Smith never yelled at anyone. It was your Grandpa Smith who made us toe the line, although it always seemed to me that he was more strict with Ettie and me than he was with Lorin and Mary. Maybe it was because they were older. Guess there are times when I miss both of them."

Miney sighed and picked up her crocheting. Ralph knew the conversation had ended. He felt Ma simply wanted to be alone with her thoughts.

Ralph went into the kitchen, took a couple of cookies, and headed back outside. Ma sure looked sad. He supposed it was because Aunt Mary's funeral would be this weekend. He knew Ma dreaded it.

Blanche had been dating Ollie Bensinger regularly. Occasionally, they saw each other during the week, always on Saturday night and often on Sunday afternoon. Ollie was a farmer and his weeks consisted of long hours in the field. He lived only a couple of miles away from his mother.

Blanche was enjoying her summer at home immensely. On Saturday nights she and Ollie often went dancing. Blanche knew her mother didn't approve; therefore, at home, she seldom spoke about dancing. However, several years ago, Pa had told her she could play cards and dance, so at least one parent had given approval. Blanche knew that with or without her parent's consent at twenty-one she would quite likely have done just as she pleased anyway. She was old enough to make up her own mind. She'd never let her life be run as Pa had always let Grandmother and Grandfather run his.

On occasion, Ralph came into the parlor in Elsie where the young people congregated but Blanche had said nothing. She was certain Ma didn't have a notion that was where Ralph was spending a good portion of his time. Dancing hadn't appealed to Ralph but he was getting pretty good at pool and he liked to play cards. Blanche wasn't sure Pa would think it proper for Ralph to do these things; consequently, she said nothing to get her brother into trouble. Blanche knew that Pa was always more lenient with her although she had never understood why. Now that she was older, she often realized that much of the time both Pa and Ma actually treated Ralph unfairly. Her brother certainly did his work well and without complaint but it seemed that neither Ma nor Pa recognized this. They just didn't give Ralph credit for much of anything. Sometimes, she even felt a little resentful because they showed so much partiality. She wondered if Ralph blamed her but if he did, he never showed it in any way. He really was a pretty good brother even if he did like to tease. However, she felt she could hold her own in that category.

It was a nice summer's evening, not too warm, with not a cloud in the sky. As usual, Ralph had given Pearl her head, and she had settled into an easy trot. Don Sherman was with him and was going to stay the night. The boys often stayed at one place or the other because they were seldom apart on a Saturday night.

They stabled Pearl and came quietly into the house so they wouldn't rouse Miney who had finally quit asking, "That you, Ralph?" every time he came in past dark. There was a lamp on the dining room table, turned down low but giving enough light for the boys to see the lunch that had been placed on the table. It was cold chicken and a generous piece of the pie. He looked at Don and a small, devilish smile appeared on his face.

"What say we see if this food is any good? Blanche and Ollie should have been home before this. It's not our fault they've stayed out so late, is it?"

"How're we to know your Ma didn't set this lunch out for us? Don't see no name tags, do you?" Don gave Rate a conspiratorial grin as he seated himself at the table.

Rate chuckled rather quietly as he slipped into the other chair and the two boys proceeded to devour the lunch.

Ralph never knew with any degree of certainty how Blanche felt about what had happened. Since they had left the dishes on the table, there was no doubt that Miney had set out lunch and it didn't take a great deal of intelligence to know where the lunch had gone. However, Blanche greeted both of them sweetly the next morning yet Ralph thought he detected something in her eyes that said she wouldn't forget. Guess he'd have to watch himself because he was almost certain Blanche intended to retaliate. At least she had said nothing to Ma to get him into trouble. Blanche was all right most of the time; at least since she was older, she no longer tattled on him. It didn't bother him that she might do something to get even. In fact, he respected her because she did her best not to let him get away with anything.

Ralph had been the one taking care of the hogs. Sure could tell the six pigs he'd bought from the fourteen Pa had brought home. Pa hadn't said a word, but Rate knew his father could see the difference in their growth. A person would have to be blind not to notice. Pa finally admitted that his pigs were quite likely wormy. After being wormed they did better but there was no way they were ever going to develop into first-class hogs. Rate felt more than a little smug as time went on and his six became hogs that would bring top dollar when sold. Why he bet his six weighed more than any eight of Pa's. It would have been nice if Pa would have acknowledged that he has the better buy after all but Rate knew his father would never say one word to give him credit for making a good choice. He guessed he might drop dead if his father ever praised him for anything, the surprise would be so great.

Grandfather Setterington came from Detroit to spend a few days. It seemed he had some business to take care of in Elsie and the surrounding area. Ralph heard his grandfather say that he had some town lots to sell in Elsie, Shepherdsville, and Eureka. He also had some notes to collect. From what was said, Rate was fairly certain Grandfather was investing in real estate in and around Detroit. It was much handier than buying up property in Clinton County and some of the neighboring counties now that he was living in Detroit. Rate had never known that his grandfather owned so much real estate, although Pa had once told him that Grandfather bought the land that was being sold for taxes. Of course, if Grandfather hadn't had plenty of money, he wouldn't have been able to take advantage of the tax sales. Sure seemed that Grandfather certainly knew how to make money. Guess the old saying, "It takes money to make money," sure applied to Horatio Setterington.

Ralph thought that while Pa had a lot more business sense than Uncle John, he was not in the same class as Horatio. Besides, he felt that Pa had a heart whereas Horatio often was simply a cold-hearted businessman. Guess maybe making a lot of money didn't necessarily appeal to Pa as long as he had enough so's he didn't owe money to anyone and could buy whatever he needed or wanted. Rate supposed Grandfather must like having plenty of money and he figured Grandmother was more than willing to help him spend it even if a good portion of what she spent was on her daughter, Ruby.

Ralph figured that if he had enough for life's necessities, he'd be satisfied. He had no need to be at the top of the social ladder and he didn't think his opinion would change with age.

Millie had decided to stack the oats by the barn to wait for the threshing rig. Since he intended to have the straw blown into the barn, it would make setting up the separator more difficult, and getting a team and wagon in the proper position to unload would have been difficult. With the stack, the bundles could be thrown directly into the separator. He'd have fewer men to line up for the threshing day too.

The oats had been cut and shocked days ago. Millie hired Jim and Merval Keenan, and Cash Waldron to help bring the oats from the field. Of course, Millie, Rate, and the hired man would work too. Horatio volunteered to pitch the bundles from the field onto the wagons. Although he was 68 years old, Millie never thought of refusing his father's offer to help.

Cash drove one wagon, Jim the other; Rate and the hired man pitched bundles to the stack. Millie and Merval made the stack. In time, the stack became so high Rate could no longer throw a bundle to the top. Millie stood partway up the stack and with a pitchfork, deftly caught the bundle Rate tossed up then tossed the bundle to Merval on top. Ralph was getting pretty tired and it became more difficult for him to toss the bundles high enough for his father to catch. It seemed the hired man was faring no better. Rate heaved a sigh of relief when his grandfather came from the field with Jim on a rather small load. He knew this was the last of the oats to be brought to the barn.

Rate looked at his grandfather in disbelief. Horatio didn't look as though he'd spent all afternoon tossing bundles of oats around. However, when they came to wash up for supper, Rate noticed that his grandfather had blisters on both hands and some of the blisters had broken leaving open sores. Rate wondered whether Ma or Pa had noticed. Seemed as though there should be something done to make certain the raw sores healed but no one said anything. To Rate's surprise his grandfather behaved as though nothing was wrong.

The entire situation made Rate marvel that although his grandfather was 68, he had worked like a much younger man. His hands must have given him considerable pain, but he had continued to work until the job was done with not one word of complaint to anyone. Rate's respect for his grandfather took a giant leap.

Grandfather was quite a man. He was certainly proud to be the grandson of Rate Setterington.

For the past few years, the dam by the gristmill had been deteriorating and now it no longer served its purpose because it allowed too much water to go down the river channel instead of through the millrace. It leaked badly in numerous places. Without sufficient water to turn the milling machinery the mill had to burn logs to provide steam to power the machinery. They used eight-foot logs but this made the milling process more expensive and it was not nearly as handy as the water power.

Mr. Harmon decided it was time to replace the old dam which consisted of felled trees, covered with clay, dirt, and planks. The new dam was made of concrete and it slanted back into the river channel. When the mill was not operating the water coming over the dam made a waterfall of some four feet or so. It was only in midsummer that the water level was low enough to be held back by the dam even if the mill was not in operation.

July had been cooler than usual but August was more than making up for it. It had been a good year for insects and the flies bothered the livestock something fierce as if the hot days weren't bad enough. Rate put a net harness over Pearl's regular harness when he drove her to help keep the flies away. The horses stood in the pasture side by side, facing in opposite directions so their swishing tails could help keep the flies from their partner's head. Sometimes Rate put an ointment on Pearl's ears to keep them from getting scabs from the fly bites.

Summer was almost over. Rate would be entering his Sophomore year and Blanche would be going to Detroit where she had enrolled for classes at The Business Institute. Rate guessed he'd miss his sister. It had seemed good to have her home for the summer. He wondered what Ollie thought about Blanche returning to Detroit. Guess when Blanche left they wouldn't be seeing much of Ollie.

It was Blanche's last weekend home. Rate knew she and Ollie were going out but he had no special plans. He wasn't just sure when the thought came but he decided he should do something as a sort of parting present for good, old Ollie.

Ma always set out lunch for the young couple just before she retired, and Rate knew Blanche and Ollie always sat at the same place at the table. Since Ma and Pa had gone to bed early, as usual, Rate came in quietly, went stealthily to the kitchen, and removed the container of cayenne pepper from the kitchen cabinet. He slipped back into the dining room, lifted the crust away from the filling on Ollie's piece of pie, and put a good dose of the extremely hot pepper on that initial narrow portion. He laughed to himself as he thought about unsuspecting Ollie taking that first bite of pie. How he wished he could watch just to catch the look on Ollie's face.

Funny thing. Blanche didn't say a thing to him the next morning about Ollie's pie. Guess Ollie must have been able to get that bite down without it strangling him. Maybe he hadn't put enough of the pepper on the pie or maybe Ollie simply hadn't wanted Blanche to know anything was wrong. Rate would love to have asked his sister if she and Ollie had enjoyed their lunch. However, Pa always said to let sleeping dogs lie and Rate decided this was probably the best policy at this time. No use to make Blanche angry with him if it wasn't necessary.

Miney knew that Blanche had no intention of letting her Grandmother Setterington know when she was returning to Detroit. Miney also knew that Millie was not aware of the situation and for once, Miney had kept her knowledge to herself. Millie had assumed Blanche would continue to live with her grandparents. How wrong he was.

Del Briggs had worked with Blanche at Netzorg's Department Store. Del had decided she was tired of a small town and she expressed herself to Blanche. After much discussion, the girls had decided Del should move to Detroit and they would room together. They went to Detroit the first of the week, which was several days before Blanche's term began at the business school to find a place to live. They were in luck. They found a large, neat room for a reasonable amount. Blanche liked the landlady; she was friendly, matronly in appearance, and didn't seem like a stranger at all. Del liked the place because it wasn't far from the streetcar line and she felt transportation would be no problem when she found a job. The girls returned home well satisfied with the day's accomplishment.

Before she was to leave, Blanche informed her father that she would not be staying with her grandparents. She explained that she and Del were rooming together. Much to her surprise, Millie simply nodded his head and said she was old enough to know what she wanted. What a relief that was. Perhaps Pa was glad to have her stand up to Grandmother. It was hard to tell because Pa shared so few thoughts with anyone--not even his wife.

A couple of days later, both girls left Elsie with a bag and baggage. Blanche had a couple of days plus the weekend before classes began, giving her plenty of time to settle in. When she knew her schedule of classes, she intended to look for a part-time job. Pa could pay her tuition and room and board but she fully intended to earn her own money for clothes and personal expenses.

After they were unpacked, Blanche gave her grandmother a call. Lovina assumed Blanche had just arrived and she sounded very pleased.

"Come right over. We have a room for you but I'm sure you know that."

"Grandmother, I already have a room. Del Briggs and I are rooming together. We will both be getting a job."

Lovina didn't respond.

Why had she put off telling her grandmother she was enrolled at The Business Institute? Mostly because she was not in any mood to have her grandmother tell her she was ruining her life by learning to be a stenographer. Grandmother had already voiced her opinion about girls who took dictation from men. Blanche knew that her grandmother would not have changed her mind; therefore, she put off the unpleasant confrontation she knew would come. There were few jobs other than teaching that Grandmother thought suitable for women. Well, Blanche had other ideas. She decided she was going to be in no hurry to pay a visit to her grandparents.

Blanche knew that sooner or later she'd have to tell her grandmother she was going to school. She figured she could use homework as a reason she couldn't visit. Grandmother might be opposed to what she was choosing as a means to support herself but Grandmother would want her to do well scholastically. After all, Blanche was a Setterington and Lovina felt Setteringtons were a niche above most people. She seemed to forget that she was not truly a Setterington but a Reynolds. She had simply had the good fortune to marry into a prestigious family.

CHAPTER 2

Shortly after Horatio had returned to Detroit, he wrote to ask Millie if he would want to buy back the north eighty. Horatio wanted to sell it because that piece of property was the last he owned in and around Elsie. Millie was dumbfounded. He had supposed that since he had farmed the property all these years it was to be his--his inheritance from his father. Of course, there had been no written agreement and now that he gave it careful thought, Pa had never come right out and said this was the way it was to be. Pa had sort of hinted, and Millie had been quick to assume. Millie felt that after all the years he had worked the land, always paying Pa a share that he had certainly earned that eighty.

Millie was furious! Pa had been the means of support for Ruby and Mac most of their married life; he'd loaned John money time after time which for one reason or another, John had never been able to repay; however, Millie had bought the farm--all 160 acres--from Pa for $3600 and had paid him every red cent. Of course, he'd sold the north eighty to John who had quickly traded it back to Pa. It was then that Pa had approached him about working the land on shares. That had been Horatio's idea and true to form, Millie had done just what he thought his father wanted.

Millie had never asked his parents for money, always made it on his own. And who was the one who got shafted? Certainly not Ruby or John. This just proved where he stood in his parents' affection--right there at the bottom.

Millie sent his father a brief note saying he was not interested in buying the eighty. In a matter of weeks, Horatio sold the place to Tabors for $2800. It was bare land with some woods. The granary Millie had moved there had long since been sold to Ezz Garrett and moved across the road. Still, it was a fair price.

Millie fumed for days. Then, he sent his father a letter giving an itemized statement of the money he had spent to put up fences on the property. He asked to be reimbursed. On the seventeenth of September, Millie received a letter from Horatio with a check for $1,114.14. This covered the loan Millie had given Horatio, plus interest, plus the bill for the installed fence. Horatio even said he hoped they would come to Detroit to the State Fair. He had no inkling as to the venomous thoughts Millie harbored. To Horatio, it had simply been a business deal.

Millie said little to anyone but both Miney and Rate realized something was wrong. Millie never mentioned his father and for the first time, no longer called his son "Rate." He would be Ralph for the rest of Millie's life. If they received a letter from Lovina, Millie refused to read it. He did not go so far as to forbid Miney to write to his parents, but by his actions, he certainly discouraged it.

Ralph wasn't sure how his mother felt about the situation. For once, she kept her thoughts to herself. He figured the quality of Ma's life would be much improved if she no longer had to contend with Lovina's constant interference. She was no doubt glad that at long last Millie would have to make his own decisions without counsel from his father. Blanche had already declared her independence from her grandmother and was doing exactly what Grandmother had been so opposed to; therefore, he supposed she would not be greatly affected by the rift between Pa and Grandfather even though she was in Detroit. Maybe she was lucky she was rooming with Del instead of living with their grandparents. Knowing Pa's stubbornness, Rate wondered if his father and his grandfather would ever be reconciled. Right now, it didn't seem very likely.

As he thought about the situation, Ralph wondered why his grandfather had not given the eighty to his father. Certainly wasn't because Grandfather couldn't afford such an expensive gift. Ralph guessed he knew how Pa felt. Pa had worked all his life to be successful and to make his father proud of him but when it counted, Grandfather had let him down. Just didn't seem fair. Yet, Grandfather's letter did not indicate that he knew how much his actions had upset his son. Grandfather certainly wasn't that dense or was he? Maybe he just figured Pa would accept anything he did because Pa had always run to him for advice on every little thing. Well, only time would tell whether or not Pa would ever find it in his heart to forgive his father.

Then, Rate wondered about Grandmother. Did Pa blame her too? If he did, Ralph felt this was unfair. Grandmother had always let it be known that when it came to business, she never interfered with her husband's decisions. Hotario did as he pleased and the less she knew about his business dealings the better.

Ralph wasn't even certain his grandfather would have told his grandmother that he had offered to "sell" Pa the property. Besides, all these years Pa had never wanted anyone to disagree with his mother in any way. He'd never stood behind Ma, but had always stuck by his mother on any disagreement. Could he now exclude his mother from his life because of something Grandfather had done?

Ralph remembered that for quite some time Pa and Uncle John had been on the outs all because of Uncle John's animosity toward Grandfather. Pa maybe hadn't suggested that he could see his father dead with no remorse but Ralph wondered if Pa had given it some thought.

Would seem kind of strange not to work that north eighty. Pa had intended to put in a field of corn and the rest would be hay. As of now, timothy hay was the best money crop a farmer could have. Guess probably Pa's income would be less even if he had had to share profits with his father.

Ralph was glad to be back in school where he saw his friends daily. The only fly in the ointment was the work he had to do before he could go to school. During the summer, Pa had decided he would sell cream to the creamery in Eureka. Ralph had to deliver the cream to the creamery located about three and a half miles from home where he sometimes found five or six rigs ahead of him. When he returned to the farm, he had to harness another horse to fit in with the team he was driving so that Pa could have a team of three--he was doing some fall plowing–harness Pearl, change his clothes then head for Elsie.

School began at 9:00. Some days he made it on time; however, on some days, he was late for his first class and occasionally missed it entirely. It was his Ag class. Rate spoke with the teacher and Mr. Harter had been sympathetic. Horatio gave Ralph to understand that he expected the class assignments to be done and all tests to be taken. Rate figured this was completely fair.

Rate didn't think his father was the least bit concerned because he was sometimes late for school. Funny thing about Pa, he more or less expected that Rate would go to school--some left school early and a good many quit after the eighth grade--but Pa didn't seem to mind if he missed a day. Rate sometimes wondered if Pa thought an education was worthwhile. Pa was forever saying, "Ignorance is a bliss" so maybe he didn't care whether or not Ralph acquired book learning. Rate knew that Pa was paying for Blanche to go to business school but then Pa had always been willing to do for Blanche. Of course, without some sort of education there wasn't much a woman could do to support herself. Maybe Pa figured Blanche meant it when she said she didn't intend to marry and knowing Blanche realized she was not about to sit around and let her father support her all her life.

The students who had to drive in from the country to go to school carried their dinner. Even some of those who lived on the edge of town did the same. The boys had a room in the basement where they could eat, and afterward, a couple of boys would put on the boxing gloves that hung there and do a little boxing. It was all done in fun, and no one got hurt. Besides, they needed something to occupy them for the hour they had for dinner. After all, eating didn't take that long.

Rate decided it was pay-back time for Bion Clement. He had never forgotten the time Bion had deliberately kicked him on the knee that had been swollen and painful from an abscess. He had told Bion he'd get even one day. Well, Rate figured that time had arrived.

Since George Lusk was a rather slick talker, Ralph decided to enlist George's help to get Bion to the basement to put on the gloves. George was tall, walked with an easy stride, and had a disarming smile for everyone. Ralph figured if anyone could get Bion to the basement, it was George. The boys knew Bion would undoubtedly be hesitant about boxing but they thought if they could get him there, the pressure of his peers would get him to box with Rate. They were certain the lad would not want the other boys to think him a coward.

Rate was boxing with another boy when George and Bion came into the room. Rate had a satisfied grin as he purposely put on a poor showing. He didn't want Bion to realize how good he was. Ralph and his partner quit and on cue George spoke up.

"Bion, why don't you put on the gloves with Rate?"

Bion looked uncomfortable. He wanted to say no but the others were urging him on. All eyes were turned on him awaiting his answer.

"I've not done much boxing. I'm not any good. Doesn't someone else want to take on Ralph?" he asked hopefully.

"Heck. You just saw Rate. He's no good either. Give it a try. I'll bet you're better than you think," urged George.

Bion finally agreed. He let George help him put on the gloves then he turned to face his opponent. The boys were about the same size, Ralph perhaps a trifle shorter and they were both slim. They looked to be evenly matched. Bion tentatively led with a right which Rate easily blocked. Since he was slow to respond, Bion's confidence soared and the chatter from the spectators served to spur him forward.

They had sparred a short time and while Bion had not landed a solid punch, Rate had been content to deflect Bion's blows without doing much to retaliate. Now he became more aggressive. Rate's punches came with more speed and much more finesse. Bion found it difficult to ward off the blows and if he did strike out, he could not hit the bobbing target which Ralph presented. Rate connected with a solid right to Bion's left eye; a few moments later a feint with the right was followed by a left hook that found Bion's right eye. Rate chuckled to himself as he easily defended himself against Bion's wild blows. After one more solid blow to the chin which sent Bion staggering backward, Rate called it quits. He looked at his completely cowed adversary with a grin of satisfaction. He was pretty sure Bion would have two black eyes come tomorrow. He hoped Bion realized why he had been so severe.

Rate looked at George and winked. Both of them felt Bion had been paid back for his cowardly act of a few years ago. Ralph was certainly glad Reverend Buffin had been such a good instructor.

Miney received an unsettling letter from Blanche. Her daughter had come down with the mumps. From the tone of Blanche's letter, she was a very sick young woman. Del had the mumps as a child, so she wasn't likely to get them again. Miney felt some degree of relief because Blanche assured her that Mrs. Morgan, Blanche's landlady, was seeing that Blanche had plenty of rich chicken broth because Blanche could eat only liquids. She could open her mouth far enough to get the tip of a teaspoon between her teeth but that was all. Mrs. Morgan had made a very tasty creamed soup which Blanche had been able to get down without too much difficulty. Blanche ended by saying that her mother was not to worry.

Miney hated for Blanche to be sick away from home. The last time was when she had had an attack of appendicitis while with Mary in Chicago. At least Blanche had been with her aunt. Now, she was with a total stranger. Of course, from Blanche's letter, it seemed as though the woman was a caring person and was doing her best to make Blanche comfortable. Still, it was not like having Blanche home where she could see to her daughter's every need.

Miney didn't realize the relationship between Blanche and her landlady. Mrs. Morgan was the motherly type without being overbearing like Blanche's grandmother; therefore, Blanche had taken an instant liking to the woman. Sometimes, when Blanche returned from classes before Del came home from her clerking job, Blanche passed some of the time with Mrs. Morgan. During one of their conversations in which the subject of boys came up Blanche admitted that she knew nothing of the facts of life. Mrs. Morgan was greatly surprised. She had thought that Blanche's mother would have explained things to her long before this. Tactfully, she told Blanche what she felt the young woman needed to know. Blanche wondered why her mother had found the subject so distasteful and so embarrassing. At long last, Blanche finally understood where babies came from and how they were conceived. She felt she owed Mrs. Morgan a debt of gratitude.

* * * * * * * * *

Alfie Clement was a neighbor some distance to the north. He had a brother, Earl, who was, for want of a better word, a tramp. He moved to wherever he could find a few days work and lived from hand to mouth, never owning much more than the clothes on his back. He had been walking past the farm in early summer when Millie had stopped him and asked if he wanted a job.

"Millie, you don't want to hire me. I'm just a tramp."

"Earl, I could use the help. I'll hire you by the day. You can stay wherever you want. If you like, you can sleep in the granary these summer months. You'd be free to leave any time but I sure could use the help for now."

Earl took the job. He was more interested in the good food Miney provided than he was in the pay. He was accustomed to sleeping in barns in his wandering. However, come fall, he said, "I don't know where to go. I can't sleep in the granary when winter sets in. I guess I'd better move on now while the weather is still mild."

Millie convinced him to stay through the winter for $6.00 a month plus his room and board. He slept in the upstairs bedroom. On the rare occasions when Blanche came home, she used the spare downstairs bedroom.

Ralph sometimes wondered why Earl couldn't take the cream to Eureka but Millie never suggested this might be an option. Rate never asked his father to be relieved of this chore to enable him to get to school on time; he was certain he knew what his father's reaction would be.

Millie would think Ralph was attempting to shirk his duties and Millie would not tolerate laziness in his son.

Ralph came into the house as soon as he had put Pearl in the stable. He headed upstairs to change his clothes before returning to the barn to do his chores. He'd unharness Pearl then and turn her out for the night. It wouldn't be much longer that the horses would spend the nights away from the barn. Fall pasture had been good thus far but that would soon end. It wasn't that the horses couldn't tolerate the drop in temperature, it was simply that they needed plenty to eat. Besides, if they remained out too long in the fall they began to put on a heavy winter coat. Nature had a way of taking care of its animals.

"Ralph, you got a card in the mail today. It's on the buffet," called his mother from the kitchen.

"Thanks, Ma. Who's it from?"

"Your grandmother, I expect. It's from Detroit, and it's not Blanche's writing."

Ma was right. It was a Halloween card from Grandmother. She wished him a happy Halloween and went so far as to ask him to come to Detroit to spend his vacation with them. He supposed she meant at Christmas. He didn't rightly remember her inviting him to visit before. Must be she felt generous toward him because Blanche had her room instead of living with their grandparents. Whatever. It was nice of Grandmother to ask. He didn't suppose he'd go, but he appreciated the invitation. He was certain Pa would have some trumped up reason why he couldn't visit his grandparents. Maybe that was why Grandmother had asked him. He was certain nothing had been said but he felt his grandmother had to know something was wrong. She must realize that Millie had no more contact with them than was completely unavoidable, and that Pa had all sorts of excuses he could drum up out of thin air for keeping his distance. Seems like both Grandmother and Grandfather would be able to understand that something had changed in their relationship with Pa. Golly, didn't they think it strange that he no longer sought their advice on anything? After all, he'd never been like Uncle John who never wanted advice from either parent.

Ralph went up the stairs and hurriedly changed his clothes. When he came back down, he went on into the kitchen, helped himself to a piece of pie and then went out the kitchen door and headed for the barn. Bruno was waiting and since he saw that Rate was eating he immediately began to beg.

"Rollover," commanded Rate. The dog quickly complied with the command. However, as soon as he came to his feet, Ralph issued the same command, "Rollover." Rate slowly ate his pie while Bruno kept up with his master by rolling over and over and over.

When Ralph had only one bite left, he told Bruno to sit. Then, he tossed the bit of pie to the dog who deftly caught it in midair. "Good boy, Bruno." Rate bent to pat his dog. Good old Bruno. He hated to think that Bruno was already getting old. There was a slight graying around the muzzle.

For some time now, Ralph had been working with Pearl to teach her some tricks. He had succeeded in teaching her to shake her head "no" on cue. He had done this by pricking her with a pin to make her shake her head. It wasn't long before Pearl understood what he wanted which, in Rate's opinion just proved what he had always known. Pearl was smarter than most horses. Teaching her to nod her head had not been difficult. Now, he was working on teaching her to walk on her hind legs. He had taught her to stand on her hind legs by tapping her front legs with a whip. Thus far, she would only take a couple of steps but he hadn't given up. With patience, he felt he could get her to walk farther. Didn't those circus horses do better than that? Rate knew Pearl could do as well if he just had patience.

Ralph kept Pearl well-groomed. He fed her eggs to keep her coat shiny. He didn't think Ma knew this but he figured Pa knew. Ma would have felt he was wasting eggs she could have sold and Ma was one who wanted every penny she could get. Pearl was kept blanketed in the wintertime as were the other horses because the stable was mighty drafty. It was either to keep them blanketed so they didn't put on a heavy winter coat or clip them.

Otherwise, the horses would sweat when working and that was a quick way to have a sick horse. The livery stable in town kept their horses clipped but this was a demanding job. Rate figured it was easier to keep them blanketed. Besides, if properly cared for a blanket lasted for several years. He and Pa had always been particular about keeping the stables clean with clean bedding, and this helped to keep the blankets clean.

Delivering their cream to the creamery after winter finally arrived was worse than before. Although Millie took the cream on Sundays, Ralph continued taking the cream six days a week. Ralph missed his agriculture class more often than he attended. Still, his homework was always done and he had no trouble with Mr. Harter's tests. He had decided it was in his best interest to complete each test and as a result, he often had a perfect paper.

In February, he had another card from Grandmother. The first sentence was to admonish him. She wrote, "Grandma thinks you might write her once in a while." Golly, he had intended to write. He'd sent a short letter thanking her for all the gifts at Christmas. Somehow, she sounded lonely. Perhaps Blanche was too busy to call and he didn't think Ma wrote to her in-laws very often. At least not since Pa was so riled at Grandfather. He supposed he'd better send her another letter. He guessed she couldn't help being such an interfering soul. Of course, she had never tried to run his life; it was only Pa and Blanche who had been awarded this honor.

When Blanche was home over the holidays, she had asked him if he knew what had happened between their parents and grandparents. Ma hadn't said much in her letters but she just knew something wasn't right. Therefore, he had told her what little he knew. Neither Pa nor Ma had said anything directly to him; it was just that he had overheard them talking a time or two.

"Blanche, Pa never mentions Grandfather or even Grandmother. It is almost like they no longer exist."

"I notice Pa never calls you Rate. If he uses a name, it is Ralph. Doesn't it seem like he'd use Rate simply from habit? Look how many years he's been calling you Rate. Talk about mind over matter."

"I know. Right now, Pa is angry through and through. I don't think he's forbidden Ma to write to Grandmother but he certainly doesn't encourage it. Ma doesn't say much either. I know Pa never reads a letter from Grandmother."

"I wonder if Grandfather ever did tell Pa that north eighty would be his?"

"I don't think so. You know that if Grandfather had actually told Pa it was to be his, Grandfather never would have gone back on his word. Of course, I learned a long time ago that you have to be very careful to listen to every word Grandfather uses. I think Grandfather said something, and Pa just assumed Grandfather meant to give him the eighty."

Blanche looked pensive, then said, "I guess that's right. Everyone knows that Grandfather's word is reliable whether it is backed up in writing or not. No one ever accused Horatio Setterington of being a liar--shrewd but never dishonest."

Blanche had said she now felt a little awkward about going over to Grandmother's place. Neither grandparent had mentioned any trouble although Blanche had noticed that Grandmother often asked about Ma and Pa which was unusual. Must be that was because Ma didn't write that often. Blanche wondered if ever the relationship would return to normal. Much as her grandmother irritated her, she discovered she did feel sorry for her. First, it had been Uncle John who didn't visit and now it was Pa. Did Grandmother deserve to have her sons alienated just because they were mad at their father?

The village decided it was time they took a step forward by providing electricity for electric lights. A few places had installed carbide lighting some years back which was an improvement over kerosene lamps or even the better gasoline lamps. However, the business men thought they should follow the example set by the larger municipalities. Therefore, two diesel engines were installed to power the generators to provide electricity.

Not everyone felt the new lighting was progress. Millie was one of those filled with skepticism. His viewpoint was strengthened when the residents discovered the new lighting was far more expensive than anyone had anticipated. Millie felt it had been a frivolous undertaking and was certain the whole idea would founder by the wayside.

Millie sold Miney's house in town and bought forty acres two and a half miles from the homestead. It had a log cabin which was falling, three large cleared fields, and a small wood lot. It would make an excellent place to run sheep in the summer along with a few head of young cattle. Millie was quite satisfied with his purchase. With this added acreage, he would not miss the eighty (which had only about forty acres of cleared land) his father had taken from him. It might not be as convenient but it would do nicely.

In March, Swarthouts left the Sherman farm and Vern and Blanche Brewbaker moved in. They had one son, Beurmann, who was about a year and a half old. Blanche was also visibly in the family way. Vern was about six years older than Ralph and as yet they didn't know each other very well. However, with farmers having to help each other with threshing and haying or possibly wood cutting, it would not be long before the two became friends.

Ralph had been on a field trip with the botany class. As usual, he was at the back of the group, wishing he could remain outside instead of having to return to classes. The weather was perfect. The sun shone brightly, most of the trees were completely leaved out and they had found signs of the early spring flowers in a few places. The temperature was mild and a gentle breeze came from the southwest. Nothing about the day was conducive to being cooped up inside a stuffy classroom.

When they were nearly back to the school house, Rate spied a garter snake almost under foot. He quickly stepped on its tail before it could slither away. He picked it up and was debating what he should do with it when he found a tin can large enough to hold the small snake. Rate carried the can under his light jacket; consequently, no one was aware of what he had.

Rate knew the next class in the science room was a class composed completely of girls. Unobtrusively, he set the can on a workbench, tipped the lid back slightly, and filed out with the group when the bell rang. However, instead of going to the study hall, he slipped into the boys lunch room where he could watch the door to the science room. He had thought of going into the furnace room where a gasoline engine powered the large fan that drove the hot air through ducts to the various classrooms when the weather was cold enough to warrant heat. Today was warm enough so he knew the engine would not be operating.

However, he knew that Charley Clement, the janitor often sat in there. Charley was a Civil War veteran who had been held in Libby Prison. Students often found Charley to be gruff and untalkative. Ralph had always wondered what he had been like before the war and if the time spent in Libby had forever changed him. If asked why he had fought he would snap, "To preserve the Union". Guess with Charley, slavery had not been an issue. Rate figured Charley, who was a stickler for rules would send him to the study hall where he belonged. The lunch room was a far better choice.

Class had no more than started when the girls started screaming and came pushing and shoving in a most unladylike fashion to get out the door into the wide hallway. Some had even run up the stairs to get as far away from the classroom as possible. Now, they looked back at the science room as if trying to decide what their next move should be.

Ralph sauntered over, stuck his head in the room now empty except for the teacher, and innocently asked, "What's wrong, Mr. Harter?"

Mr. Harter was medium height, slender enough to be classified as skinny, and his long, thin, boyish face held a perplexed look as he turned toward Ralph. "There's a small garter snake in here. I haven't the slightest idea where it came from but it certainly frightened those girls. Never heard so much screaming and all over a harmless little snake. I haven't been quick enough to catch the little bugger."

"Want some help?"

"Aren't you supposed to be in class?"

"Naw. I've just got study hall. Here. I'll see if I can get him for you."

The snake *was* elusive but with both Ralph and Mr. Harter pursuing the reptile it was soon caught. Mr. Harter took the poor snake to the outside door, released it and watched it slither away where it disappeared under some bushes.

He thanked Rate profusely for his assistance. While Ralph was able to keep his face expressionless, his eyes danced and he laughed to himself. Those silly girls had looked funny falling all over themselves to get out of the classroom. You'd have thought that poor little snake was some big monster. They didn't look any too happy to be going back to class. The way they behaved, they seemed to be afraid they might find another snake. Sure had turned into a fun day.

Jessie McDougall was a grade ahead of Ralph but they were the same age. She lived on a farm east of Elsie. Rate had taken her to a couple of school parties; he found her fun to be with.

They had gone out on a Saturday night but Ralph was always careful to get her home before midnight--the curfew set by her parents. He had seen Jessie home as usual; then, as soon as he left her yard he promptly went to sleep knowing that Pearl would take him home.

The next thing he knew, he was cramped from his position on the buggy seat. Golly, it sure looked a lot lighter than when he went to sleep. The buggy wasn't moving. Hadn't he woke up when Pearl got him home? He began to look about him, noticed the rosy glow to the east then realized where he was. Pearl was tied to the hitching post in Jessie's yard, stamping impatiently. What a predicament. He sure hoped Mr. McDougall wasn't an early riser like Pa. He'd hate to try to explain his presence at this hour.

Rate quickly untied Pearl and headed for home. As soon as they turned onto the road, he gave Pearl her head, and the mare broke into a run. He slowed her to a fast trot while they went through the village even though it was too early for townspeople to be up and about and the streets were deserted.

Pearl kept to a fast trot much of the time but occasionally, she ran for a short distance. She was eager to get home too. Rate was content to let her set her own pace. What had happened? He had left the McDougall yard before midnight, so how had he ended up back at the McDougall hitching post? Then, a possible scenario came to mind. He knew Ollie Bensinger often rode with Dr. Russell, the local veterinarian, when Doc had to make a call at night. He surmised those two had met him on the road and Ollie had at once recognized Pearl and the rig. Ralph figured Ollie had turned the mare around, took her back to McDougall's and tied her so she couldn't leave. Ralph never knew this for certain but he firmly believed that Ollie had gotten even for the cayenne pepper in his pie.

When Ralph arrived home, his father was already in the barn. He wasn't sure what his father would say but he lost no time changing his clothes so he could return to the barn to do his share of the chores. It was that time of year when the manure had to be cleaned out of the sheep shed and the large piles of manure--one by the horse stable and one by the cow stable--spread on the fields where they would plant corn. They were a little behind with this task because it had been such a wet spring. Usually, clearing out the manure piles was a slow process. The manure had to be forked onto a wagon flat rack and then tossed off in such a way as to be more or less spread evenly over the field.

This year was to be different. Will Fizzell, a neighbor to the south, had bought a manure spreader--the first in the neighborhood. He let it be known that he would rent out the machine for a dollar a day. While Millie was often skeptical of anything new, he decided to rent the spreader this year partly because they were behind with their work. It was much quicker to load manure into a spreader then drive over the field with the spreader forcing the manure out the back in a pattern much wider than the spreader itself. Even at a dollar a day, Millie figured the time saved would make it worthwhile. Ralph chuckled over Millie's decision. Sometimes, Pa was difficult to figure out. Ralph would have been willing to bet that his father wouldn't have wanted to try out this "new contraption." Seemed Pa hated hauling manure more than he disliked other jobs around the farm.

The school year drew to a close. Ralph had completed ten years of schooling. However on the last day of school, the superintendent A.O. Jones called Ralph into his office. Ralph had no idea why he had been summoned but he thought Mr. Jones looked particularly solemn.

"Ralph, I've been going over your attendance record. It seems you were absent from your agriculture class more than you were present."

"I know but it couldn't be helped." Rate patiently explained the situation. "Mr. Harter made sure I did all the assignments. I took and passed all the tests."

"Be that as it may, it doesn't alter the fact that you missed an unacceptable amount of class time. Therefore, I have decided that you cannot be given credit for this particular class."

"Not given credit! How can you make such a judgment? I didn't miss even a single question on the final exam. Others sat in class every day who didn't do nearly as well. Do they deserve credit more than I do?"

"Ralph, your performance on a test has nothing to do with anything. Do you deny you missed class more often than you attended?"

"Of course I don't deny it. I just don't think you have the right to disallow a credit that I've earned and Mr. Harter has given me. Talk to Mr. Harter. He'll explain."

Ralph had been standing in front of the superintendent's desk during this verbal exchange. He did not fail to notice the set expression on Mr. Jones' face. With a sinking feeling he knew that he had failed to sway the man's decision.

The superintendent shoved himself up out of his chair and as he leaned forward his hands on the desk, he once more pronounced his decision. "There is nothing more to say. You *will not* be given credit for your agriculture class. I have made up my mind. There is nothing further to be said."

"It's the wrong decision, Mr. Jones, and you know it."

Ralph doubled up his fist and struck the superintendent with enough force to knock the man back into his big swivel chair. Ralph took great delight in the look of surprise on the man's face. Pompous ass! Ralph said nothing more but strode out of the superintendent's office and on out of the building. It was the last time he was to enter the building as a student.

Neither of Ralph's parents were overly concerned over what had happened. Ralph had glossed over the part about striking Mr. Jones. While Miney did not approve of this action, Millie merely nodded his head in agreement. He seemed to understand what had driven his son to commit the deed.

Since Ralph would not return for the eleventh grade, he had no idea what he was going to do come fall. He didn't want to be dependent on his parents. As it was, he still did his chores but he sometimes worked a day or two for someone else to have a little pocket money. He had asked his father what he thought of Michigan Agricultural College.

Millie had been completely outspoken when he answered. "It's a gol-durn fool notion for anyone to go there to study how to farm. What is there to learn that hasn't already been learned from the old-timers? I've farmed all my adult life and I've had a good return most years. What else should I know?"

"Well, I've read where they have new ideas about feeding cows to increase their milk production. They also have a commercial fertilizer which will boost yields from all the crops. Mr. Harter says there is a lot to be learned. For instance, we don't burn our wheat stubble like some of the older farmers. Mr. Harter says that plowing the stubble under returns nutrients to the soil; therefore, the following crops do better."

"Knew that man was filling your head with foolish notions. It's all a lot of fol-de-rol. Pure nonsense. All the fertilizer one needs is to spread manure on the fields. Of course, it pays to rotate crops, and it helps to rest a field for a few years by using it for pasture or hay. Can't see where no man who has never farmed a day in his life can tell the rest of us how to farm. No, sir, studying agriculture is a complete waste."

That was that. Ralph had been giving some thought to taking classes at MAC, but he now knew that his father would never consent. Guess when Blanche came home, he'd ask her for her opinion about him going to school somewhere. Seeing as how she was attending business school, Ralph felt she could give him sound advice. Well, summer was just beginning which meant he had plenty of time to decide what he should do come fall.

Ralph was on the Ridge Road headed *west* on a moonlit night; he was keeping Pearl on a fast walk while he conversed with his female companion. He knew from Pearl's actions a rig had pulled up behind them. Pearl hated having another horse this close.

"Who've you got in the buggy?" It was his father's voice. Must be he and Ma had gone over to Aunt Lorin's after they did their shopping. They weren't usually out this late.

Rate gave a little chuckle before he called out an answer. "You'll have to look to find out." His father was driving Nell, and she couldn't hold a candle to Pearl when it came to speed.

Millie accepted the challenge. Ralph heard the crack of his father's whip accompanied by a yell at Nell. Ralph merely let Pearl have her head and she surged forward as if pursued by the devil himself. Both rigs raced down the road, swaying slightly but with Ralph lengthening the distance between them.

Ralph could hear his mother's voice begging her husband to slow down. "Millie, you're going to kill us. You're going to kill us. Please, Millie, please slow down," she implored. Rate knew she was half crying from her tone.

Ralph did feel some compassion for his mother. However, he was totally satisfied because his father never found out it was Hazel Bachelor in the buggy with him. Hazel hadn't been afraid and she thought the situation as humorous as Ralph did. It wasn't often that Rate bested his father on anything so he took particular delight in winning this time.

CHAPTER 3

R alph had brought in the mail which consisted of a couple of letters. He hadn't been interested enough to look at them to check on who they were from; he had simply handed them to his mother. Then, he became aware that Ma was speaking, informing Pa they had "received a letter from Mother Setterington." Pa didn't let on that he even heard his wife, simply continued reading yesterday's *Toledo Blade.*

Ma had scanned the letter, then she began reading it aloud. Golly, Grandmother said that she and Grandfather would be moving to California soon–permanently. At least this news had Rate's attention.

Lovina was not very specific but it seemed that Mac had decided his fortunes lay in California--the land of opportunity--not Michigan where his great talents had never been fully recognized. Of course, if Mac and Ruby moved to California, Lovina had to follow since she refused to be separated from her only surviving daughter. Besides, she now doted on Lois as well. Miney's voice trailed off as she read the part where Lovina said she and Horatio sent their love to all.

At first, Millie merely grunted when Miney read the letter aloud. After a few moments, he said, "I'll bet dollars to doughnuts that Mac has some get rich quick scheme which will never pan out. It surprises me that Pa goes along with Mac's hair brained notions. I guess it is easier to get along with Ma if they continue to coddle Ruby. They always belittled John and made fun of Grace but Mac is no better. Without Pa's help, he'd be in the poor house. I've never felt he had any business sense. At least when he was down and out, John could always find work and he was willing to do manual labor, not afraid to soil his hands."

This was a long speech for Millie, especially now that he so seldom mentioned either of his parents. Miney realized how much he resented the way his parents had always taken care of Ruby. It didn't seem quite right but there was nothing anyone could do to make the situation better. No wonder Millie had been so disappointed and upset with his father over the north eighty. It seemed as though Millie was never given any consideration simply because he had always worked hard and had been completely responsible.

Personally, Miney had always thought Mac was lazy. He and Ruby got along well but Miney figured that was because Lovina saw to it that her daughter wanted for nothing. Ruby and Mac had always lived beyond their means. Miney supposed they were bringing up Lois to expect the best of everything. Sure didn't fit with Miney's frugal background. Miney wondered if Mother Setterington had told Blanche. If so, it seemed odd that Blanche hadn't mentioned it in her letter of a couple of days ago.

Rate didn't figure the move was of much concern to him. Since Pa had been so angry with Grandfather, he had not seen his grandparents, so he guessed he wouldn't miss them. While both Blanche and Ralph were surprised to learn their grandparents were moving to California, Blanche wondered if there was some ulterior motive which Grandmother had not divulged. She had always seemed to be perfectly content in Detroit and Blanche had heard her say more than once she was tired of moving all around the country.

Blanche liked Aunt Ruby well enough but she had always felt Uncle Mac was completely lacking when it came to having common sense in business matters. Add to that the fact that he was lazy, liked to put on airs about how important he was, and Blanche found him to be not very likable. All he seemed to want from life was to be rich without doing any work. Then, there was Lois. Grandmother spoiled the child and Aunt Ruby did nothing to prevent it. The older Lois became, the more obnoxious she was. At least Blanche figured Lois got Grandmother out of *her* hair a good share of the time. In reality, Blanche had never liked confrontations with her grandmother. It was just that there was no way she was going to let Grandmother run her life. Blanche wondered if Lois would ever reach the point when she would resent having her grandmother interfere in her life.

Sometimes, Blanche wondered what Grandmother's parents had been like. Grandmother was not one to talk much about her family. Blanche wondered if Grandmother's parents had tried to run her life the way Grandmother tried to run the life of everyone with whom she came in contact. Because Grandmother had so often irritated Blanche, she had never asked her questions. Now, when

Grandmother was moving such a long way from Elsie, Blanche wished she knew more about the Reynolds. While Grandmother had been born in New York State, why had she been teaching in Canada? So many unanswered questions.

Lovina had called Blanche after she had sent the letter to Millie and Miney. Although she tried to sound very upbeat about the move, Blanche felt her grandmother was not quite as enthused as she would have Blanche believe. When she and Grandmother had sort of been at odds since Blanche was studying to be a stenographer and Lovina highly disapproved of such a position. Blanche felt her grandmother secretly hoped Blanche would get a job she wouldn't like or that the company would think her incompetent after a brief period and fire her. Blanche felt it was very difficult for Grandmother to accept she had a granddaughter who was capable of making her own decisions. It seemed as though Grandmother had never taken an interest in Uncle John's girls. They sure were lucky. Blanche at once felt contrite because she knew her grandmother cared about her even if she did have an irritating way of showing it.

Once again Millie built an addition onto the house. While Miney had liked all the cupboard space Millie had put in when he added the kitchen, he had not seen fit to make the room very wide. There were times when Miney felt cramped in the narrow space. It seemed as though the stove took up such a large part of the available space, it left little room for the cabinet and work space.

Now, Millie decided instead of the narrow north porch. He would put on a wide one like the porches to the south and east. He would extend the walls of the kitchen as far as the well curb on the north. He eliminated the east kitchen door and put in a window instead that was high off the floor but was wide and gave a lot of early morning light since it faced the east even if a porch did shade it. In the southeast corner, he installed a pitcher pump to bring water from the cistern and he put in a narrow sink. This meant that the wash dish could set in the sink and the dirty water no longer had to be thrown outside. The drain from the sink simply emptied under the house but this served the purpose well enough.

Miney was quite satisfied with the results. The room was now wide enough to accommodate the stove without it making the room seem cramped. The door to the north opened directly onto the boards covering the well curb around the pump. The door had a half window which, along with the window to the east, made that corner well lighted. There was also a window to the north and one to the west. My how the ventilation did help on a hot summer's day.

For the past year or so, Rate had sometimes chummed with Suzie Fry, a relative newcomer to the vicinity who was only about a year younger than Ralph. His given name was Francis but no one called him Francis except maybe his mother. Everyone, young and old, called him Suzie. Rate figured if anyone said Francis or Frank, Suzie wouldn't have known they were referring to him. Suzie had a stepfather, Mr. Rivest and a stepbrother, Russ. The boys were about the same age.

Ralph had been in town on a Saturday night when he happened to meet Suzie and Russ. The boys were rather provoked with Russ' father. It seems the gentleman had bought a new buggy and the boys had asked to use it. Mr. Rivest had told them no. He had come into town with the new buggy and left it at the livery stable.

"Rate, wanna come with us?" asked Suzie, his round face breaking into a grin.

"Where to?"

"To the livery stable," replied Russ and both boys gave him a mischievous grin.

"Don't tell me you are going to do what I'm thinking." Ralph looked at first one then the other.

"Guess that depends on what you're thinking. If you mean are we gonna help ourselves to the old man's new buggy and leave our old one for him to use, you'd be right as rain," answered Suzie.

"Have you thought about how mad he'll be?"

"More or less, but we're still gonna switch buggies, aren't we, Russ?"

"Sure are," replied Russ.

"Count me out. You don't need my help. You can get into trouble all by yourself. What're you gonna do after you make the switch?"

"Haven't thought that far. Maybe we'll just ride around. Might find a couple of girls who'd like to take a ride in a spankin' new buggy."

"I'd be careful if I was you. Mr. Rivest just might see you."

"Naw. Pa always goes to the pool hall and spends his time there. We'll stay away from that part of town," explained Russ.

Everyone knew old man Rivest had a terrible temper. Rate wondered how severe the punishment for the boys would be. He was certain Mr. Rivest would see nothing humorous about the situation. Rate figured it would be quite entertaining to be there when the old man discovered the switch. He'd sure raise the roof.

* * * * * * * * *

Blanche had written that she had a new friend whom she had met at business school. Her name was Frances Ryan. She was ever so much fun and had kept telling Blanche that she wanted Blanche to meet her "pig-eyed brother." Now, wasn't that some description? It seemed her brother was a motor man on a streetcar.

Well, to make a long story short, Frances had talked her into going with her for a ride on her brother's streetcar shortly before he would be finished for the day. Her brother, George, certainly looked good in his uniform. He had acknowledged the introduction but that was about all he had time for. However, when they came to leave, Frances had gone down the steps first and before Blanche could follow her, George had closed the door and sent the streetcar surging forward towards his next stop. Well, what was Blanche to do? She was not very familiar with this part of town thus she had been forced to ride with him until his replacement took over. She had tried to be angry with him but he certainly had the way of the Irish. He had been so witty, she had found it impossible to stay upset. Of course, being a gentleman, he had escorted her back to her rooming house.

She had seen George a few times since. He said he did not expect to work on a streetcar all his life. Blanche felt certain that with his wit, intelligence, and willingness to work, he would accomplish much. She had discovered that she truly enjoyed his company. He could always make her laugh.

George and Frances got on well together, partly because they both liked to tease. George called her Mickey but Blanche had no idea where the nickname had come from. They had a sister, Mildred, whom they both called Mil. Blanche had met her and she seemed much more serious than the other two.

Miney reread the letter. Was Blanche truly interested in this young man? She had never had this much to say about any of the others she had gone with *even* though a couple of them had certainly been interested in her. Well, she supposed Blanche was old enough to become attached to a young man because Miney felt certain Blanche would eventually marry even though she had always maintained marriage was not for her. Well, Blanche was already older than Miney had been when she and Millie were married.

Rate had learned there was going to be road work done by the bridge over Maple River just north of the Stafford school. He asked Millie if he could have the use of Gyp and Nell so he could earn some extra money. Since this was a slow time for field work, Millie was agreeable. Rate was offered $3.50 for himself and team for a ten hour day. It seemed a fair enough wage.

Ralph had been working for several days, and while this was not the most rewarding work he had *ever* done, he reasoned it was still better than picking strawberries as a kid. He laughed to himself when he thought of all the time he had spent picking strawberries for Tillotsons for so little monetary reward. At least he was now earning as much as most of the other men.

Ralph had been given the job of cutting pieces of sod and loading them on a gravel wagon. He had about half a load when something scared the team,and they took off, scattering sod and dump boards as they went. (The bottom of a gravel wagon consisted of boards about eight inches wide and two inches thick; they rested on a 2x6 between the wheels so that when the load was dumped, not all of the gravel had to be shoveled off. When the sides were removed, the dump boards could be turned up sideways, allowing the gravel to fall to the ground.)

The ground was uneven and the wagon could not withstand the strain. Something snapped! The team now had only the tongue and front wheels bounding behind them. The noise frightened them further. If other men had not made the effort to stop them the half-crazed horses would have gone right off the approach which was still under construction. Ralph breathed a sigh of relief when he saw them stopped. Had they continued, both horses would quite likely have broken a leg or sustained other injuries which would have necessitated putting them down. Rate figured he was pretty darned lucky. Of course, Pa should be understanding since more than once he had had a team run away. At least Ralph hadn't left the team to stand without him being with them even if his proximity hadn't helped.

When this job was completed, Rate and Don Sherman were to take a load of gravel to the Page school from the gravel pit located on the Ridge Road where the road curved. The school was about a mile and a half west and then south a half mile or so. Everything was going fine until they had the wagon loaded. Ralph spoke to the team as usual. Nothing happened. He slapped them with the lines, yelled a little louder but neither horse would tighten a tug. Don moved off to get a switch from a group of willows. The team pranced a little as if they knew their refusal to pull was going to bring dire results. Ralph spoke to them again and when neither horse responded, he cracked both of them on the rump with the switch. They danced but still made no move to pull. It took a few more solid whacks before the team gave in and pulled the wagon onto the road. Rate stopped them to allow Don to clamber aboard. When Ralph spoke to the team, they moved off as though nothing had happened. One just never knew about horses; sometimes, they could be as defiant as people.

One of the final jobs for the road work crew was to put in a culvert near the Page school. Rate, Don Sherman, and Cash Waldron were assigned this job. They had stumbled into a bumblebee's nest by the side of the road; consequently, they had put a large hunk of sod over it to keep the angry bees contained. Since they wanted to finish the job as soon as possible, they were a little annoyed when two Mead boys from a nearby farm came to watch and were constantly in the way. Suggestions that the boys go home fell on deaf ears. The boys continued to be a nuisance.

Finally, Don said, "Why don't you bring that piece of sod over here?" He pointed to the sod covering the bumblebees.

Both boys willingly grabbed the piece of sod. They had no more than raised it a few inches when the angry bees began to swarm. The boys dropped the sod and took off for home on a dead run. The bees swarmed after them.

"Guess they won't be back for a while," laughed Don.

"Now, wasn't that kind of a dirty trick?" asked Rate. His eyes twinkled showing that he found the situation humorous.

"You have any better idea? Guess no one ever taught them to stay out of a working man's way. They asked for it. Heck, we were just fortunate that we had such a good method available for getting rid of them. We'll be all set if those blamed bees don't decide to return."

Both young men laughed as they continued to work. They spent the next day there to finish the job but no one from the Mead farm came to annoy them. Ralph did wonder if either boy had been stung but he guessed he agreed with Don: they had asked for it.

Blanche came home for her birthday. Ralph asked her if she felt he should go on to school. Blanche thought it was a good idea because she felt an education certainly never hurt anyone. She asked him if he truly wanted to leave the farm. Rate admitted that he didn't rightly know. He had learned about new ideas in his Ag class but there was no way he could try out any of those ideas because their father was against anything new. He didn't think he should go in debt to buy a farm but he needed a means of making a living. He didn't intend to act as Pa's hired hand all his life. Blanche promised to look into a suitable school, one that would fit his needs. Rate was not enthused about living in Detroit; therefore, he told Blanche he'd prefer a school located in a smaller city.

Clinton County was one of the many counties in the state that had a fair in the early fall. Rate and Don Sherman had gone to St. Johns, the County seat, in the early evening to the fair. They had gone on the late grandstand since there had been two shows.

When they left the fairgrounds, it was almost midnight. There was no moon, the sky was black, and when they got away from town, it was difficult to know where they were. As Rate said, it was darker than a stack of black cats, and to make matters worse, it started to rain.

Don let the horse have its head, hoping the animal would know how to get them home. Ralph wished he had driven because he had a great deal more faith in Pearl's ability to get home than he did in Don's horse.

The horse picked its way slowly and had made a couple of turns. The boys had no idea where they were. In the blackness, they could see nothing that looked remotely familiar. Finally, after what seemed a long period, they saw a house with lamplight showing from one window.

"Rate, I'm going to stop here and find out where we are" said Don. He handed the lines to Ralph and climbed out of the buggy. The rain had lessened by now, but it was still too dark to see much.

Don was gone only a few minutes. He climbed back into the buggy without saying anything.

"Well?" asked Rate.

"They said we were at some place called Rochester Colony. Rate, where in hell is that?"

Ralph started laughing.

"What's so funny?"

"You. Don't tell me you've never heard of the Colony."

"Course I've heard of the Colony. It's a few miles south of your place. What's that got to do with anything?"

Ralph laughed again as he said, "The whole name is *Rochester* Colony, you idiot. Now, do you know where we are?"

"How in heck was I supposed to know there was a name like Rochester tacked on it. Go ahead and laugh. How'd you know?" he asked suspiciously.

"I don't know. For anyone who has lived around here all his life, I thought it was common knowledge."

"Well, it isn't", replied a disgruntled Don.

Don turned his horse left at the next crossroad and in moments, they had crossed the river. At least Don and Ralph both knew where they were--just a few miles south of the Setterington farm. It wasn't long before the horse became more animated as though he knew they were getting near his stable which meant food and rest. Ralph chuckled inwardly. Pearl would have known where her stable was from the moment they left St. Johns. Just proved that he drove the smartest horse.

* * * * * * * * *

Ralph had become good friends with Vern Brewbaker now that they were close neighbors and sometimes shared work. Farming necessitated neighbors working together especially at threshing time, corn husking or silo filling time. There were other times when neighbors gave each other a hand; it saved the expense of hiring someone to help. While Millie often had one or more hired men, Ralph felt that Vern could not afford such luxuries. He now had two young sons--Wilson had been born in April--as well as a wife to support, and Ralph felt Vern was not the best of farmers. He rented the farm and Rate had no idea what the terms of the rent were.

Vern liked to hunt almost as much as Rate did so when Vern asked Ralph to go hunting with him on his parents' farm, Ralph readily agreed.

Vern's younger brother Carl, wanted to go with them. He was about eight years younger than Vern and a year or two younger than Ralph. He was short in stature, so Ralph looked upon him as a kid. They good naturedly let Carl tag along.

It was chore time when the three returned. Carl hurried to the barn while Vern went to the house for a few words with his mother. Rate was getting the horse hitched to the buggy when he heard a commotion in the barn. He went to see what was wrong. What he saw astonished him.

Elzie, the eldest son, was yelling at Carl, berating him because he was late arriving at the barn for chores. Ralph had heard angry words before but what terrified him was that Elzie was holding the tines of a pitchfork just an inch or so from Carl's throat. Elzie had the boy backed into a corner where there was no chance of escape.

Rate quickly assessed the situation. Since Elzie was shouting, it was an easy matter for Ralph to quietly come up behind the man. He quickly locked his arms around Elzie, pinning his arms to his side. Elzie began to curse Ralph as he struggled to free himself. Rate held on tenaciously while Carl scooted out of harm's way.

Elzie was raving at Ralph like a demented man when Wilson Brewbaker, the father, came into the barn. "Let him go" he said quietly to Ralph.

"Not until he quiets down" replied Ralph. How'd he know what this man would do? He sure was some different from Vern who was mostly good natured and never showed much of a temper and wouldn't have hurt a fly if he did. Ralph had never seen anyone as out of control as Elzie seemed to be.

"Make the son-of-a-gun let me loose," yelled Elzie.

"You heard what he said, Elzie. Quit struggling and shut up." Wilson scarcely raised his voice but it somehow held an unmistakable tone of authority.

A moment more and Elzie did as his father ordered. As soon as Elzie complied with Wilson's instructions, Ralph dropped his arms and stepped back, eying Elzie warily. He had no idea whether or not Elzie would turn on him. However, Elzie behaved as though nothing unusual had happened and moved off to continue with his work.

Ralph said goodbye to both and got in the buggy. He noted that Carl had temporarily disappeared. Vern was returning from the house and reached the buggy only moments after Rate. He knew nothing of what had transpired, and Ralph said nothing. The incident had somewhat shaken Ralph. He wondered if Elzie would have harmed Carl had he not intervened. Wilson had not seemed unduly concerned. Perhaps Elzie's temper had flared up at other times. Ralph felt sorry for Carl. Elzie must be twelve or fifteen years older than the boy, old enough to be more understanding and certainly to have more self-control.

Ralph saw Elzie from time to time at Vern's but no mention was ever made of the incident. Rate wasn't sure how he felt about Elzie. He was a good looking man, tall and slender. Vern was short like his father and heavier set, however, Vern had a better sense of humor. Well, thought Ralph, perhaps it just seemed that way because he was better acquainted with Vern.

Ralph had no way of knowing that Vern's sister, Edith, often visited them. If either of the boys were sick Vern would fetch Edith to help with their care. She had said nothing to anyone but if Ralph came to see Vern while she was there, she usually tried to get a look at him from a window or doorway. She thought he was very good looking, even handsome. While she viewed him from afar, she was too shy to approach him or speak to him. She was content to gaze from the safety of the house. Besides, if Vern thought she was interested in Ralph, he would tease and quite likely he'd tell Art and she just knew that brother Art would tease her unmercifully. Better she keep her thoughts to herself. She was especially careful not to let her sister-in law, Blanche, notice her watching for Ralph. She just knew that Blanche would be likely to mention it to Vern. Never giving it a thought that Vern would be quick to tease. Blanche didn't think like Vern and Art.

Even though Edith was past eighteen she had just graduated from Eureka-they had only ten grades. She had never had a real beau. There was a time when she had had a crush on one young man but he had never been particularly interested in her. The family had often teased her about Frank Stabell, a teacher at Eureka, telling her it was easy to see that he was sweet on her. At that time, since a teacher only had to go one year to County Normal to be able to teach they were often only a few years older than their older students. Edith had never believed what her family said and had simply put up with the teasing. However, she was certain that a good looking young man like Ralph was already keeping company with someone; therefore, she would just observe from a distance.

* * * * * * * * *

Rate and Don Sherman had gone to some doings in Ovid. Both had driven. Don had a new buggy which had cost him the astronomical sum of $75. It had taken quite some time for him to save that enormous amount. He was proud of the buggy and wanted to show it off to friends. After driving around a bit, they had left their horses and buggies at the livery stable.

It was late when both young men returned to the livery stable to hitch up their horses.

When both were ready to leave, Don yelled, "Race ya!" He cracked his whip and his horse took off.

Of course, Rate could never refuse a challenge; therefore, he gave Pearl her head. Knowing Pearl and her aversion to having another horse ahead of her, Rate was confident she would pull ahead in short order.

Ralph passed Don just before the road made a rather sharp curve to the west. He and Pearl negotiated the curve safely but moments later he heard a cracking sound, like wood splintering. He pulled Pearl in and looked back to see what had made that sound.

Don had not made the curve. His buggy had swung off the road and hit a huge oak tree that grew close by the edge of the road. The new buggy was in shambles.

Rate carefully turned Pearl and went back to his friend. Don was disconsolately looking at the wrecked buggy.

"You all right?" asked Rate, a worried tone to his voice.

"Guess so. Maybe a bump or two but Rate, just look at my buggy. Think it can be repaired?" he asked hopefully.

Ralph got down to observe the buggy more closely.

"Don't know, Curly. It looks a mess but Mr. Besley is pretty darned clever with such things.

It's in such bad condition you can't drive it home. Let's see if we can get it out of the way and I'll take you home. You can tie your horse to the back of the buggy. We can come back tomorrow with a wagon to get it and you'll just have to see what Mr. Besley thinks."

"Rate, that's $75 gone like water through a sieve", lamented Don.

"You knew that tree was there. Why didn't you hug the inside of the turn?"
"How in the heck do I know? I just wanted to beat you and Pearl for once."

While Ralph felt some degree of sympathy for his friend, he also found the situation funny. He hoped Don could have the buggy repaired but Rate thought that possibility was quite unlikely.

Fall was well on its way. The fieldwork now consisted of harvesting corn for either the silo or the crib. Rate was on his way home from Elsie when he decided to stop at Vern's to see how his friend was coming with cutting a sizable field of corn. As was often the case, Vern was behind with his fieldwork and the corn for the silo had not yet been cut.

Vern and Elzie were just coming from the field, and Elzie's right hand was a bloody mess. Vern hastily explained that he had heard Elzie yelling and when he reached his brother, he discovered Elzie's hand was caught in some gears on the corn binder. Vern had managed to get Elzie released from the binder and had tied the team to a fencepost but he needed to harness a horse so he could drive Elzie to the doctor. Vern looked almost as white as Elzie which made Ralph wonder if Vern was truly capable of getting his brother the three and a half miles to Elsie.

"I'll drive you. Pearl's faster than any of your horses. Have you got a towel or something to wrap around his hand? He's losing a lot of blood."

Vern got some heavy material from the house and the three of them headed for Elsie. They went to the office of Porter and Bell, and luckily, both doctors were in. They looked at Elzie's hand and both agreed that his forefinger would have to be amputated. At the word "amputate" Vern blanched even whiter and looked as though he might faint. The doctors sent Vern to the waiting room saying they had no time to spend looking after him.

Dr. Porter gave Elzie ether and when he was under Dr. Bell prepared to do the amputation.

"Ralph, think you can help by holding Elzie's wrist? I need it to be held steady. Even though he's out, he could move and I need the hand to be immobile."

"Just tell me what to do."

"You're not going to let this make you feel faint, are you?"

"Not me, Doc. I'm fine."

Ralph found the entire procedure interesting. He was amazed at how the muscles contracted during surgery. Watching them reminded him of his mother frying frog's legs, and how she'd hated to have those legs jump in the pan. At least Dr. Bell seemed to know what he was doing. He left a flap of skin from the finger to cover the raw wound. When he was done only a small amount of blood seeped between the stitches. While Dr. Bell bandaged the hand, Rate was reminded of the time his leg had been sliced open by Pearl's newly shod forefoot. At least these doctors had been much more careful about clean instruments. Both doctors had scrubbed their hands before surgery and even asked Ralph to wash his hands; therefore, he figured Elzie's hand would heal without any trouble. At least he hoped so. He'd not wish for anyone to go through the process of getting proud flesh burned off.

The last time Blanche had been home, she had suggested that Ralph might like to go to Cleary Business College in Ypsilanti. She knew he was good with figures; therefore, she reasoned he would have an aptitude for bookkeeping. This was a far cry from farming but she felt working with numbers might interest him.

Ralph looked into this idea and learned that he could begin a term there on the first of January and finish the last of June or the first of July. He would have the other six months to help Pa on the farm or work to earn money for his stay in Ypsilanti. The college was not really a large one and Ypsilanti was certainly much smaller than Detroit. When Rate told his father of his decision, stressing the fact that Blanche had suggested this, Millie made no objection. Neither did he offer any monetary assistance. Ralph knew his father was paying for Blanche's schooling but he wasn't completely surprised that this benevolence did not extend to him. Oh well, he'd manage on his own. He really didn't want to be beholden to Pa anyway.

It was getting to be the time of year when farmers began to think of butchering. The weather had been unusually cold, the days not warming much although there had been only a sprinkling of snow. Thus far, an odd year indeed.

Claude Conklin stopped by to ask Rate if he wanted to help butcher a steer for Herb Putman, a neighbor about a mile to the north. Ralph knew Claude would likely give him a dollar or two, so he readily agreed. Besides, he liked working with Claude.

They discovered that Herb did not have the steer locked in the barn; it was running loose in a back pasture. Rate wondered why Herb hadn't had the foresight to have the animal in the barn since he knew what time Claude was coming. Besides, at this time of year, there was nothing to eat in the field. To remedy the situation, Herb gave both Rate and Claude a rifle, stationed them where they could shoot the steer when he drove the animal up from the pasture. He figured this would work better than attempting to get the steer in the barn when the animal knew his comrades were back in the field. Both Ralph and Claude remained hidden. Time dragged for Ralph but then he heard Herb's shout and could hear the steer approaching at a fast trot.

Just as the steer came within range, it took a turn away from where Ralph was hidden, providing only his rump for a target. The animal was headed straight for Claude. Rate heard the crack of Claude's rifle and expected to see the steer drop. However, the steer had not been hit, only scared. How could anyone miss a target that large and that close, Rate asked himself as he watched the steer jump the barnyard gate with an ease that astonished everyone, and take off down the driveway. The frightened animal turned north on the road with all the speed it could muster.

Claude, Herb, and Ralph went after the crazed steer. They were north of the little town of Bannister when they finally caught up with him. The poor animal was so tired from his exertion, he allowed Herb to get a rope on him to lead him back to the farm to meet his fate.

Ralph knew that Vern was supplementing his farm income by hauling ice for Clinton Creamery. Since his fieldwork had been finished weeks before, Vern could well afford to take the time away from the farm. Besides, he could certainly use the extra cash.

Although it was well into December, there had not been the usual amount of snow. As a result, wagons were still in use instead of sleighs. There was more than one team hauling ice from the Maple River channel just above the dam at the gristmill. The men drove their teams onto the millpond ice and backed up to the hole where the ice could be picked up as it floated down from the ice cutters further upstream.

Vern backed his wagon up to where he expected the blocks of ice to float down. Someone had scraped a bunch of slush into the hole, camouflaging the true extent of how far the hole extended. Since Vern thought it was solid ice, he jumped off the back of his wagon. He went right out of sight. Others had seen what happened and they were there to haul him out as soon as he surfaced. A horsehide robe appeared from somewhere to wrap around him while they took him to the gristmill to dry off.

Ralph came along just as the group was crossing the road. There was a long, low shed, open to the east by the north drive to the mill where farmers could stable their horses to keep them out of the worst weather. Sometimes when they came to the mill, they had to wait because others were ahead of them. They appreciated having a place to put a team while they waited. The farmers could always go inside and chat with other farmers while they waited. Ralph quickly decided to put Pearl in the shed so he could go into the mill where Vern could explain what had happened.

"Rate, don't you dare breathe one word of this to Blanche. She'd fuss like everything and I'd have to quit this job. The pay may not be all that much but it helps."

"Supposing you get a bad cold or even pneumonia. How will you explain that to her?" demanded Ralph.

"I'll think of something", Vern said with an unaccustomed worried frown.

Ralph was sure he would.

Blanche would believe whatever her husband told her and Rate was certain that Vern would come up with some kind of story, plausible or not. He hoped his friend didn't get sick. Vern was lucky he had not been in the water long. His thick outer clothing had prevented the cold water from soaking his winter underwear. It was only slightly damp. Of course, his wool stockings and shoes were wet since the water had gone down the tops of his arctics.

Knowing how adept Vern was at convincing his wife of just about anything made Rate chuckle. One night, Vern had shown up at the barn after dark to see Ralph for a few minutes. Ralph had been quick to ask, "How did Blanche ever let you come down here? Everyone knows she's deathly afraid to be alone after dark."

"Oh, she's fine. I left the lantern burning in the stable so she thinks I'm still doing chores. She'll never know I was gone." Vern chuckled. "What she doesn't know won't hurt her."

"Vern, sometimes you amaze me. What if she goes to the barn to see what is taking you so long to do chores?"

"She won't. She's afraid to stick her head out the door after dark and she'd never send the boys to find me. I'm safe."

This was not the only time Vern did this. He never stayed long. Rate figured Vern was just lucky Blanche never found out he was putting something over on her. She had a temper and Vern's shenanigans would certainly have made her angry.

Blanche had written that they had two weeks off from classes at Christmas; therefore, she would be home for the holidays. Miney was quite relieved. She had not wanted to face the holidays without her daughter home. Blanche had seldom been home since she started classes in September. She seemed to be having a delightful time from the tone of her letters. She often mentioned Frances Ryan and sometimes she spoke of going some place with George. Miney felt that Blanche was becoming quite enamored with this young man whom she and Millie had not yet met.

When Blanche arrived at the depot in Elsie, she was met not by her parents or brother but by Ollie Bensinger. Somehow, this rankled her. She had only written to Ollie once or twice since going to Detroit. They had been casual letters to a friend, nothing to give the man hopes for anything more than friendship. Why was he here?

Much to her surprise, Ollie had brought a diamond ring and fully expected her to accept it. This irritated Blanche because never once had he suggested marriage. Had he done so, she would certainly have discouraged that line of thinking right from the start. He had been someone to squire her around when she had nothing better to do but he certainly didn't fit the pattern of a prospective husband.

Blanche stared at the ring then looked up at Ollie's face, glowing with expectation. She had better choose her words carefully.

"I'm sorry, Ollie. I can't accept this. There is no way I shall ever come back to Elsie to live. My life is in Detroit now. When I finish school, I'll get a job in Detroit. Coming back here would not work for me." There was no doubting her sincerity.

Ollie's chagrin showed on his face. He expressed his regrets. She supposed she should feel sorry for him but she didn't. He had simply assumed too much. The ride to the farm was rather a quiet one. Neither had anything they wanted to say.

Blanche's thoughts were on a happy, fun-loving Irishman. She wasn't certain George would ever propose since he felt he was responsible for his mother and sisters. However, Frances would soon be through school, and with a decent job, she would assume part of the financial burden. Blanche was in no hurry to be married; however, she certainly was going to have a good time for the next few years and she truly hoped George Ryan would play a prominent part in her life.

As the time drew near for Ralph to leave for Ypsilanti, he wondered how well he would like living away from home. Blanche had always been the one to be gone but except for staying overnight at Sherman's, he had never gone anywhere without a parent. Sure would be different. He could make all his own decisions without Ma there to voice an opinion. Not that Ma was anything like Grandmother but she was one to give her honest thoughts on his activities or his choice of clothes. He thought he just might miss his mother's cooking since she put some really tasty meals on the table for the family.

Ralph wondered if Pa would miss having him around to work. Pa never said anything but Ralph figured his father appreciated what he did to help. He sure hoped Pa would drive Pearl some of the time and that he'd let her run if she was so inclined. She needed to be driven regularly and Rate knew he wouldn't be home often enough to give her the exercise she needed.

Then, there was Bruno. The dog had always liked Pa but Ralph figured Bruno would miss him. Pa had never really paid much attention to the dog. Ma would see that he got enough to eat so that was no problem. Ralph guessed he'd miss having his dog by his bed at night. There'd also be no one to share his cookies or part of his pie. Guess he'd have to come home fairly often just to see his dog.

CHAPTER 4

Ralph moved to Ypsilanti the weekend before his term began at Cleary. He had already made arrangements for his room and board with a young couple, Clint and Grace Reeve on North Adams Street for the sum of $3.50 a week. Their place was only a short distance from Cleary. He had not met Clint but he was favorably impressed with his landlady. She moved with grace even though her girth was more than ample; she seemed to be a jolly sort and Rate liked that.

He dreaded to go down for his first meal because there were other boarders--all of them were girls. However, he was to discover that Grace was a good cook and he could hold his own with teasing girls. Clint was a Linotype operator in a printing office; therefore, he was rarely there for dinner (the midday meal). He always made it home for supper and Ralph welcomed the presence of another man.

On a blustery Monday, Ralph began classes at Cleary. He sat in Mr. P.R. Cleary's office (Originally, he was Patrick Rogers O'Cleary but he had long ago dropped the O and adapted the use of only his initials.) looking at the drawings which decorated Mr. Cleary's wall. They were made with continuous ovals and Rate marveled at the work. The one he liked best was the picture of a horse. Mr. Cleary wrote out Ralph's schedule and gave it to him expressing the hope that he would find his time at Cleary enjoyable.

Ralph did not look at what the man had written until he was in the corridor. My gosh, he'd never seen such awful writing--it could justly be called chicken scratching. He took it to a teacher in the first classroom he found that wasn't full of students. The man deciphered his schedule for him. He also told Rate that Mr.Cleary had once been a beautiful penman, but now he had writer's cramp and

Ralph had seen the results. Mr. Cleary had made the drawings in his office many years ago. Ralph had not known about writer's cramp before and it was hard to believe someone who could make those drawings could no longer write legibly.

Ralph had to take penmanship, even though he thought it a complete waste of his time. After all, he had been writing for years. They had to have a new point for their straight pen every single morning. Mr. Kriegbaum made certain of this. Ralph thought it a needless expense and with his tight finances, he didn't need any additional expense.

Ralph needed a job. He had been looking for almost six weeks when he finally found a job at the Traveler's Cafe just across from the train station. He was to be taught to be a short-order cook. Since he could eat his meals at the restaurant--they were included in his wages--he no longer paid board to his landlady. His room was a dollar fifty.

Ralph tried out for baseball at the college and made the team. He was told that one of the rules the college set forth was their players could not play for any other team for money. The coach assured the players the rule was strictly enforced. Rate didn't figure this would apply to him thus he gave the rule little thought.

It was April Fool's Day and Mrs. Reeve had invited Rate to have supper with them. He figured a good, home-cooked meal would taste pretty good. Restaurant food was all right but there wasn't the variety to which he was accustomed; therefore, he accepted the invitation. He did have some misgivings because he knew his jolly landlady could also be a practical joker.

The whole group sat down as usual. One of the dishes was dumplings. Ralph was the last person to whom the dish was passed. He had seen Clint take something from his mouth that seemed to come from the dumplings; consequently, he did not take any. When the others began to eat, all of them began to extract something from their mouth. They finally figured out what had happened. Grace had stirred bits of cotton batting in the batter for the dumplings. Everyone took the joke good-naturedly but they threatened to get even. Ralph felt a little smug because he had been the only one to miss out on the "treat." He was almost certain this had been why Grace had invited him to the meal. Guess the April Fool's joke had been on her where he was concerned.

The restaurant had been abuzz about the sinking of some ship but Rate had been too busy to pay much attention. Since he worked in the kitchen, he never heard the whole story on much of anything. However, when he returned to his rooming house, Clint gave him the news. The supposedly unsinkable *Titanic* had struck an iceberg in the North Atlantic and had rapidly sunk. The loss of life had been great: 1,513 lives to be exact. The *Titanic* had been on her maiden voyage and while she was indeed a luxury liner, she had not been equipped with a sufficient number of lifeboats. As a result, the women and children were the first to be put into lifeboats, separating families. Stories abounded. Some went so far as to say men were caught disguised as women attempting to win a spot on some lifeboat. It was said that throughout the near hysteria, the band kept playing "Nearer My God to Thee" until the ship finally went under.

Ralph listened to Clint as he told of the disaster. Ralph made a few comments since it seemed to be expected. However, in his room, when he gave it thought, he felt the San Francisco earthquake and fire had been much worse. The Californians had had no choice, whereas those aboard the luxury liner had chosen to be on the ship. He felt compassion for families who had lost loved ones but with his father's fatalistic view, he thought what was done was done. No one could change any of it.

Ralph was contacted by the manager of an independent baseball team. The man asked Ralph if he had ever pitched. Ralph admitted that he had occasionally pitched for his high school team. The manager made him an offer. Pitch for him on Sundays and he would get $5.00 a game. Wow! If Rate gave the college rules any thought it was certainly a fleeting one. Besides, who'd ever know? He readily accepted the offer. The only fly in the ointment was that he had to provide his own uniform. Naturally, he could not wear the one he had been issued from the college. However, he had a friend who might loan him his uniform for Sundays since Royal never played on the Sabbath.

Ralph had played a couple of Sundays. He hadn't done too badly because they had won both games. The last one had been a close one, 3–2. Next Sunday, they were to travel to Belle Isle for a game which would be the furthest they had had to travel thus far.

When the two teams began warm-up, imagine Ralph's surprise when he recognized a kid named Norwood on the other team. Rate didn't know the boy's first name since he was always called Chief because of his American Indian heritage. Chief also played for the Cleary team.

Rate managed to see the young man off to one side. He grinned and said, "I won't say anything if you won't".

Chief grinned back, and said, "Deal."

Neither of them ever spoke of the encounter to anyone. Rate surmised that Norwood needed whatever money he could get. He probably didn't earn as much as Ralph because he was an outfielder but when money was tight, every little bit helped. Once, he had asked to borrow a dime for carfare to his rooming house.

The Cleary team had a catcher who was also a student at the County Normal. However, he came to Cleary to take up typing only because for some unknown reason he wanted to play baseball for Cleary. His last name was Tenny and the players quickly dubbed him Typewriter Tenny. His first year, Cleary beat the Normal but they were not always this lucky.

Some of the fellows often went swimming in the Huron River above the dam. Ralph had gone there with a friend. They swam across the river but on the way back, Rate got a severe cramp in his leg and could no longer swim.

Ralph called out to his friend explaining the situation.

"Ralph, I can't help you. I'm getting pretty tired and figure I'll be lucky to make it myself. I'll get help if I can."

Ralph discovered that he could turn over on his back and float. However, this didn't make the cramp any less severe, and he wasn't certain how long he could float. He tried to look up at the clouds, just anything to take his mind off his predicament. Golly, what was taking Ray so long? Hadn't he been able to make it to the shore? Well, he'd wait a little longer, then he guessed he'd have to try to move toward shore using just his arms. After what seemed an interminable length of time, Ralph thought he could detect the sound of paddles.

"Ralph, we're here," shouted Ray.

There was a canoe rental place on the shore and Ray had come back out in a canoe with a couple of fellows to help. Realizing there was no safe way to get him into the canoe, Ralph turned over and held onto the rear of the craft to enable the young men to tow him to shore.

Golly, he'd heard of swimmers getting cramps and drowning but he hadn't truly believed the stories. Now, he knew cramps could be a very serious matter. He wasn't certain what would have happened if Ray hadn't been able to get help. Once he was on land, he had walked up and down and massaged the calf to work the cramp from his leg. He knew of nothing he could have done to bring relief while he was in the water and he rather doubted if he would have been able to make it to shore using only his arms. Oh well, as Pa was forever saying all's well that ends well.

When Rate came home for the summer, the first person he saw that he knew was Old Sam Packingham tilted back in a chair on the railway station platform. Sam seemed like a permanent fixture around Elsie and Rate chuckled to himself as he greeted the man. Rate remembered how Sam had liked to tease him about the Garrett twins. Sure knew that he was home and nothing much had changed.

While he had been content in Ypsilanti, Ralph was glad to get back to the farm. He was also glad to be with his long-time friends. New friends were fine but he had shared so many experiences with the friends from home and they were just special.

Ralph figured his father hadn't been too good about keeping the buggies clean in his absence. The one he normally used was particularly dirty. Pa had probably used it on a day when there had been rain because it was spattered with mud. Rate decided he would drive back to the river by the Page place. He tied Pearl under the shade of a tree several feet up the river from where he worked washing the buggy. Just before he came to get her, she started pulling, fighting the rope that held her. She had never done this before. Ralph attempted to quiet her and make her stop without success. Finally, being thoroughly disgusted, he took out his jack-knife and as the mare pulled backward her feet braced, tugging with all her might then he cut the rope. The sudden release sent the mare over a six-foot embankment where she landed on her back in the swimming hole. It was the first and last time she ever fought the rope when Rate tied her anywhere.

Ralph played ball for the Elsie Independents. He had had to buy himself a uniform which had cost a whopping $9.00 but he guessed it was worth it. Ed Hawes was hired to take the team to Maple Rapids, St. Johns, Ovid, Laingsburg, and Bannister but when they played at Ithaca, Corunna, or Durand they traveled by train. Ralph enjoyed the camaraderie almost as much as he enjoyed playing the game.

Don Besley, whose father made carriages and light wagons, had been in Rate's grade in school. Don also played with the Elsie Independents. Since he was exceptionally fast, He made an excellent center fielder. He was a small man, short in stature and slim; consequently, he was difficult to pitch which made him a good lead-off man because he often drew a walk. Putting Don on first was as good as putting him on third because he routinely stole bases.

The Independents were playing at Bannister. True to form, Don had drawn a walk and had advanced to third base. Bannister's third baseman was a big fellow named Whitman. He made Don look like a midget. Don had taken a sizable lead off base and when he returned, he somehow stepped on the man's foot. Whitman bristled, feeling Don had done it on purpose. Rate edged over to take his friend's part if Whitman threw a punch. He was close enough to hear what Don had to say as he looked up into the big fellow's face.

"L-l-look. Y-y-you wouldn't hurt me. Y-y-you can't r-r-run fast enough."

Whitman burst out laughing and the tension was broken. Rate heaved a sigh of relief. This was not the first time Don's audacity had gotten him out of trouble and Rate figured it wouldn't be the last time.

Seeley Finch was one of the town's barbers. Rate and Suzie Fry had stopped in the barbershop to chew the rag as Rate explained since they could see he had no one in the chair. While they were talking, Seeley happened to look out the window and spotted a member of the Salvation Army headed for his shop.

"The Salvation Army is on its way. They always expect a donation. Suz, tell them the owner's not here". With those instructions, Seeley disappeared into the back room.

Rate and Suzie looked at each other and gave a knowing grin.

Seeley was right. The woman gave them a little spiel and then asked for a donation, whatever could be spared.

With no hesitation, Suzie stepped over to the cash register and took out a fifty cent piece. "I hope that will help," said Suzie solemnly.

"Thank you for your generosity. The Lord will bless you", said the woman as she left the shop.

She was no more than out the door when Seeley came charging in from the backroom, fairly breathing fire.

"Suz, what in heaven's name is wrong with you? I told you to tell her the owner wasn't here. I sure as heck didn't say for you to give her money! How much of *my* money did you give her?" he demanded.

"Gosh, Seel, I was sure you said to be generous. Rate, didn't you think that's what he meant?"

"Absolutely. Why if we'd known what a cheapskate you were, we'd simply have sent the poor woman on her way. Suz only gave her a measly fifty cents."

Ralph and Suzie could contain their laughter no longer. Seeley glared.

"Fine couple of friends you are," complained Seeley. "Bet you wouldn't have been so generous if it had been *your* money."

Rate had been to town on a Saturday night where he had been at the pool hall with friends. It was after midnight when he started for home. As was his custom, he promptly went to sleep knowing Pearl would take him home. He awoke with a start. Pearl was on a dead run and it was the swaying of the buggy which had aroused him. Rate said nothing, nor did he try to slow her. He felt no danger, and he was curious, wondering what the mare was going to do. After a short time, she slowed, then stopped altogether, listened a moment, and then moved forward at an easy trot. Ralph knew she had heard some horse pull up behind her and since she never wanted any horse to pass her, she had made certain she kept well ahead. Pearl sure was a gem. He guessed he'd never have another horse that smart.

"Pa, did you get Nell bred while I was in Ypsi? I haven't noticed her coming in heat since I've been home."

Nell was a sorrel, and because the mare had had the reputation of being a bad actor, Millie had bought her dirt cheap. At some time, she had reared up and come over backward. This maneuver had broken a bone in her rump giving her a deformed look. Will Fizzell had owned her and since Ab Day was working for Will, he was the one who was supposed to drive her. Ab couldn't handle her. Will's son, Alton, took the mare figuring he could make her behave as she should. No such luck. Alton fared no better than Ab.

Millie bought the mare, and for a time, used a kicking strap over her rump so she couldn't rear up and he checked her uptight. If a horse can't get its head down, it can't kick with its hind feet. When it had come Rate's turn to drive her, he used neither the kicking strap nor the check rein. If he had her on a buggy, he let her run. She was a very good workhorse once her bad habits had been altered.

"Had her bred last month. Art Hawkins came around with his dapple-gray stallion and since the fee was reasonable, thought we'd see what kind of a foal we'd get from her."

Ralph knew that the mare would foal in May of next year. He'd still be in Ypsilanti at that time but he too wondered about the temperament of any foal dropped by her. Nell was a smart one but she also had a stubborn streak and often hated having to do what men expected of her. One always had to be watchful because she took advantage of every opportunity to do as she pleased. Rate had always viewed her as a challenge. Perhaps a foal would have some of her characteristics. Sure would be interesting.

Blanche was coming home for the weekend much to Miney's delight. She had thought by now she would have become accustomed to Blanche being away. However, this did not seem to be the case. She readily admitted that Blanche was usually good about writing but it was hardly the same.

Blanche arrived on Friday evening. Both Miney and Millie had met her train and they had returned to the farm immediately.

Saturday was a beautiful sunny day; therefore, Miney and Blanche drove into town to do some shopping. The day seemed all the brighter to Miney because Blanche was with her. Miney needed to buy some dress material and she needed material for a couple of aprons; it was always nice to have Blanche's opinion on which material to buy. Millie never minded waiting for her while she was buying groceries but became impatient sometimes while she shopped for the other notions like thread, buttons, embroidery floss, crochet cotton, or material for dresses or aprons. He never understood why it should take much time to make the wisest choice of material. Miney felt he tolerated buying groceries because he always had a whopping big appetite but he could never quite understand why these other items were important too. Guess maybe he simply didn't realize that a woman needed to make dresser scarves, pillowcases, as well as dresses, his shirts, and her aprons just for starters.

As luck would have it, Blanche and Miney met Ollie Bensinger on the street. Since she couldn't avoid him, Blanche spoke pleasantly. They talked for a few minutes about inconsequential matters.

Then, Ollie looked serious as he said, "Blanche, Nellie Graham is wearing your ring".

For a moment, Blanche didn't know what to say.

"I'm glad for you Ollie and I hope you and Nellie will be very happy. She will make a good farmer's wife because she is very capable. I was never cut out for farm life--at least not after I had lived and worked in the city."

At this awkward moment, they then parted. Blanche did hope he would be happy. Ollie was all right as a friend but Blanche could in no way imagine herself as the wife of a farmer. Besides, Ollie had never been half as exciting to go with as George Ryan. Somehow, George often made her laugh; his Irish wit was contagious and if she had been the least bit disgruntled over something, he could always make her spirits soar. Thus far, George Ryan was in a class by himself. Besides, she liked his family as well.

Rate had finally achieved his goal with Pearl. After putting her harness on in the barn. He would bring her outside, crack his whip and she would walk on her hind legs to the buggy. He always held the thills up to allow her to walk into position then drop to all fours where he could put the thills in place. Just proved he was right when he had always contended Pearl was as smart as any circus horse.

Ivan Clark liked to play checkers and he often came over in the evening to play a few games with Rate. He wasn't very good as yet but he was still pretty young, only about nine or ten. Not being like his father, Ralph sometimes let the boy win. He figured it just made Ivan try all the harder to win more games.

Millie bought a new spike tooth drag. He intended to put out a small field of wheat and at this time of year when there had been less than the usual amount of rainfall the ground was difficult to break up. The heavy clay turned over in hard lumps. The old-timer's theory that it was best to "dust in your wheat" sure did apply to this year. The field had been gone over with the disk immediately after plowing and then it had been rolled, hoping to break up some of the lumps. After all, wheat needed a good seedbed if it was to do well. Now, Rate was using the disk again while Millie used the new drag.

Millie had left his team unattended while he walked over to where Rate was just making his turn. Rate had no sooner pulled up to see what his father wanted when something spooked Millie's team and being tired of standing they took off across the field. The drag bouncing every which way behind them only served to frighten them more.

"No need of me winding myself trying to catch them", was Millie's observation. When the team finally gave up their run, Millie walked over to them. Both of the horses were fine but the drag hadn't fared as well. There was not a single tooth left in it. Ralph was quick to note this but he wisely said nothing. Would Pa ever learn not to trust a team to stand?

Millie shook his head as he observed the destruction. Then he said, "Don't that beat all?" He made no further comment.

It was getting to be the time of year when field corn had to be cut and shocked and silos filled. It was a busy time for farmers.

Not everyone had a silo, so farmers had to go farther away to find someone to exchange work with or they had to hire someone for the day. Shocking corn after it had been cut was also time-consuming; therefore, Millie often hired extra help during this season.

Millie's brother, John, was down and out which was no surprise to Millie. John's financial status went up and down like a bouncing rubber ball. Since Millie harbored such ill feelings toward Horatio, his brother was once again in his good graces. Perhaps he now understood why their father seemed to bring out the worst in John, mostly because John did not live up to Horatio's expectations. Of course, what good had it done him to try to live his life exactly as his father saw fit? None. Pa had robbed him of that north eighty without giving it a second thought.

Millie felt sorry for his brother's family so he gave John a job. John stayed with Millie all week and went home for the weekends. He owned a forty-acre farm about ten miles north which was in the sand country and wasn't very productive, to begin with. John was not cut out to be a farmer. Millie wasn't certain what John was best fitted to be, he only knew that his brother certainly didn't have an aptitude for farming.

John had a buggy that was so rickety, he often walked beside it instead of riding. Ralph figured his horse was so old and feeble, the buggy was probably all the poor beast could pull. The horse would get down in the barn and could hardly get up. John would grab the poor horse by the tail, hit it with a shillalah, lift the hindquarters and say, "Get up. Get up, or you'll never hear the whippoorwills holler again." With all the exertion it could muster the old horse would be able to stand. Then, John would give the horse a reassuring clap on its rump as though he understood the effort.

Although Ralph chuckled at the words, he found the situation far from funny. Ralph wondered just how long it would be before the horse simply dropped dead. Of course, he marveled that his Uncle John was strong enough to lift the horse's hindquarters. Ralph had always figured Pa was pretty strong but Uncle John was certainly the stronger of the two.

Millie bought a new corn binder. Ralph wondered if his father would have any better luck with this piece of equipment than he had with the drag. The metal seat was fastened to a piece of U-shaped metal that was like a steel spring, and located in the back of the seat were gears and a drive chain. These were all open with no covering to protect them from anything.

The weather had turned quite frosty; consequently, Millie had recently purchased a warm coat for every day. His old one showed plenty of wear and was even patched in several places. He had put on this new coat because there was a stiff wind out of the north and Millie knew that without physical activity it would be mighty cold riding that corn binder.

It was the first time Millie had needed to use the new binder. Millie's 235 pounds depressed the seat much farther than a normal-sized man; therefore, he hadn't made a complete round when his coattail got caught in the drive chain and gears. There was no one around to give him any assistance. The coat had pulled tight so rapidly, by the time he had the team stopped he couldn't unbutton it to get it off and he certainly couldn't drive further. Millie knew he had to get himself out of this predicament. He managed to work his hand into his pocket to get his jackknife. He then proceeded to cut away at the offending coattail. At first, it was hard work because the tightly pulled jacket restricted his movements; however, with each little cut, the work became easier. Finally, he was free. He looked at the ragged portion of the coat which protruded from the gears. Sure had made a mess of his coattails.

First the drag and now the jacket. Ralph thought both incidents were rather humorous but he kept his thoughts to himself and said nothing. Miney was very upset over the coat. It wasn't something she could repair--too much of it had been haggled off. Such a waste of money. Miney never had Millie's fatalistic attitude that what was meant to be, would be and a person was powerless to change it; therefore, she felt the trouble had been caused by Millie's carelessness.

One evening, after supper, John told his brother of a run-in with the law which had him riled. It seemed that a man named Zack Freedom had stolen lumber from the property joining the back of John's forty acres. Trouble was the thieving sneak had hauled it off across John's property. John had been arrested and had been hard-pressed to prove his innocence.

Ralph had listened to his uncle relating the incident to his father. He could understand why Uncle John was so angry. Uncle John may have had faults but Horatio had taught him well; as a result, he was completely honest. It was just that Grandfather's business sense was completely lacking and Uncle John's devil-may care attitude did not help him to get ahead financially. He liked what pleasures life offered but was too carefree to worry about making a good living or worry about tomorrow. He could dance all night but when it came to certain types of work his feet always hurt. Of course, Aunt Grace had never seemed to mind their lifestyle.

Since Millie hadn't needed John for a few days, he hired out Naegles to fill the silo. John was dumbfounded when he saw Zack Freedom was there, also hired by Naegles. To make matters worse, both men were to stay the night and they were expected to sleep together.

John told Mr. Naegle, "If I have to sleep with that son-of-a-gun, I'm gonna cut his throat".

They gave John another bed.

John related the incident to Millie and Millie understood how his brother felt. It was bad enough that John had to work with Zack. It was a wonder John hadn't punched Zack out. Millie was certain his brother could have dropped the man with one well-aimed blow. Maybe John had, at last, learned to control his temper.

CHAPTER 5

Wilson Brewbaker came to ask Ralph to help fill the Silo. He also hired Don Sherman. In the morning they were due at the Brewbaker farm, Ralph drove. When they turned into the Brewbaker driveway, Wilson's daughter Edith was out sweeping off the sidewalk at the back of the house.

Don said, "I'm going to make a date with her".

Rate gave a chuckle, tossed the lines to Don and jumped out of the buggy. By the time Don had taken care of the horse and carriage, Ralph had already asked Edith for a date. He was to pick her up for church on the coming Sunday. Taking the young woman to the church was an established and appropriate place to go on a first date.

Edith was in seventh heaven and she was properly impressed that Ralph had asked her to attend her church. Just showed how well brought up he was. While she had only spoken with Ralph a few times, Vern talked of him so often she truly felt as though she knew him.

Of course, she had never allowed herself to believe he might ask her out. Edith knew she was very plain looking and she had been so ill, the doctors thought it might have been infantile paralysis. She had been forced to wear a lift on her right shoe. Still, she did have a small, eighteen-inch waist, and she had lovely, thick dark hair. She wore glasses and she felt this certainly did nothing to enhance her looks. However, she felt being asked out by Ralph Setterington was near a miracle. She was at once ecstatic about the coming Sunday and yet apprehensive. Would Ralph truly like her? She certainly hoped so.

That first date had been even more satisfying than Edith had ever imagined. She had felt extremely proud to have Ralph by her side, knowing there were those in the congregation who were quite dumbfounded that Edith Brewbaker was being accompanied by a young gentleman. And gentleman, Ralph was. Seemingly without thought, he made all the gentlemanly moves that some men never seemed to acquire.

After church, Ralph had dinner with the Brewbaker family. This was also an accepted way for the woman's family to get to know the young man. The Brewbakers treated him as though this was a common occurrence. Ralph was to discover that Alice Brewbaker was indeed a mighty fine cook. He didn't fail to notice how Elzie ate very little and only soft food painstakingly prepared by his mother. Ralph remembered that as a child, Elzie had taken a sip of lye, thinking it was cider and as a result had always had trouble eating.

After dinner, Ralph and Edith went for a drive. Ralph told her that he had spent part of the year attending Cleary and would return for classes the first of the year. He didn't mention what his plans were, if indeed he had any for when he finished school. Edith didn't feel that she should be so forward as to ask. Perhaps when she knew him better, she would feel they could discuss what he expected from life. As it was, she felt from what Vern had said Ralph enjoyed farming. Seemed odd that he was attending business school.

Most of the men Edith knew did not have schooling beyond the eighth grade. Cousin Lee Brewbaker was attending the University of Michigan but the family and others had hinted this was because Lee was lazy, and didn't want to soil his hands with honest work and they laughed behind his back. Of course, Edith felt this was an unfair assessment. Lee was her favorite cousin and she would have approved of whatever he wanted to do. Besides, Lee liked literature and poetry. Edith could certainly understand this since she liked literature and she found poetry, beautiful. She had always found it easy to understand. Why their examination when they had completed the eighth grade had covered all the chapters of Longfellow's *Hiawatha*. She had liked the work so much that she could quote many lines throughout the book. Sometimes, Edith wrote a verse or two, she found writing in rhyme and meter was easy if she put her mind to it.

Ralph made arrangements to see Edith the following Sunday. This time, they would go to the Baptist Church in Elsie, the one Miney attended and the one Ralph had been brought up to attend, although, since his sixteenth birthday, his attendance had been sporadic at best. Edith was a little apprehensive. She just knew that the Setteringtons dressed better than the Brewbakers. She could tell that Ralph's suit was of far better material than her father or brothers. Since she had not met Miney, she wondered how much better Miney's dress would be than hers. Well, she guessed it didn't matter. Her dress was always well-pressed and neat; the cost of the material was irrelevant, Edith told herself.

A few days after Millie had had the silo filled, he complained that he hurt around his waist where the band of his trousers came even though they were held up by suspenders. A couple of days later, the pain was so great, he could scarcely move, and when tiny blisters put in an appearance, Miney said it was high time he went to the doctor. Even though he seldom saw a doctor, rarely took any kind of medicine, and prided himself on always being "fit as a fiddle", for once Millie did not object. He always bragged that he had never had a headache although he sometimes admitted his head hurt. Rate figured to anyone else it was a headache but his father never took any aspirin to make the pain go away. Therefore, rate figured his father must be in more pain than anyone had realized since he was willing to see a doctor.

The diagnosis was shingles. There wasn't a lot the doctor could do. He said they did not know what caused the inflammation. It had to run its course; with some, it was a matter of days, with others a matter of weeks and in rare instances, it was months before all the pain was gone.

Millie, it turned out, was one who had to tolerate the disease for several weeks. Since the chores were more than one person could handle, Herb Putman was hired to do the milking while Rate took care of the horses, hogs, and sheep.

This was a trying time for Miney. Millie did not like the forced inactivity and there were times when the pain was so intense he could hardly tolerate even his clothing touching the affected area. Miney knew when he was short with her it was the pain speaking. She felt helpless.

Miney found Millie to be even more uncommunicative than usual. This was especially difficult for her since he was in the house the entire day. He hurt too much to walk more than was absolutely necessary. The first couple of weeks were the worst but it seemed to Miney that Millie was never going to get back to normal. It was so odd. Millie had never really been sick since they were married. She felt she was sometimes not as understanding as she should be but this was because she knew of no way to help him through this trying period. Each night she asked God to give her the strength to meet her obligations with as little resentment as possible.

Ralph decided he needed a new winter overcoat. He fully intended to buy one but without the presence of his mother. Instead of going to Owosso, as the family usually did, he intended to go to St. Johns to Clark & Hulse. They were related to the Brewbakers and Edith had told him they carried a very good line of men's clothing and were reasonable in their prices. After all, he'd be nineteen in a short time, plenty old enough to choose his own clothing without his mother tagging along to give her opinion.

He had gone south to the Colony then over to the State Road and into St. Johns. He told the clerk what he wanted. The man measured Rate's chest, then brought out a coat. The sleeves were a little short. However, the next coat fit perfectly. Ralph hadn't even asked the price, simply said he'd take it. Ma would certainly have asked whether or not they had something cheaper. Rate simply wanted a coat of good quality that fit, he didn't care about the price or color.

On the way home, he was sort of daydreaming, letting the horse pick its way. He had gone east from St. Johns intending to go to Elsie before he went home. The road was really rough, ruts cut several inches deep in portions of the surface. Suddenly, before Rate realized what was happening the horse jumped the shallow ditch; the buggy tilted ominously then righted itself as the horse kept going but now they were on smooth land by the fence. Luckily the level portion was of ample width to accommodate the buggy. Rate figured the horse wasn't as dumb as he'd thought at first. Anything was smoother than the ruts in the road. All he had to worry about now was finding a place where it would be easy to return to the road.

Some of the merchants in Elsie banded together to hold a raffle with a goose as the prize. As it turned out, a man by the name of Jack Pierce won the bird. Don Sherman, George Lawrence, Suzie Fry, and Ralph decided to sort of borrow the goose not to keep permanently but just long enough to cause a little excitement around the village. Trouble was that Jack had a watch dog tied up outside in the yard. But as luck would have it the dog knew who George was since he delivered groceries to the Pierce's home.

"Hey George, since the dog knows you, he more than likely won't bother you like he would the rest of us," said Don, showing a mischievous grin.

George scowled as he contemplated his companions. He was slightly taller than Ralph but heavier by ten or fifteen pounds.

"What you're sayin' is you want me to do the dirty work." George couldn't deny the fact that the dog was accustomed to having him come there. He simply wanted them to know that the idea did not appeal to him.

"Not at all, George. The rest of us will be waiting for you just across the street," explained Suzie.

"What's the matter, George? It's a simple task," laughed Ralph.

The boys finally agreed.

All went well. The dog never barked and they made off with the goose who didn't seem to mind being carried. George said the goose had hissed a couple of times initially but when held has remained quiet.

"What are we going to do with it?" asked Don. "We never got that far in our planning."

"We need to put it somewhere where it's not gonna get loose and runoff," said Suzie. "You have any ideas, Rate?"

All eyes turned to Ralph. He thought a moment, then a smile spread across his face as he looked from one companion to another.

"What about Seel Finch's barbershop? Seeley would sure know where the goose came from. He might even have a good idea how it got from Pierce's to his shop but he wouldn't say anything. It would be easy to see that the goose was well-fed in his back room."

They all thought this was a terrific idea. If anyone discovered the goose, Seeley would have to explain how the goose got in his shop. He'd undoubtedly have to do some fast-talking but they figured Seeley would rise to the occasion.

Later the next day, one by one, the group stopped by to chat a short time with Seeley. No mention was made of any goose. The boys were completely baffled and collectively, they wondered what had happened to the darned goose.

"Sure we got the door closed tight?" asked Don.

"Checked it myself", said Rate.

"If Seel thought it was us, would he keep quiet just to get our goat?" asked a puzzled George.

"Naw. He'd do a little yellin', berating us for tryin' to cause him trouble. Even though he'd not squeal on us, he'd sure as heck let us know he was on to us" said Suzie. Rate and Don nodded in agreement.

The boys were not only perplexed but they felt guilty. They knew the goose had been slated for thanksgiving dinner and thanksgiving was only a couple of days away. Jack had made it known that his goose had disappeared but other than that, no one seemed to know anything about the theft. The boys were considering pooling their money to buy a replacement. This prank sure hadn't turned out as they had expected. The best-laid plans of mice and men thought Ralph. Sure as heck applied here. No use to worry about what had gone wrong now.

The morning before Thanksgiving, the goose was discovered tied to a tree in Jack's front yard, honking his displeasure at being restrained. Now, the boys were more perplexed than ever.

All four were together when they ran into Ernie Buehl who was several years older.

"You boys hear about Jack Pierce's goose? Said it was tied in his yard this morning. Isn't that surprising?"

The boys eyed him suspiciously. That smirk on his face certainly was there for a reason. Besides, how'd he known so much so soon?

"Ernie, you know more than you're lettin' on." Accused Rate.

Finally, after a little prodding, Ernie admitted that he had seen them take the goose, so he had followed them. He put the goose in an empty corn crib where he saw that it was properly fed for the couple of days he had it. He had planned all along to return the goose but he had wanted the boys to stew a little first. He chuckled to himself at the thought of being able to pull off a prank on the boys.

John had returned to Millie's to husk out the corn in the south field which had been cut and shocked long ago. Ralph wasn't sure why his father did this because, in other years, he had had the cornhusker set up in the yard. Rate sort of suspicioned it was because Uncle John needed the money and he figured his father was a soft touch sometimes even though he would be quick to deny it.

John husked from one shock at a time. A shock was made up of several bundles that had been dropped from the corn binder. He tossed the golden ears in a pile by each shock. It was Ralph's job to pick up the piles to transport the corn to the corn crib.

When Rate had shoveled off his last load for the day, he put the team in the barn and came to the house expecting supper to be nearly ready.

John was sitting by the kitchen stove but there was no sign of Miney and it was obvious that no supper had been started. Rate saw that the fire was low and John had done nothing to change that because when Ralph looked in the firebox, there were only a few coals there. Rate knew his father would arrive shortly since it was almost six o'clock and since Ma always had their meals on time, he wondered what had happened that she did not have the meal nearly ready.

"Where's Ma?" asked Ralph.

"Guess she's gone to a bee. Saw her run down the road a while back", replied John who is completely unconcerned.

This didn't tell him much except that Ma had gone toward Petersons. Rate figured he'd better rustle up some food. Uncle John had an appetite as big or bigger than his father. Sure seemed odd that Ma hadn't said anything to anyone. At least with dry wood, the fire was beginning to burn well. Ralph looked in the cupboard and in the safe in the cellar to find what he could get that would cook in a hurry. He didn't expect any help from his uncle or his father. At least there was plenty of bread to slice and they'd make do with the eggs and bacon he'd found. It wouldn't take him long to have a meal ready. He even found a pie for dessert.

Ralph was to learn later that his mother had indeed gone down the road to Petersons. It was the fourth of December and Ada had given birth to a daughter whom they named Thelma.

Ralph continued to see Edith often. She was beginning to dread the time when he had to return to Ypsilanti. She just knew that it would be out of sight, out of mind. She often thought about how different their lives had been. Not only had Ralph gone to Detroit frequently but he had also been as far away as Chicago. He had been up north to Big Rapids and even to Traverse City and to many other small towns in the State of Michigan.

Edith's travel had been very limited. Her folks had taken her to Grand Rapids once and she had been to Lansing since the interurban had been in operation. They had relatives living there and her folks looked upon relatives as important. She had never eaten in a restaurant because the people they visited provided their meals. Of course, they went several times a year to St. Johns, occasionally to Elsie and regularly to Eureka. Edith had never been to a theater to see a stage play. Ralph had seen numerous plays including *Ben Hur* in Chicago. Since she knew the plot of *Ben Hur* she could not readily imagine what that must have been like seeing it on stage. How wonderful it must have been.

It truly amazed Edith that one so worldly could be interested in her. Maybe he wasn't really interested, only needed a diversion for the balance of the year, the time before he returned to Ypsilanti. It was a dismal thought but she felt it was a distinct possibility. Edith fretted over this but she said nothing to anyone. She did not want anyone to know her true feelings. She enjoyed each outing with Ralph even though the weather was not always the best. The weather was cold as expected and there had been some snow. She supposed it would not be long before the buggies were put away in favor of cutters. Ralph always saw that she was amply covered with a heavy blanket and even a horsehide robe. Sometimes, when the weather was really raw, there was warm soapstone for her feet. She appreciated his thoughtfulness.

The weekend before Rate was to leave for Ypsilanti, he asked Edith if she would wait for him. Edith wasn't certain whether or not this was a proposal of marriage but she readily said she would. She asked no questions, afraid of the answer. Ralph promised to write and he asked her if she would write to him. This did much to bolster Edith's spirits. Perhaps Ralph did care. She fervently hoped so since she now realized she had fallen hopelessly in love with him. She hoped she hadn't assumed too much. She could think of nothing more wonderful than for Ralph to have meant that he was indeed serious about her.

It was Edith's and Ralph's last evening together. They had not been out very late since Ralph was to take an early train on the morrow. Mrs. Brewbaker had set out lunch for them before she retired. There was a piece of cold chicken, one of Edith's mother's rolls with butter and honey, and a piece of apple pie. Edith didn't feel particularly hungry but Ralph seemed to enjoy the food. Must be the cold air gave him an appetite. Edith was glad one of them was enjoying the fruits of her mother's labor; Edith believed the lunch was a way of saying "thank you" for an enjoyable evening and she could hardly blame Ralph for her mental state.

Edith had given Ralph a small picture of herself but Ralph had left the picture still on the table where they had eaten their lunch. Since Ralph hadn't taken the picture, she assumed he hadn't cared enough to want it. Then, why had he asked her to wait for him? She was near tears when she went up the open staircase to the bedroom she shared with her sister, Edna.

Imagine Edith's surprise when she received a card from Ralph, dated the fourth of January, apologizing for forgetting the picture and asking her to send it to him at the restaurant. Once more, her world righted itself and she felt he did care.

Ralph and Edith corresponded regularly for the most part. There were letters and cards, most of it were rather impersonal. While Edith sometimes hoped for more, she told herself that she was fortunate because Ralph wrote it all. From the tone of his letters and cards, he was busy. He was taking an advanced course in what he called double entry bookkeeping, for every debit there had to be an equal and opposite credit. Edith was not certain what all this meant, she just knew that it was a time consuming course.

Thus far, Ralph hadn't mentioned coming home for a weekend. Before he left, he had indicated he would come home more often than he had last year. He had remarked rather casually, "I have more reason to come home this year." Edith had not known whether or not to take him seriously. She had learned early that Ralph liked to tease. Of course, she was accustomed to being teased; her brother, Art, was a great hand to tease as was Vern and Carl. Garth was following their lead now that he was older. However, her brother's expressions usually were a dead give-away whereas Ralph always had a completely wide-eyed, innocent look.

* * * * * * * * *

There had always been a good-natured rivalry between the Normal and Cleary. Groups from each institution often played pranks on their counterparts but most of the deviltry came under the classification of good, clean fun. No one from either school set out to harm anyone or damage property. There had been plenty of snow of late and Ralph knew a bunch of students from the Normal had been using the steep hill by Cleary as though it was their private hill for sliding. He felt that sooner or later some of the Cleary boys would do something to show the Normal students they were operating on turf controlled by Cleary.

Rate came out of the building where he had had his last class for the day. To his surprise he found a toboggan unattended leaning against the wall of the building. With a chuckle, Ralph jumped on the toboggan and had a glorious ride to the Masonic Building which was almost a mile away. Once he stopped, he stood the toboggan up against the building in plain view. He did not doubt that its owner in all probability a Normal student would be along shortly to claim his property. Ralph also knew that the owner would quite likely be accompanied by several companions, none of whom would feel any too friendly toward the person or persons who had made off with the toboggan. The thought of perhaps being stuck head first in a snowbank had little appeal; therefore he lost no time in leaving the scene.

Winter had been colder than usual but with the arrival of February, the weather moderated. They had had little snow for the past month. Ralph decided he would go home for the weekend. He had not been home for six weeks. Although Edith had not complained in so many words, he could often read between the lines and knew she was keenly disappointed.

Rate came home on a Friday evening in the middle of February. He advised Edith and had set a time when he expected to call on her. While she had seemed glad to see him, he wondered just how much she had missed him. He had no way of knowing that Edith felt if she showed her true feelings, her conduct would be much too forward. After all, nice girls did not throw themselves at a man.

In spite of the late hour Ralph had kept on Friday night, he was up early to give Millie a hand with chores. He decided that since he was not seeing Edith until the afternoon, he would go skating on the millpond. He hadn't skated much last winter, and thus far, he had not been skating this season.

There were not many skaters as yet. Ralph strapped on his skates and took off. Sure felt good. He decided to skate upriver a ways. He knew he couldn't go too far because his ankles would tire easily, something he hadn't considered earlier. He stopped to talk with an ice fisherman, went a little further, then decided he had better head back before his ankles gave out entirely.

He was just coming onto the millpond from the channel when his skate runner caught on one of the leather thongs which held his skate in place but had become loosened. Down he went, head first, sliding on his belly and outstretched hands. He cussed a little under his breath while he retied the thong. When he reached the edge of the millpond by the road, a group of young boys was just coming onto the ice. All except one had a pair of skates dangling over their shoulders.

Rate quickly removed his skates, walked over to the skateless boy, and said, "Here, kid. Here's a pair of skates, a little used, but still in pretty good shape. I don't need them any more."

The kid's face lit up like a Roman candle as he stammered his thanks. Rate hoped the kid would get as much enjoyment from the skates as he had.

When Edith received a card from Ralph the very first part of the following week, she felt he must have enjoyed the time spent with her. He even made mention of her lack of sleep. Well, he had stayed later than usual Saturday night; however, it seemed their time together had been far too short. Still, she was glad he had come home, and she figured she had better count her blessings.

A few days later, on the twenty-first of February, to be exact, her sister, Gladys, gave birth to a son. Gladys said she had never realized just how painful giving birth could be. Edith thought Gladys was exaggerating because they all knew how Pa had always coddled her. However, a few days later, it was evident that Gladys was not regaining her strength; in fact, she seemed to be going downhill. Edith knew her mother, Alice, was very concerned. Then, the doctor took Alice aside and said, "There is something definitely wrong, and if I can't find the cause, Gladys is going to slip away from us."

Edith and her mother stayed the rest of the afternoon because Alice was so concerned about Gladys. When it came time for Gladys to nurse the baby, tears ran down her cheeks although she said nothing. Alice asked her why she cried and Gladys admitted that it hurt so much, she could hardly tolerate the pain.

The next morning, Alice informed the doctor. Gladys never nursed Gordon again. She had an infection in her breasts and it was several days before the doctor declared her out of danger and on the road to recovery. Her husband, Don, was upset with the woman who had been taking care of her. Gladys had told her of the pain when Gordon nursed but the woman had thought Gladys was simply making up a story to gain sympathy; therefore, neither she nor Gladys had mentioned this to the doctor. The lady felt the pain was just something Gladys had to endure. She didn't realize her silence had almost cost Gladys her life.

Another month passed, and Ralph made no mention of coming home. Then, Edith received a card telling her he had no time to write more because he had to press a suit and his overcoat. He was going to Detroit for the weekend. He failed to mention whether or not he was going to visit his sister. For a moment, Edith wondered if he was going to see another woman.

Then, she felt this was a ridiculous thought because if that was the case, he certainly would not have told her of his plans.

Edith chuckled at the thought of him pressing his own clothes. Goodness, she didn't think any of her brothers were that capable. Of course, none of them had lived away from home. Vern had moved out when he and Blanche were married. The other five were still at home where they expected their mother or sisters to do such work. Gladys had married in 1910 which left Edith and Edna. Since Edith was older, this usually meant such a task fell on her. She didn't mind. Nevertheless, she would like to have been a mouse in a corner to watch Ralph.

Shortly after this, Edith received a letter that at first hurt her feelings, then made her angry. Ralph had written: Absence makes the heart grow fonder--fonder of another person. Had he found someone he liked better? Then she thought of what a tease he was and decided teasing was what he was doing. Wait until he came home. Two could play this game.

CHAPTER 6

Ralph had moved the first of May. His landlady had moved from Adams Street to Florence which was actually nearer to the Normal than it was to Cleary but Ralph had decided there was no need for him to look for other accommodations. He liked Grace and Clint, and he knew they liked having him as a roomer.

Rate was at baseball practice. It seemed as though his shoulder was a little stiff. He remembered that it had been tight after practice yesterday. He took the mound and threw a few pitches to Typewriter Tenny. One of the students stepped up to the plate. Rate tried a curveball but it didn't break as it should; his fastball wasn't any better. With each throw, his shoulder felt worse. Finally, he walked over to the coach and explained why he was doing such a poor job. Since their season was just beginning, Ralph thought he might better quit and give someone else a chance to play. The coach was understanding and wished him well.

Once again Ralph dropped a card to Edith explaining that he didn't have time to write because he was going to Detroit for the weekend. Edith felt he certainly had made plans with his sister and quite likely the man she was dating but Edith wondered if there was another woman to make a foursome. She knew that Ralph and his sister enjoyed going places together because he sometimes mentioned that Blanche had come to Ypsilanti to visit on a weekend.

True to her promise, Ralph received a letter from Miney informing him that Nell had dropped her foal, a colt. Millie had named the little rascal Buster. He was a strawberry roan, a color one did not often see around Elsie. Seemed rather odd since Nell was a sorrel, and his sire was a dapple gray. Ralph could hardly wait to get the time to go home to see the colt. He had always liked horses, and he was curious as to what kind of a colt Nell had produced. Rate wondered if the little fellow would be as stubborn as his Ma.

Ralph hadn't decided whether he should go home for Decoration Day or not. He had half expected that Blanche was going to visit but then he had a card from her saying she wasn't coming until the following weekend. From what she said, she had been having a mighty fine time. Not only did she spend time with Frances Ryan, Addie Pulford, and Nettie Daugherty but she also seemed to be keeping pretty steady company with George Ryan. Ralph had met him and found him likable. Certainly was a far better choice, in his opinion than Ollie Bensinger. George was a good conversationalist. They could always find some topic of interest to both to discuss. Of course, it was George's sense of humor that Rate really appreciated. George liked to tease as well as the next person. Rate wondered if at last, his sister was serious about a man. Sure seemed likely.

Ralph went home since they did not have classes on Decoration Day. It was late Thursday evening when his train got in, a little behind schedule as often was the case. He decided it was too late to visit Edith. He had not told her he would be home, he hoped she hadn't already made plans for the weekend. However, from what Vern said, Edith was a homebody and seldom went anywhere except to visit family members or to some club meeting with a group. He guessed she had never really had a beau which was fine with him.

Ralph went to the Decoration Day parade. There were only a handful of Civil War veterans this year. He could remember when he was very young there would be thirty or forty of them. He remembered Andrew Call who had died in 1900 but Rate had always looked for him as wel as Charley Dodge and Charley Clement. There were only a few Spanish American veterans. He guessed in a few years there wouldn't be any veterans to march. Perhaps there would no longer be a Decoration Day celebration.

Rate had been glad to see Nell's foal. At this time, the colt looked to be all legs. He had a well-shaped head, dainty ears, and a wary look in his eye as though he had not made up his mind if he could trust these humans. Rate thought there was a look of intelligence in the way the colt eyed him. Sure was a good looking little fellow. He had a deep body and a broad chest so he should develop into a sound workhorse. Pa was lucky Nell had produced such a fine colt.

Ralph figured his luck was good because he found Edith at home. She told him she probably wouldn't be writing for several days because she was going to Lansing for a week or so to visit her cousin, Carrie Crawford. She told him that Carrie was a very interesting person. She had lived in Grand Rapics for a time and had visited Ludington, Muskegon, and other places on the west side of the state. She had also taken trips to Canada and had gone as far away as Syracuse, New York. It was not difficult to understand that Edith was slightly envious of her cousin and yet Rate realized Edith would never have had the courage to have lived and traveled on her own. In many ways, she was shy and very unsure of herself. Perhaps that was what he liked about her; she needed someone to take care of her.

* * * * * * * * *

Since Ralph was going swimming, he decided to take the landlady's coach dog (Dalmatian) along. The dog would have followed Ralph anywhere. Several young men had met to swim up the river to the railroad bridge which was a mile away. The dog was having a high old time swimming in circles, going first by one person, then another.

After a time, one of the fellows noticed the dog was slowing down. "Ralph, I think that dog has worn himself out. He never gonna make it."

Within moments of this remark, the dog came alongside Ralph for a few minutes then with an effort jumped on Ralph's back. The suddenness of the added weight momentarily drove Rate under but with a solid kick and stroke he resurfaced with the dog laying crosswise his back. "Claude, you darned fool. I'm not going to give you a ride to the bridge. If you hadn't been so stupid, you could have made it on your own."

With a shout to his friends, Rate headed for the river bank. When the dog realized they were nearing the bank, he jumped off Ralph's back, swam to the bank, and climbed out on dry land where he immediately shook himself. Ralph didn't want the dog to get lost so he gave up his swim for the day. Crazy dog. See if he'd take the dog the next time he went somewhere.

Edith had a letter from Ralph explaining that the reason he hadn't written was that he had been sick. He didn't say what had been wrong but told her he had missed over two weeks of school which he had to make up at the end of the term. He assured her he was feeling better but still could not eat much. She had been expecting him home at the end of June, but now it seemed that it would be the middle of July or later since the school always had a few days off for the Fourth. She was greatly disappointed.

Ralph was feeling much better, so that he decided he would go swimming; however, he had not realized how quickly he would tire.

His illness had sapped his strength much more than he realized; consequently, he hadn't stayed in the water as long as he would have liked. On the way back to the rooming house, he stopped his bicycle on a bridge over the river to rest a few moments. He looked down through the crystal clear water to the riverbed. What was that floating on the water? Certainly didn't look like any seaweed. Golly, it looked like the long hair of a woman. He tried to look from a different spot on the bridge and thought perhaps he could see the outline of a body partially hidden from this angle by a rock. He guessed he'd better tell someone. He looked around. Since there was a mill only a short distance away, he decided to ride over there. He advised the first man he saw of what he had discovered. The man promptly called the police who requested that Ralph remain where he was until they arrived. They needed to have someone show them the exact spot where he suspected there might be a body.

When Ralph showed the two officers where he had seen the floating hair, they went down the embankment to the river bank where they found a fully clothed, slightly built, elderly woman whose long hair had come loose from her braid and flowed out onto the water. She had a rope tied around her waist, the other end was fastened securely to a tree on the bank.

One of the officers thought he recognized her as a sort of recluse who was known to show signs of insanity. Some of her neighbors were afraid of her although she had never done anyone any harm. The officers theorized she had used the rope to keep her body from being carried down the river when she intentionally drowned herself. Ralph thought that while they might think she was crazy, he figured she had certainly known what she was doing when she committed suicide. Didn't seem like a crazy person would have had that much forethought.

Ralph was undecided about his future. His course at Cleary would be finished in the middle of July. He had already had an interview with Standard Oil Company and with Michigan Central Railroad. Both had offered him a position, and both offered him a starting salary of $15.00 a week. After a time, there was some likelihood of advancement. However, both job opportunities were in Detroit where rent and just about everything else was higher than in Ypsi. Rate figured that after board and room, laundry, and the clothes needed to work in an office, he wouldn't have much left. At least not enough to entice him to live in Detroit.

Consequently, after careful consideration, he came back to Elsie to the farm, still undecided about where his life should go. He knew there were plenty of times when his father could use his help but he knew he should find a job to give him a steady income. If he was ever to begin farming for himself, he would need money for livestock and machinery. He was certain he could find someone with fields to let if he had the means to put in a crop. He figured Pa would quite likely loan him a piece of machinery now and then but he needed a good team of workhorses to make any sort of a start. Well, as Pa always said, take one step at a time.

Ralph had been home only a matter of days when his mother asked him if he would drive her to the funeral of Ralph Boone's mother. The family had moved away from Elsie several years ago and Rate had not been bit sorry to see them leave. However, Mrs. Boone's body had been returned to Elsie for burial.

Rate sat beside his mother only half-listening to the words of the preacher. From where they sat, he could see Ralph Boone's profile. Rate recalled the promise he had made that someday he'd be big enough to pay Boone back for shoving him down the stairs at school when he had been on crutches. Rate had a little half-smile for a moment as he thought, Boone, I think we're of a size now. I'll bet I could take you easy, only I guess now is not the time nor the place. At least Brownie and I gave you the drubbing you deserved but I'd sure like to do it on my own. Oh well, some things were just not meant to be.

Even though Rate no longer attended Sunday School and did not attend Church regularly, the minister had asked him if he would play on the Sunday School baseball team. They played only a few games and since they needed a few more players it did not matter that Ralph no longer attended because after all he was still considered a member. Ralph was happy to play ball anytime, anywhere. He already had a suit from last year which was still in excellent condition. He had bought one that was just a trifle large in the event he grew a little even though that was unlikely at his age.

The Sunday School Class was to play at Mccurdy Park in Corunna on the Fourth of July. Millie told Rate he could only go if he got his cultivating done. Even at nineteen, Millie still felt there were areas where he could regulate what his son could or could not do. Playing baseball did not have a high priority in Millie's world.

Ralph managed to get his work done; therefore, he left Elsie with the Baptist team. The game was a tight one. Both pitchers had been doing an excellent job. The hits had been sporadic and the score was tied, 1 to 1. Rate had had only one hit and that had come with no one on base. It was now the last of the ninth.

Rate was playing center field. The count on the batter had reached full count: three balls, two strikes. The windup, the pitch, and the crack of the bat. Rate knew from the sound it was a well-hit ball. He started to run. With luck, the ball would drop in front of the fence at the back of the field. However, luck deserted Ralph's team. The ball sailed a considerable distance over the fence. Ralph could see it but there was no way he could scale the fence in time. The home team had won by 2 to 1. Rate simply walked off the field. Let someone else risk tearing his uniform climbing over the fence. The ball belonged to the other team; therefore, he told himself it was no skin off his nose if they couldn't find it.

Rate looked around Elsie for a job. Because of his experience in the restaurant in Ypsilanti, he found employment at Johnson's Restaurant for the wage of $15.00 a week, seemed to him this was the amount everyone offered but at least here his meals were included. However, the hours were longer than what they would have been working as a bookkeeper. He sometimes opened the restaurant at 5:00 in the morning and some days he was there when it closed at 8:00 in the evening. He often had an hour or so for dinner, but he still put in ten to twelve hours a day. On Saturdays, the restaurant was open from 5:00 a.m. until 2:00 a.m. Sunday morning. He had every other Saturday evening off, and because the restaurant was closed during the day on Sundays, he had Sundays to himself.

At least by living at home, the money he made was pure profit. He could still help his father by transporting grain to the mill to be ground for feed for the hogs or milch cows, and he could do field work on his free Saturdays. The long hours cut down on his social life since after 8:00 was not a proper time for a young man to come calling. However, he could see Edith on Sundays, and on his Saturday off, they could go some place for entertainment.

Rate had been disappointed because Millie had sold Pearl to the Army just before he came home from Ypsilanti. Pa figured $150.00 was a good price for her since she was getting on in years. Still, Rate missed Pearl. He'd always thought of her as belonging to him. Now, he mostly drove Dory who didn't have a brain in her head although she was a good looker. He guessed what bothered him the most was that Pa had never asked his opinion about selling Pearl, simply had sold her and let Ralph learn of her sale after he came home. Had he had the chance, he would have worked to pay Pa for the mare. Course Pa would have had to give him time, and he supposed Pa felt the entire $150 in his hand was better than his son paying him in weekly installments. Still, it kind of rankled. Seemed that in some ways Pa took after Grandfather. Business came first and to heck with a person's feelings.

Blanche came home for a visit. She had finished her schooling and was now working for the Michigan Machine Company. She hadn't told Ralph what wage she was getting, and he didn't ask figuring that if she wanted him to know, she would have told him.

However, he did get a kick out of hearing her describe some of her experiences while on the job. She had been there only a few days when she was called to take dictation from the boss' son who was a brash young man probably no more than two or three years older than herself.

"Well," said Blanche, "I was settled with my pad ready whenever he was ready. When he began dictating, he took off like a house afire. There was no way I could have kept up with him. He must have been going over 200 words a minute. I just sat back in my chair, and when he came up for air, I said firmly, "When you can dictate at a sensible rate of speed, I'll take dictation. Otherwise, I won't. And I looked him straight in the eye. After what seemed like an eternity, he laughed and started over. Since then, we've been getting along just fine."

Ralph could just imagine his sister asserting herself. Those brown eyes wouldn't have wavered one iota. Blanche could take care of herself, that much was certain. Perhaps she did have something of Grandmother in her.

Millie had nodded in silent agreement as though nothing else was to be expected of his daughter. After all, she was a Setterington to the core.

Miney was the one who found the situation difficult to accept. All she could think of was that Blanche had shown those characteristics which certainly came from Mother Setterington. Miney knew that she would never have had the backbone to stand up against a young man especially when that young man was the son of the owner. It was at moments like this that Miney was at a complete loss to understand her daughter. Of course, the whole episode had turned out well, and Miney was truly proud of her daughter's capabilities even if a huge chunk seemed to have come from Lovina. At least Blanche had not inherited Lovina's propensity for interfering in other people's lives. Miney felt truly grateful for that.

Sometimes, Ralph could spend time with Edith when she stayed with Vern and his family. He could stop in there for a short time on his way home from work. He was never certain if Edith visited often because this gave her a chance to see him or whether it was because she thought so much of her nephews. One thing was certain, Edith dearly loved children.

Edith had told Ralph that if either of Vern's boys were sick, Vern always came to get her. He always said Blanche felt better with her there. However, Wilson could be quite a problem and had been even before he was a toddler. He hated to take medicine of any kind because he said it tasted awful. Of course, he was right about the taste. Anyway, he would simply refuse to open his mouth no matter if they cajoled or threatened. Edith had come up with the idea that she would hold his nose, and when he opened his mouth to breathe, Blanche would give him a spoonful of the medicine. The first time this didn't work because Wilson wouldn't swallow; therefore, when they tried it again, as soon as the liquid was in his mouth, Edith blew in his face to make him swallow. It had worked. Edith admitted that she sometimes cried after such a session, telling her sister-in-law,

"Blanche, he will just hate me. I know he will." Blanche always laughed, and said her fears were groundless.

Ralph felt Blanche was right because it sure seemed to him that Wilson adored his "Aunt E." In fact, now that Wilson was a little older, they sometimes took him with them for an outing. Edith found it delightful when strangers often thought she and Ralph were married and Wilson was their son. Neither felt they should set the record straight. Edith felt proud to have people think Ralph was her husband.

Beurmann could have gone with them, but he never seemed to want to accompany them any place. Ralph got a big kick out of the kid now that he was four. That kid had the biggest bump of curiosity he'd ever seen. Beurmann asked questions about everything. Trouble was if you gave him an explanation, you knew that no matter how well you had explained something, as soon as you were done, he'd say either "Why?" or "What for?" There were times when it did get irritating, partly Ralph guessed, because a person simply ran out of ways to explain something especially to a four-year-old.

Rate had stopped in at Seeley's barber shop for a haircut. Since no one else was in the shop, Seeley brought up a subject that had been bothering him.

"Rate, do you know Laura Pickett?"

"Not well, but I know her. I think she's staying with her sister who lives a couple of blocks north and east a couple of houses. Right?"

"She's the one. Sure is a fine looking woman. I'd like to date her, but that older sister won't let her go any place with me."

"Well, if you didn't drink to beat sixty, it might help. What's Laura say? Don't tell me she'd be interested in you." A note of disbelief crept into his voice.

Seeley ignored the tone of Ralph's comment. "She would be interested if I had half a chance. I can't make time if I can't keep company with her."

"Does she know how much you drink?"

"How in heck should I know? Maybe I wouldn't drink as much if I could spend time with her."

"Why are you tellin' me all this?" asked Rate. The suspicion in his voice was unmistakable. The chair was turned so he was facing the mirror; therefore, he could watch the expression on Seeley's face even though the barber stood behind him.

"Well, I've got this idea, but I'll need your help," he admitted.

"Knew there had to be a catch somewhere. What's on your mind?"

''Perhaps you could pick her up like you was taking her out. I could meet you by the school and then she'd go with me. Sounds like a good idea, don't it?'' Seeley asked hopefully.

"What makes you think her sister would let her leave with me? And how is she gonna get back home? Look kinda odd leavin' in one buggy, but comin' back in another, wouldn't it?"

"Why'd her sister have anything against you? You don't drink. Heck, you've got a job, and you've got a good reputation. I'll see that she gets home. Laura says her sister goes to bed early, so that likely wouldn't be a problem especially if she thought Laura was with you. C'mon, Rate, can't you do this for a friend?"

Gosh, Seel sure did look serious. Well, why not? Laura's sister sounded pretty bossy just because she was older and married. Laura was old enough to know her own mind.

"All right, Seel. We'll give it a try. I'll do it once, then I'll decide whether to do it again. I'm makin' no promises."

As it turned out, Rate picked Laura up several times and took her to meet Seeley. The first night, she wasn't gone long, and Laura's sister was pleased that Ralph had brought her sister home so early. Finally, Laura decided they were not to be dictated to, and she and Seeley sat down and explained the situation to Laura's sister. Ralph felt a sense of relief since he no longer had to help Seeley and Laura pull the wool over her sister's eyes.

One day Mott Bates came into the restaurant while Ralph was clearing off tables from the dinner crowd. He came over to Ralph and asked, "Rate, aren't you somehow related to a Glen Curtis?"

"He's a cousin. He was Ma's sister's oldest boy. Why?"

"Well, when we were in Florida this year, there was a Glen Curtis playing in a checker tournament. He was pretty good too. He looked older than you."

"I think he's a few years older than Blanche. He left home when he was only about sixteen. Guess he didn't want to stay around after his ma died. I never really knew him. Didn't know they had such things as checker tournaments."

"I didn't either. It was held by some checker association. He was good. He won both games I saw him play."

Rate guessed he would tell his Ma about Glen. She hadn't heard from Glen in ages, and then it was to ask for some money. Pa had sent him a few dollars to get him to another town where he said he had a job waiting for him. Of course, Uncle Doc wrote occasionally, and he wrote to Blanche, but since Aunt Ettie died, they had not been close.

Rate didn't think Ma had forgiven Uncle Doc for Aunt Ettie's death. Just because Aunt Ettie had died in childbirth, he had never understood why Ma thought Uncle Doc was to blame. That would be like blaming the bull if a cow died after having a calf. It didn't make any sense.

Rate was working late one Saturday night at the restaurant. Things had been rather slow for a Saturday night. It seemed as though time dragged when business was sporadic. Right now there was only one couple at a table by the window. They were likely to be leaving soon.

Just then, the door banged open and Stirling Blayney came stumbling through the door and up to the counter where he slouched onto a stool. Ralph knew at once that Stirling had had plenty to drink. All Stirling wanted was a cup of coffee. Ralph served him and started to move away, but Stirling began a conversation. Ralph had always liked Stirling even though he was much older. Rate remembered the time he had gone out to visit Stirling, who lived on Maple River Road, because Rate wanted to see the birch bark canoe some Indians had given Stirling when he was only a lad.

Stirling was on his second cup of coffee when Billie Carl, slightly worse for drink, came in. Billie chose a seat near Stirling, and shouted for coffee. Since Stirling and Billie struck up a conversation, Rate moved off to finish doing some dishes.

Voices were raised, and Ralph moved closer to the two perpetrators. Billie and Stirling were having a strong disagreement over something. It looked like they might come to blows. Ralph interceded, and gave a sigh of relief when both men left, promising to head for home.

Ralph's shift was over. Just before he left, Billie Carl came back in still in a belligerent mood. At least he was alone. Rate stepped out into the night where he saw a shadowy form with his nose up to the window, looking into the restaurant. It was Stirling Blayney. Ralph hesitated. He wondered if Stirling had any idea of re-entering the restaurant to continue his argument with Billie.

Stirling straightened up, looked at Ralph, shook his head, and said, "If that son of-a-bitch ain't goin' home, I am." With that, he turned and left.

Ralph chuckled to himself. At least there would be no confrontation tonight.

Millie decided he needed more room in the barn than the existing hip roof gave; thus, he figured to install a gambrel roof. The original barn had cost one hundred dollars, but Millie figured that the changes he wanted would cost more than that. Seems as though the price of everything kept edging up although it didn't seem as though farm prices rose as steadily. Why the master carpenter would get a minimum of $1.25 for a ten hour day while the men of his crew would quite likely receive $1.00 a day, and any master carpenter would likely have three or four men working for him. Besides, the gambrel roof would require a lot more rafters, roof boards, and shingles than did the old roof. It would be a costly project, but Millie felt the expense would be worthwhile in the long run.

Millie decided he'd change the horse stable too. Instead of one door on the south side, he'd have one on the west opening onto the barnyard, and one on the east to lead to the driveway. Since their return to the farm, he had put a gate between the barn and a shed so the livestock no longer came to the house for water. The old picket fence needed a lot of repair; consequently, Millie felt he was better off to tear it down. Miney said that confining the cows and horses away from the house certainly cut down on the fly population. Besides, it was nice having some lawn in front of the buildings as well as around the house. Millie still used the center portion bordered by the circular driveway to grow potatoes. Miney didn't really mind although Blanche had mentioned that it would look nice if that was also lawn.

After much thought, Millie decided to build the second silo. Corn grew well on his clay loam, thus he'd have no trouble producing enough corn to fill both silos. Millie had learned that when cows were fed silage, their milk production increased. Therefore, he felt the silo would pay for itself in a very few years if only the price of cream stayed at a reasonable rate. Seemed like a good investment to him.

Ralph had learned in Mr. Harter's Ag class that silage increased milk production; therefore, he found it rather humorous that Pa had discovered this. The first silo had been built just to augment the hay required because there were years when the hay crop was not as bountiful as it was in other years. Millie had reasoned silage would be a big help because they almost always had a good corn harvest. Rate could have told his father that by giving the cows silage, their milk production would increase. However, Rate knew his father would never have believed him; he would have put the information down as some fool idea Mr. Harter had dreamed up.

Rate decided to stop to see Vern. He was headed for Elsie, but he had plenty of time. Vern's wife, Blanche, was on the back porch shaking rugs. Rate spoke to her, and she told him that he'd find Vern fixing fence around the hog pen.

Ralph said, "I suppose those two leather heads are giving him help."

Blanche glared at him and gave him to understand in no uncertain terms that her sons were not leather heads, and she would appreciate it if he showed a little more respect. After all, her sons were both intelligent children, very normal. Rate laughed because she was so irate.

"If they are so bright, then why did I find them with their express wagon drawn up behind Daisy tying knots in her tail? You know how mean she is and that she is a kicker. It's a wonder she didn't blast away at them. One hit on the head and she could easily have killed them."

"I knew nothing about that," she admitted. "I can't be with them every minute. Did you explain to them that what they were doing was dangerous?"

"I simply told them that if I ever caught them doing this again, I'd give them the trouncing they deserved. Of course, Beurmann asked why, and yes, I did explain to them why what they were doing was wrong. I told them Daisy is not to be trusted and they were lucky she hadn't kicked their brains out."

"I just hope they realized you were serious," responced Blanche, a worried frown creasing her forehead. She hated to admit that there were times when she found her sons difficult to manage. They had no fear, and their curiosity was great.

Ralph moved off toward the hog pen to locate Vern. For some reason, Vern never actually repaired the fence around the hog pen. His idea of repairing was to use a board to prop up the fence where it leaned. Trouble was, the fence always leaned into the pen; consequently, Vern propped it up, and the hogs came along a short time later and knocked the prop down. Rate figured it would have saved a lot of time if Vern had only replaced a couple of fence posts. It seemed that Vern's hogs were always getting out, but the only time this bothered him was if he was sick. To hear him tell it, his hogs were never out except when he was too ill to put them back where they belonged. Then he would lament, "My hogs are out, my hogs are out. Why did they have to get out when I'm so sick? I just can't get them in until I feel better."

Rate never failed to find the situation comical.

In many ways, Vern was a poor excuse for a farmer. Ralph guessed that not everyone was cut out to be a farmer, and Vern was one of those. He wasn't as bad as Uncle John, but nearly so. Ralph felt that with Vern's gift of gab, he'd make a good salesman. He was a likable person, and could talk with anyone. It was true that he often embellished a story, but he didn't out and out lie, at least not about anything important. Besides, he was basically honest. This characteristic was important to Ralph. He could go along with Vern's fudging the truth when he was teasing someone as long as he didn't mislead people on important matters.

* * * * * * * * *

"Pa, have you noticed that the rims on the wagon are getting awfully loose?"
"Can't say as I have."

"Well, you should take a look at them. I'm off next weekend, so I could soak them for you. Thought it would be best to get it done before we get bad weather."

The wagon wheels were made of wood and covered with steel rims. Over a period of time, the wood dried out, and as a result, the rims loosened. Some farmers soaked the wheels in water, but Millie had always preferred to soak the wheels in hot linseed oil because the results were better. By using the oil, the process didn't need to be done nearly as often.

"Reckon you'd best get some linseed oil before then. I've got some, but not near enough. Guess probably it would pay to get it done before the fall rains come. I'll give them a look to make sure."

Rate chuckled to himself. Pa would never admit that he knew as much about wagon wheels as Pa did. If he hadn't mentioned it, Pa would likely have kept putting off the task simply because it was not the most enjoyable work to do. Pa was forever saying, "Never put off until tomorrow what you can do today." It just seemed that Pa was very selective where this applied if the task was something he enjoyed, or whether it was something he disliked doing.

Although Millie never actually admitted the wagon wheels were in dire need of soaking, he told Ralph that if he wanted to bother, he could do the job come the weekend. He gave Rate the money to buy the linseed oil needed. Ralph chuckled to himself because it was so difficult for Millie to admit that his son was as knowledgeable about things pertaining to farming as he was. Pa just hated to give him credit for knowing much of anything. One thing was for certain, when he could afford to farm on his own, he'd never run to Pa for advice like Pa had always been quick to run to Grandfather. He would certainly be his own man. If he made mistakes, he would have no one to blame but himself.

Fall sort of crept up on the countryside this year. It had been unseasonably warm one day, and it seemed that the next it had been cold and blustery. The leaves had turned color overnight, and while the maples along the road were brilliant, and each woodlot displayed its red, golden, and orange finery, the condition did not last long. Some days, the fierce winds whipped the branches unmercifully, and soon the limbs were stark and bare.

Ralph had always liked harvest time even if it did mean a lot of work. He found it rewarding to see the fruits of one's labor. If the growing season had been good– the right amount of rain combined with warm days and nights to promote growth– the yield was generous. Of course, a farmer was at the mercy of the elements, but Rate figured the risk was worth the effort.

There was a good layer of tracking snow, and Vern asked Rate to go hunting with him. They took Bruno along since there was nothing that dog liked better than to chase rabbits. They went to the forty acres which had been the first farm Wilson Brewbaker had owned. While the barn was still in good condition, the old house was falling in. Ralph and Vern pried up boards from a bedroom floor to enable Bruno to chase out the rabbits holed up there. Two rabbits took off, and Rate stepped out of the ramshackle house to shoot. Just as he shot, a man stepped out from the corner of the house. Rate's heart was in his mouth. He had not known anyone other than he and Vern was around. The man, who was the minister of a church in Eureka, was not hurt, but the close encounter had visibly shaken him. Ralph picked up a dead rabbit to show the man what his target had been.

Ralph figured the man must have heard him and Vern ripping up the floorboards, and Bruno's excited barking would have been difficult to ignore. Seemed to Ralph that the man should have announced his presence. At least there had been no harm done, but somehow, Rate's desire to hunt had left him for this day. He and Vern called it quits and left for home.

November brought plenty of snow with strong gusty winds that whipped the snow into huge drifts. It was time to get out the cutter arid sleighs because it sure seemed that winter had come to stay. Maybe it was payback for the light winter of last year.

When Rate showed up for work Monday morning, the folks in the restaurant were talking about the news that had come in over the wire at the railroad station. It seemed that yesterday, November 9, a great catastrophe had struck on the great lakes. Eight ore carriers had been sunk as a result of the heavy winds which had produced monstrous waves. Thus far, there were deemed to be more than 250 dead. The news report seemed to believe the count would go higher. (The final tally was 270 lives lost.)

While Ralph enjoyed swimming as much as anyone, he had never thought service in the Navy, Coast Guard, or Merchant Marine was an option. He thought drowning was an unenviable way to die. He was certain other methods were much easier, and certainly less painful.

Even though the roads were horrendous at times, Ralph continued to see Edith whenever he could. They sometimes stayed at her place or drove only the short distance to visit Edith's sister Gladys, her husband, Don, and baby Gordon. Ralph got along well with Don because they could always talk farming. Of course, this gave the young couple very little time to themselves, but Ralph didn't mind. In some respects, he thought Edith was lucky to have so many brothers and sisters. Garth was only twelve, but Rate got a kick out of him, and he realized Edith was particularly fond of her "baby brother."

Because the weather had been extremely bad, Edith's younger sister, Edna, had been forced to stay in Eureka with their cousin, Carrie Burk, in order to attend school. Wilson did not have a driving horse that was shod, and to take a horse that had not been shod out on these icy roads was inviting disaster.

Edith confided to Ralph that Edna was becoming quite homesick. She had never been away from home for this long a time, and even though she was very fond of Carrie, Edna missed her family. Carrie had one son, Lawrence, who was about Garth's age, and while Edna liked him, she looked upon him as just a kid. As a result, she felt very lonely.

The whole family was fond of Carrie because at one time, she and her brother, Frank, had been part of Wilson's family, but that was before Edna's time. Frank and Carrie's mother had died, and their father had remarried. Neither Carrie nor Frank could get along with their stepmother; therefore, Wilson had taken his niece and nephew to be a part of his family. Carrie had been with them until she was married in 1893. Edith was too small to remember Carrie living with them; however, Frank hadn't been married until 1901, thus she could remember him staying with them. Since Carrie had always lived in Eureka, and Frank had bought a grocery store there, the family had seen them quite often. Edna had been named after Carrie whose middle name was Edna, then Garth's middle name had been because of Carrie's husband, Milton Burk.

This was Ralph's weekend off, and it was early Saturday evening.

"Why don't we go bring her home?" asked Ralph.

"You mean it?" asked Edith wondering if he was just teasing.

"Why not? It's not far. We can take her back late tomorrow afternoon, if you think she'd like to come home for such a short time."

"She's so lonesome, she'd come for an hour," laughed Edith. "Well, give her a call."

Ralph and Edith drove to Eureka to get Edna. She was waiting impatiently by the window almost afraid to believe she was really going home. She was usually quiet around Ralph, but this night, she rattled on almost non-stop. In her own mind, she thought that Ralph was the most wonderful person she knew. She hoped he and Edith would have the good sense to get married. She would certainly welcome him into the family as a brother-in-law.

CHAPTER 7

When spring put in its appearance, Millie made Ralph an offer. If he'd work at home, field work and whatever else needed doing, Millie would pay him a decent wage. Of course, that would mean Ralph would have to quit his job at the restaurant.

Rate knew that some work had to be done on the forty if they intended to pasture the sheep and young cattle there. Fences must be in good condition if a farmer didn't want to spend time chasing livestock when it got out. Rate knew there were places where the old fence had to be repaired, a few broken posts replaced, and much better gates were needed. Besides, Pa wanted to tear down the old log cabin that stood near the road. He intended to salvage some of the lumber. The rest would be used in the stoves.

Since the sheep and young cattle would be pastured on the forty, Rate knew that Millie intended to plant more corn so he'd have enough to fill both silos. After careful thought, Ralph decided working outside would sure be better than being at the restaurant, and he would have more time to spend with Edith. This was indeed a pleasant thought; therefore, he accepted Millie's offer.

There were times when Ralph wished his father would let him have more say in how they ran the farm. However, he realized this was an idle wish. Millie became more set in his ways with age, and Millie simply rebelled at anything he thought was a "modern" idea voicing his opinion that the old tried and true methods were the best. Ralph would liked to have tried some of the concepts he had learned in Mr. Harter's class. Well, some day he'd be farming on his own and could then put those ideas into practice. Until then, he'd keep his mouth shut and do as his father wished.

Crops were planted on time since the weather had been most cooperative. Although Millie said nothing to Ralph, to himself he acknowledged that he was glad his son had decided to help him with the farm work instead of working in that infernal restaurant. Ralph did his work thoroughly and efficiently, and Millie never had to check on him as he did with hired hands. Now that there was a lull between planting, cultivating corn, and haying, he'd set the boy at some of the small repair jobs that he had been putting off. Ralph had done a creditable job repairing fence on the forty. At least none of the livestock had got out as yet.

Nell foaled again the latter part of May, another colt and another strawberry roan. Rate thought Monarch was a little smaller than Buster, and perhaps his conformation was not as good as Buster's. Still, Pa was lucky Nell had produced two such fine colts.

Ralph had always known that Dory didn't have a brain in her head, and she had certainly proved that Saturday night. He had gone to sleep as soon as they left the Brewbaker driveway. Rate figured he would wake up when Dory stopped in their own yard. Apparently, he hadn't.

Rate awoke because the buggy jolted to a stop. Where in heck was he? Dory was pawing the ground, thoroughly impatient to be off. There was almost a full moon in the cloudless sky; consequently, Ralph could get a pretty good look at his surroundings.

He was at Vern's, That stupid Dory had left their own driveway, gone up the road to Vern's, and had tried to go between an apple tree and the windmill. There had been ample room for the horse, but the space was far too narrow for the buggy. Ralph checked to make certain the buggy was not caught on anything, then standing in front of Dory, made her back slowly and carefully. Dumb mare!

The next day, he was even more disgusted with the mare. Apparently, she had brought him home all right, but since he hadn't awakened, she had taken a turn around the driveway, then stopped again. By the looks of the tracks, she must have done this a dozen times before she decided to go up the road to Vern's. Guess this made him realize all the more what a gem Pearl had been. He sure wished Pa hadn't sold her. Of course, Pa, horse trader that he was, never formed an attachment for any horse. They were only a means of making money. Rate vowed he'd never be like that, he would feel loyalty to a horse that served him well.

Ralph did not always show interest in foreign affairs. He usually had a general idea what was happening at the local level and even the national level in politics. Since he was not yet old enough to vote, he reasoned there was not much he could do about what man was put in office. Besides, since he was making decisions which affected his future, he figured he had enough to occupy his mind. Seemed to him that there was always unrest in Europe, that none of those countries could get along.

Then came June 28, 1914. A Serbian nationalist assassinated Archduke Franz Ferdinand of Austria along with his wife in a place called Sarajevo, Bosnia. What an uproar that caused in the European community. Ralph knew little about royalty, thus he was not certain why all the hullabaloo. We had had presidents assassinated without much commotion. Guess Europe was just different than the United States.

Of course, Austria wanted some sort of restitution, and when none was forthcoming, declared war on Serbia on July 23. This began a chain of events which was the beginning of what would be called the World War--the war to end all wars. By August 4, Great Britain had declared war on Germany. They said it was because Germany had declared war on Russia and France and had invaded Belgium. At this time the Allies--Great Britain, France, and Russia were pitted against the Central Powers--Germany, Austria-Hungary, and Turkey. What a mess! Ralph hoped the United States would keep her nose out of the fracas. In the past, the U.S. had interfered in the problems of other countries. He fervently hoped this would not be one of those times. Because he knew young men who had been killed in the Spanish American War, he had resented that war terribly. He agreed with Pa. War was a complete waste of lives as well as money. It brought only heartache to the average person who had no control over what the leaders did.

Ralph and Edith now spent every Saturday evening and Sunday afternoon together. Since the time when he had asked Edith if she would wait for him, he had said nothing further to indicate he might have marriage on his mind. At times, Edith wondered about his intentions. She knew he was not seeing someone else, but she still harbored the fear that Ralph would not wish to marry a simple farm girl. She felt she was perhaps too homely for someone as handsome as Ralph.

It was a Sunday afternoon and Edith and Ralph had gone for a ride. The day was pleasant, not too hot and a gentle breeze made it extremely comfortable. Edith was mildly surprised when Ralph produced a pipe and carefully filled it from a small tobacco can. She knew he smoked, but he rarely smoked in her presence.

She picked up the tobacco tin which Ralph had placed on the seat between them, and said, "You know I don't approve of you smoking. I think I'll just throw this can in the ditch."

"You do, and I'll kiss you," he said with a tantalizing laugh. His eyes danced.

Edith hesitated just a moment. Was he bluffing? One way to find out. She gave the tobacco tin a heave to the side of the road.

Rate gave a devilish chuckle, called "whoa" to the horse, then he put his hands on Edith's arms, turned her to face him, and leaned forward to give her a kiss squarely on the lips. Edith wondered if he had expected her to put up some resistance. She hadn't because she had really wanted to be kissed.

Ralph got out of the buggy and retrieved his can of tobacco. He nonchalantly drove on; however, Edith noticed that he put his unlit pipe in his pocket. Perhaps he did care what she thought.

From that time on, Ralph usually gave her a kiss before helping her out of the buggy when they returned from an outing. There were times now when he held her hand as they drove. Edith enjoyed the feeling of her small hand in his. Would he ever introduce the subject of marriage?

With the advent of harvest time, there had not been enough work to keep Ralph busy all day; therefore, Millie had agreed to let him work on a threshing rig to earn extra money. Although he said nothing to anyone, Ralph had an ulterior motive for this. He would draw none of his wages until the threshing season was done. By then, he figured he might have enough to buy Edith a diamond ring. While he had never exactly come out and asked her if she would marry him, he felt certain that she would. At least she had never given him any indication that she saw or wanted to see anyone else. She always seemed content to be with him.

* * * * * * * * *

Alton Fizzell, who lived about a mile and a half from the Setterington farm, had asked neighbors to help move a small barn. Rate and Dave Watson were sitting together on a pry board waiting to let the barn down on the new foundation.

"Dave, have you any fields you want to let out?" asked Rate.

"If you had a housekeeper, I'd rent you the whole farm."

"I can get the housekeeper," replied Rate with a grin.

"Thought maybe you could. Word gets around you know. Talk it over with her, and let me know what you decide."

Ralph went to see Edith the next day. He didn't come right out and say, "Will you marry me?" Instead, he asked her if she thought Dave's proposition was a good one. He explained that he had money enough to buy a good team, and before March, he would be able to buy some cows. He figured his father might give him a hog or two, and it wouldn't take much to have a few chickens. They might not have much furniture, but they could get the important pieces. Edith had never seen him this serious.

Of course, she agreed. She had been making linens for her hope chest for some time now, and she had saved a few dollars to put towards their furniture. Besides, she thought her folks might give them a rocker or a chest of drawers.

Actually, Edith was walking on air. She had fantasized about being Ralph's wife for a long time, and now her dreams would come true. She didn't suppose she was formally engaged because Ralph had given her no ring, but she could name others who had never had an engagement ring, merely a plain gold wedding band on their wedding day. Besides, they would have so many expenses, she was certain Ralph could not afford something as frivolous as an engagement ring. Better they spend their money on cows from which they could make a living.

Ralph drove directly to Watson's from the Brewbaker farm. He told Dave he would rent the farm. They agreed that the place would be available the first of March since this was the time when farming changes were usually made. Farm field work did not begin until the last of March, or if the weather was bad, the first of April. Ralph felt quite satisfied. Dave had told him that he would have a lease written up so there would be no doubt concerning the obligations of each party. This was fine with Ralph although he believed Dave's word was good.

It was mid fall, and the pesky crows were so plentiful they flew in huge flocks. When they settled, they would literally cover an entire field. Millie and Ralph often shot a few to scare them off. If they remained this thick, next year would be a bad time for corn fields. Crows go right down a row of corn where the green shoots are just poking above the ground. They pull the corn and eat the kernel at the bottom; the green stem is simply left on the ground to wither and die.

Near the end of the fall season, Rate and Millie decided the fifteen acres in the back field across from the woodlot should be broken up. It had only been used as pasture thus far. The trees had been logged off years ago, and as of now, there were a few rotted logs dotting the landscape from trees blown down long before the Setteringtons had owned the farm. Millie had burned out most of the stumps a few years ago. Some thorn brush, and undoubtedly a huge rock or two besides plenty of small stones covered the land. It would be a tremendous job. Still, both Millie and Ralph felt it was time to add this virgin land to the available cropland.

It was getting to be the time of year when livestock that had been out on pasture for the summer should be brought home. Rate noticed a flock of sheep coming along the Ridge Road. Since this was unusual, Ralph ambled up the road for a closer look. He noted there was a grub wagon, a man, and two dogs immediately preceding the flock. About half way back along the line of sheep, there were two more dogs, one on each side. It seemed as though the line of sheep was never ending. The rear was brought up by another man and two more dogs.

Ralph could hear Vern shouting, so he made his way through the close knit sheep to find out what had Vern so upset. It seemed that Vern had 18 sheep, and he had just discovered that his sheep had got out and were now mingling with the strange flock. Vern was always one to react with near hysteria when something went wrong instead of calmly looking for a reasonable solution. Ralph was the one to explain the situation. Vern's ranting had been a muddled confusion of words which the man had found impossible to decipher.

When the man at the rear understood the problem, he shouted a command to the dogs with him. Quietly, the dogs bunched the sheep together so they could actually walk on the backs of the sheep. They would cut out eight or ten sheep, and one of Vern's would be with them. One dog was a pretty farm collie who was still a pup, but he understood every command and worked diligently. To Ralph, who loved dogs, it was a beautiful sight to watch these intelligent, well-trained dogs work. It was easy to tell which sheep were Vern's because farmers usually marked their sheep with a splash of paint on their back. Sheep often got out and mixed with a neighbor's flock, and this was the way farmers identified their own.

Ralph helped Vern put his sheep in a shed where they would be safely contained until the huge flock had moved on. The man told Ralph they were bringing the sheep from a pasture up north to Elsie, and then to Vernon. There were 1800 sheep in the flock. Rate had never seen so many sheep in one flock before, nor was he ever to see such a sight again.

A few days later Ralph was to learn the sheep men had rented a hay field from Bert McKinstry, Edith's uncle, to keep the flock penned over night. In the morning, the hay field was bare, the hay eaten down to the ground. What had seemed like a good way to make a few extra dollars had been a most unwise decision.

Ralph and Millie went to an auction where Ralph bought a team of horses along with suitable harnesses. He had one field on the Watson farm that he intended to plow this fall if the weather held. Dave Watson had given him a good price on a plow, a disk, and a drag. Now, Ralph's biggest worry was having enough money for seed come planting time. Millie had given him a cow due to freshen in the spring. Ralph rather hoped his father would give him some seed corn as well. However, one never could outguess his father which meant there was nothing on which he could really rely. Ralph would never have asked his father for anything. Whatever Pa gave him would have to be because Pa himself had wanted to give him something.

Millie was in the barn getting a team ready to do some field work. The west barn door was open, and just as Millie took a harness off the pegs to throw on a horse, the colt, Buster, came tearing in through the open door. Quick as a wink, he was entangled in the harness. Ralph helped his father extricate the colt.

When done, Millie asked, "Do you want this colt?"

"Sure, I'll take him."

"I want him just a little longer."

Millie picked up a whip and then took Buster in on the barn floor. When they came out a short time later, Buster would follow Millie anywhere.

"I've taught him this much. Now, he's yours."

Little did Ralph realize then the challenge the colt would present. Ralph often remarked that Buster was too smart for his own good. Their relationship was always a battle of wills. Ralph knew it would be at least another year before he broke the colt to drive, but he was glad to have him. Gosh, Pa had really been generous. Maybe, just maybe Pa was making up for the money he had given Blanche for her education. First the cow, and now Buster. Yup, when he wanted to, Pa could be all right.

Rate and Millie were over to the forty sawing some lumber when Ralph's two great uncles, Uncle Vest and Uncle Albert, visited from Canada. One of Uncle Albert's boys, John, lived in Maple Rapids now; therefore, Rate supposed they had come to visit him, and since they were that close had decided to visit Pa. Ralph remembered Blanche telling about Uncle George and Uncle Albert visiting Grandfather when she was young and had been staying a few days with their grandparents. Ralph had not met any of them before. They were large men, and like Grandfather, stood ramrod straight. Blanche had always maintained Uncle Albert and Uncle George were much less serious than Grandfather, and Ralph found this to be true about Uncle Vest too. He wondered what the rest of Grandfather's family was like. Since they lived in Canada, he didn't know them. In fact, he didn't believe Pa had seen all of his aunts and uncles. Some different from the Brewbakers who seemed to have plenty of relatives whom they saw frequently.

On the fourth of November, Miney had a telegram informing her that her brother in-law, George Curtis, had died the day before. Miney was a little surprised that Glen had taken the time to inform her. She had not heard from her nephew for over a year. Miney knew she should call Blanche even though it was long distance. Blanche had always been fond of "Uncle Doc" and they had written to each other after Ettie died. Miney had always blamed George for Ettie's death since her sister had died in childbirth, and Miney had found it difficult to forgive. Sometimes, she was a little put out because she just knew that Blanche had liked George more than she had liked Ettie. Well, even though Ettie was her own sister, Miney had to admit that Ettie was different in many ways. Lorin was different too, but not in the same way as Ettie. Mary had been the only one of the girls who had been like Ma, and everyone old and young alike, had liked Ma.

Miney tried to be a good neighbor and follow the teachings of the Bible. She knew she sometimes fell short of her goal, but at least she tried. She hoped Millie felt she was a good wife. At least he never said anything to indicate he didn't. Miney gave a sigh of sadness. With both George and Ettie gone along with Jap and Mary, she realized her family was getting smaller. Of course, George had been 65, at least he had had more of life than poor Ettie.

Seemed like the katydids had begun hollering early this year, and as everyone expected, a killing frost had come six weeks later. However, snow had held off and Rate had done his fall plowing on Watson's. Now, it was time to start on the fifteen acres for Pa.

First of all, Rate pulled the thorn brush and burned that. He found a few old stumps that Pa hadn't burned, and these had to be taken out and burned along with the old, half-rotted logs. It was time consuming, and the hours of work showed little in the way of progress.

Finally, the day came when he started plowing. The field was 80 rods in length and he plowed it east to west. As he had surmised, there were plenty of small stones from watermelon size to the size of a bushel basket. It was going to take a lot of time to haul them off the field. With all the stops he had to make to get rid of debris, he could only make four rounds in half a day. Since the walking plow made only a 14 inch furrow, this did not make much of a dent in getting the field plowed.

Then came the day when the plow point hooked onto a rock that would not budge. Ralph dug around it and was surprised at the size. The stone was almost round, but he had no idea how deep it went. He plowed around it for the rest of the day. When Ralph told his father about the size of the stone, they decided to use dynamite to get it out of the ground where they could put a log chain around it and have the team haul it out of the field.

Ralph and Millie tunneled the earth away from the stone far enough to allow them to place the dynamite under the stone. Because Millie never took any unnecessary chances, he had plenty of fuse. He lit the fuse, and both he and Ralph moved still farther away. Kaboom! The two men watched in disbelief as the stone rose about ten feet above the land surface, then dropped back into the same hole.

Millie looked at Ralph, and said, "Now, don't that beat all?"

"What now, Pa?"

Millie looked perplexed. "Don't rightly know. Think it's too big for a team to pull?"

"It looked pretty big, Pa. Is there a way we can set the dynamite to split a chunk of it off?"

"We can give it a try. Don't rightly know what else to do."

Instead of setting the dynamite in the middle as before, they positioned it nearer the perimeter. At least this time they achieved the desired results. A portion split off the stone, and they were able to put a log chain around it. The team had no trouble snaking the smaller piece out into the lane where it was left along the north fence. That piece was soon joined by the other slightly larger one. Numerous smaller stones, that had to be hauled off the field before it could be fitted and planted in the spring, would soon be filled in around them.

In early November, a snow storm dumped a good four inches of snow on the countryside. Ralph decided he could plow through the snow. However, he knew that dirt would freeze to a cold plow share, so each day he took an armful of straw from the barn to burn on the plow share to take the frost out of it. This method worked fine and the plowing progressed in spite of the snow.

Ralph went to pick up Edith on a Saturday afternoon. Edith told him that her sister, Edna, wasn't feeling real well. It didn't seem like a cold, but she had a slight fever. Ralph was in the house only a few minutes since Edith was ready as usual. Rate had always liked her promptness, probably because he had always hated having to wait for his mother.

When Ralph went to see Edith on Sunday, he could not go in the house, only look through the window. It seems they finally knew what was wrong with Edna. She had the mumps.

A couple of weeks later, Ralph felt lousy. He was glad he was through with plowing that back field even though he still had some stones to pick up. He hoped he felt better by Monday. He didn't. He felt worse. He had a good case of the mumps. He was swollen on both sides. Darn that Edna. He knew she was the one who had given the mumps to him. Didn't seem like he'd been with her long enough to catch anything. He couldn't even help Pa with the chores. Ma watched him like a hawk. Since Vern had had mumps as a child, he came to visit although he was far from sympathetic. Although Ralph had plenty of books to read, the inactivity proved to be difficult. Living on a liquid diet didn't bother because Ralph was often a very light eater even when doing hard, physical labor.

Finally, Ralph was past his bout with the mumps and resumed helping Millie with chores. He also spent time picking up the last of the stones from the back field since the early snow had melted and only a light dusting had taken its place. Miney admonished him not to stay out any longer than necessary in the cold because he might take a chill, and a chill could bring a relapse. Ralph took his mother's coddling in stride. Ma was happiest when she had someone to mother. She was like a mother hen with small chicks. Ralph realized part of this excessive concern was because she could no longer smother Blanche with her well-meaning attention.

Vern had decided to butcher a sow. Rate figured the animal weighed at least five hundred pounds, too fat for Rate's taste. While Millie ate fat meat with relish, Ralph had never acquired the taste for fat and usually trimmed the fat from his portion much to Bruno's satisfaction. Of course, a little fat marbled in with beef made the beef juicy and tender, but Rate figured the only reason to have a fat hog was to have plenty of fat to try out for lard.

Since Rate was well again, he offered to help Vern with the butchering. The sow was safely penned in a shed. When Rate arrived at Vern's, his friend already had a fire going under the large, black, cast iron kettle, nearly full of water, in which they would scald the hog.

When the water was hot enough, it would be time to kill the hog.

"You intend to stick her?" asked Rate. Sticking a hog meant the animal was placed on its back and the long, slender blade of an especially sharp knife was inserted into the body at a point where it pierced the heart. Death was almost instantaneous.

"Not me. Even though I've watched Pa do it countless times, I just never got the hang of it. Didn't I ask you to bring your rifle?"

"No. Thought you had one."

"Well, I do, but Garth wanted to borrow it to go squirrel hunting, so I let him take it. He hasn't brought it back as yet."

"Give me your axe," said Rate.

Axe in hand, Rate approached the sow who was warily watching their approach. Ralph hit her a resounding blow right between the eyes. Instead of dropping as expected, she stood straight up, gave a terrified squeal, turned, and crashed through the boards on the side of the shed. The hog ran wildly with both Vern and Rate futilely attempting to get her into a pen. They chased her for the better part of an hour before she was worn out enough to go into a pen and plop down in complete exhaustion. The men gave a sigh of relief since they were getting winded themselves. Rate thought hogs were much more difficult to drive than cows.

The fire had long since burned out, and the water was too cold to scald properly. As a result, they had to shave instead of scrape most of the carcass. Initially, Vern had been extremely upset, but now that they were actually getting the work done, his attitude improved. He could finally laugh with Ralph, who always had a good sense of humor. Since they worked well together, it made the time pass more quickly.

Sometimes, Rate felt that Vern's luck was just naturally bad when it came to farming. Seemed odd since he had lived all his life on a farm. His father was a good farmer, thus he must have been taught well. Maybe it was being on his own that he couldn't handle. Rate certainly hoped he would be able to do better when he started farming on his own. He didn't expect to farm exactly like Pa because he intended to put into practice some of what he had learned from Mr. Harter. Then, he'd see who was right, Mr. Harter or Pa. At least he would be open to new methods, willing to try anything that might improve his income. He'd not be like Pa and automatically be against anything Pa termed "modern."

Ralph turned twenty-one on the eighteenth of December. He decided he had better register so he could vote in any upcoming election. He registered as an independent, but over the years, he was much more likely to vote for a Democratic candidate than a Republican. This put him at odds with most of the community, but Ralph never cared. He was always to maintain that he voted for the man, not the party. He was careful to learn how the candidates felt about the issues, then he made up his mind accordingly.

When Christmas came, Ralph gave Edith a diamond ring. It had taken his entire wages from working on the threshing rig; however, he felt it had been well worth the money when he beheld the glow on Edith's face when she saw the ring. Just for a moment, she was completely speechless which delighted Ralph.

In fact, Edith was overwhelmed. She thought she had never seen anything quite as beautiful as this ring. If she had ever had any doubts about whether or not Rate truly loved her, she had none now. She felt the ring must be terribly expensive. All she knew was that the ring had cost Rate his wages from working on the threshing rig, She had no idea how much that was, and she was never to find out. Rate could be mighty secretive when he wanted to be.

After the first of the year, Ralph and Edith set the date for their wedding, the eleventh of March. There was no question about who would be best man. Since Don Sherman was Ralph's best friend, he filled the bill. Edith was a little undecided about who she should ask to be her maid of honor. She felt she wanted a relative. Since Thelma Turner had often dated someone Ralph had brought home for the weekend from Ypsilanti, to make it a foursome, Edith felt Ralph knew Thelma better than her other cousins; therefore, Thelma was a logical choice. Besides, Don knew Thelma and Edith felt this would be better than having a best man and maid of honor who were perfect strangers.

It was to be a small wedding at the home of Edith's parents with only family and a few close friends invited. There would be no wedding trip, but neither Ralph nor Edith seemed to mind. After all, they would have plenty to do to get settled.

On the seventeenth of January, Vern and Blanche were blessed with another son. They named him Wendell Holbrook. He was a beautiful baby, and when Edith held him, she longed for the time when she might hold a baby of her own. Children were what made life worthwhile.

While Edith wanted children, she hoped she and Ralph would not have any until the second year of their marriage. She was not that certain how this was to be accomplished because it seemed that her mother was rather vague about the relationship between a husband and wife. However, Edith truly felt a man and woman needed time to become accustomed to each other. She had often heard the expression from the older women: You never know a man until you've lived with him.

When Wilson learned that his beloved Aunt E was getting married, he was distraught. He was almost in tears when he asked, "What should we do when Wendell gets sick?"

The question thoroughly disgusted his mother.

"Let him die, I suppose," Blanche retorted.

Edith felt sorry for her nephew; therefore, she patiently explained that just because she was getting married, did not mean she wouldn't be around if he needed her. And yes, if Wendell became sick, she probably could come over in the daytime to help care for him.

This explanation seemed to satisfy the little fellow, and he went outside to play. Edith laughed because Blanche was still disgruntled. Poor Wilson. It was hardly his fault he thought his parents incapable of taking care of a sick child. After all, Blanche and Vern had always been quick to seek her assistance if either boy was sick; therefore, Wilson simply accepted the idea that Aunt E was a most important person. He loved his baby brother, and his concern was natural. Actually, his reaction gave Edith a good feeling because she loved Wilson dearly. She tried to show no partiality, but Wilson was definitely her favorite. Perhaps it was because Wilson had always been such an affectionate child whereas

Beurmann had always been an independent soul. It was almost as though he had been born older than his years.

Ed Clark came to see Ralph. It seemed that Ed's old Curly, who was past thirty, a very old age for a horse, was not expected to winter through. His teeth were so bad, Ed felt he would quite likely die of indigestion--a very painful death, now that he could no longer be on pasture. He had begun to lose weight even though Ed had tried to give him the best hay. Ed told Ralph that if he would kill Curly and bury him, he could have the hide to make a robe. Rate thought this was a good deal.

The ground was frozen down about four or five inches; therefore, Ralph built a fire where he wanted to dig the hole. As it turned out, he had over estimated the size of the hole needed. Because the ground was partially frozen, he had dug diligently, not wanting to keep building a fire to keep the earth thawed. When it was time to drag Curly into the hole, Rate laughed to himself. He'd spent a lot more time digging than was necessary since it looked as though he could have put at least two more carcasses along with poor old Curly and still had room.

Ralph sent the hide to a company in Three Rivers to have it tanned and made into a robe.

Neighbors gave Mr. and Mrs. Watson a going away party. As was customary, the coats were all piled on the bed in the spare bedroom. The next day, Dave came to warn Edith that Mrs. Watson had found three bedbugs on the bed the next morning. They all knew they had very likely come from Jeff Walker's family. Edith had gone to school with Jeff's wife, the former Mae Cordray, and it was difficult for her to understand why her friend's family was so dirty. People often joked about the Walkers, saying the bedbugs were ready to carry the house off. When Walker's house burned a few years later, someone in the crowd that had congregated suggested there was a big loss of life in that house when everyone knew all the family had got out safely. Many laughed because they realized the person was speaking of bedbugs.

Edith and Ralph went shopping for furniture. They had $135.00 to spend. With this amount, they bought a dining room table and six chairs, a buffet, a library table, a matching bed, dresser, and commode for the guest bedroom, as well as a dresser and bed for their bedroom. Millie and Miney had given them a commode, a kitchen table they no longer used, and a rocking chair. The Brewbakers had given them a small rocker with no arms and a couple of straight chairs for the kitchen. Both Ralph and Edith felt they had enough to get started. Watson's had left both the kitchen stove and the stove in the living room which was generous of them. Later, Ralph bought another large rocker at an auction.

While Edith had numerous linens she had made over the past few years, she was pleasantly surprised when her mother gave her some pillow cases which had wide crocheted lace made by her grandmother McKinstry. Edith decided they were too precious for everyday use, but she was glad to have them. Then, too, Miney had given her a few crocheted pieces and a couple of dresser scarves. Edith had made a wool braided throw rug from the material in old coats; she had made a crocheted rug as well from cotton stockings. All of these things would help to make a house a home.

The sixth of March, friends gave a shower for Edith. It was here that she acquired much of her cooking utensils, dishes, and even some pieces of silverware. Most of the gifts were accompanied by a few lines of verse (see appendix) which were generous with their advice on how best to handle Ralph after they were married. All the verses were definitely from a woman's point of view. It was all in fun, and the ladies enjoyed themselves.

If Edith had any doubts about this marriage, it was because she felt inferior to Ralph's family. Mrs. Setterington used her well enough, but Edith sometimes wondered if Miney truly felt Edith was good enough for her son. His sister, Blanche, was friendly, but here again, Edith felt Blanche had accomplished so much more than she had; Blanche was much more sophisticated. Blanche's beau, George, was easy to get along with, and he had a terrific sense of humor. When he was around, Edith usually felt at ease. Mr. Setterington was not one to talk much, but he was always polite, and she just guessed that he was not really much of a talker, especially with a woman.

Ralph's family was not like hers. There just weren't many relatives. His Aunt Lorin was the only aunt on his mother's side, and on his father's side there was an aunt in California and an uncle in Flint whom she gathered was sort of the black sheep of the family. His Setterington grandparents also lived in California. Rate had indicated that his father and grandfather had had a falling out a few years back, but he had not given her any more of an explanation. Rate didn't seem to know his uncle's children and he had never spoken of visiting them or vice versa. At least she had met Aunt Lorin, and although Aunt Lorin seemed a little odd, Edith liked her. She often referred to Rate as "poor little Ralph," and Edith often wondered why. It was obvious his aunt really cared for him.

There weren't many cousins either. Edith knew that Rate's Aunt Mary had had at least one son and two daughters. The youngest daughter was Blanche's age. Aunt Lorin had only had Georgie, and although Aunt Ettie had had two sons, Rate said they had seldom seen them. Seemed strange since there were cousins galore on the Brewbaker side of the family and even a few from the McKinstry side. Because many of the families were large, Edith had first cousins almost as old as her parents. No matter. They were still cousins and she enjoyed them. Of course, some who were nearer to her in age were very special. Edith thought she was fortunate to have so many relatives. Family gatherings were always something to enjoy. It seemed as though there were always cousins from somewhere visiting Wilson's family. Some stayed a few days while others stayed for weeks. Edith knew her parents welcomed them, each and every one. Family ties were strong.

Edith believed large families were nice although she had always planned to have only four children. Of course, she wanted two boys and two girls. Some of the older women always said you should "fill up your beds as you go." Therefore, she had felt it would be best to have the two boys first. She had planned all this long before she knew where babies came from. Now that she was about to be married, she still felt she would like four children. She was certain Rate would be a good father. He was good with her nephews. A lot depended on whether they could make enough as tenet farmers to support a family. Edith didn't ask for much, and she had been taught to be frugal, but she certainly didn't want to be as poor as some folks she knew. She had often heard her father declare that someone "didn't have a pot to piss in nor a window to throw it out of." Well, she and Ralph were certainly not going to be in that category. Ralph was a hard worker, and she knew he'd be successful as long as he stayed healthy.

Blanche had taken time off from work and had come home from Detroit on Wednesday to be present for her brother's wedding. George Ryan had come with her. If she had had any doubts before, Miney now knew that Blanche was indeed serious about this young man. The important thing was that Miney was glad to have her daughter home for a few days. At least Blanche didn't expect to return to Detroit until Sunday. It seemed to Miney that she never had much time to spend with Blanche; however, she reminded herself that she should be thankful for what little time she had.

Since Blanche seemed happy, that was all that mattered. As the time went by, Miney could certainly see that Blanche and George got along well. My, thought Miney, George was certainly different from the other young men with whom Blanche had kept company. While Miney liked George's quick wit and his sense of humor, she sometimes was at a loss as to how to respond to him. He certainly made her laugh often, and she was certain George was sweet on Blanche. Well, perhaps he would be the one to make her daughter happy. If so, he certainly had her approval.

CHAPTER 8

When Ralph went to the barn to do chores, he noted the sun was coming up in a cloudless sky. This gave him a good feeling because today was the eleventh of March, his wedding day. Edith set such a store on old sayings, and he knew she truly believed "Happy is the bride the sun shines on." As for himself, he had never put any store in those old adages. However, he was glad to see the sun for Edith's sake. As expected, the air was crisp and cold, but without a wind, it was very pleasant.

Ralph was to leave early for the Brewbaker farm because Rev. Robinson had said there were some forms to be filled out. The rest of his family would come in time for the ceremony.

When Rev. Robinson asked Ralph for the marriage license, Ralph reached for it in the inside pocket of his suit jacket. There was nothing in the pocket. He knew that was where he had put it. Then, he remembered that his jacket had hung on a chair in the dining room while he tied his tie and put in his cuff links. Blanche! She had been in the dining room when he took his jacket from the chair.

Ralph stammered something to the surprised minister about he must have left the license at home, but he'd be back shortly. With that feeble explanation, he rushed out of the house without a word to anyone else. As soon as the horse made the turn out of the driveway into the road, he urged her to a run. His anger was building with each passing minute. By the time he turned into the Setterlngton drive, he was furious.

He slammed the door behind him as he strode into the dining room. His mother was just coming from her bedroom. Before she could say anything, he demanded angrily, "Where in hell is Blanche?"

"Ralph! Such language. You know I don't approve. Whatever is wrong?" Miney looked puzzled.

Ralph never swore in her presence, and she had never seen him look this angry.

Just then, Blanche came from the parlor where she had undoubtedly heard his demand.

"Something wrong?" she asked sweetly.

"You damned well know there is something wrong. Where in hell is my marriage license?"

"How should I know?" was the innocent reply.

"I know you sure as hell took it. I want it now, and don't give me any fol-de-rol about not knowing where it is."

"Perhaps it was that paper I found on the floor after you left." Blanche moved to the buffet, picked up a folded piece of paper, waved it in the air, then held it out to her brother. "Could this be what you're looking for?"

"You know damned well it is!" growled Ralph as he grabbed the license and stuck it in his pocket.

"Really, Ralph, you should learn to take better care of important papers. Isn't it lucky I found it?"

"Sure, and the damned thing just jumped right out of my pocket."

Ralph glared. Blanche gave him a sweet, innocent smile in return.

"Tsk, tsk. Such language, and you know Ma doesn't approve of swearing," she said reproachfully.

Rate gave her a venomous look and left.

Blanche gave a chuckle. She really hadn't thought Ralph would be that angry. Usually, he had a better sense of humor. Guess maybe he had the wedding day jitters. Oh well, she was certain he'd get over his anger. She wasn't one bit worried about their relationship. She and her brother might not always show how much they cared, but they really did enjoy each other's company. Blanche felt this would never change even if Ralph was angry now.

While the parlor of the Brewbaker house had been festooned with wide, twisted strands of crepe paper, little else had been done for decoration.

Edith's dress was white lace over a satin lining. A narrow, stand-up collar of organdy circled her throat. The sleeves came only to the elbow; the toes of her shoes peeked from beneath the gentle folds of the skirt. A satin sash accented the smallness of her eighteen inch waist. She wore no jewelry. The only color was an artificial rose worn in the center of her bosom. While not a beautiful bride, she was radiant. It was obvious that this day was indeed the fulfilment of her dreams. She wore her heart in her eyes as she gazed up at her handsome husband-to-be.

Ralph looked completely serious. Even the twinkle was absent from his eyes. He looked mighty nice in his dark suit, snow white shirt with a four-in-hand tie held in place by a gold stick pin. The lock of hair that so often fell down his forehead was combed safely in place.

The wedding went off without a hitch. At least Ralph's good nature had returned before the ceremony. However, he promised himself that he would do something to get even with his sister. Right now, he had no idea what that something would be, but he was certain he would eventually think of some way to retaliate. Blanche would expect him to do something to get even, and he wouldn't want to disappoint her.

The bride and groom opened their wedding gifts, and in the late afternoon left for the Watson farm. Ralph had chores that would not wait.

Edith's mother had given her daughter food for an evening meal and enough for breakfast the next morning. Edith had already purchased staples for the pantry, and because she had helped her mother can fruits and vegetables last fall, Alice had given Edith a few jars to help tide her over until there would be garden produce in the summer months.

The young couple retired early since Ralph had early morning chores. Edith was already in bed when Ralph came to the bedroom. He had seen to banking the living room stove for the night.

Ralph slipped into his pajama tops, but just as he went to remove his trousers, he stepped behind the foot of the bed. Edith felt like snickering. She would never have thought Ralph could be so modest. Although Edith knew very little about the relationship between a husband and wife because her mother had found it a difficult topic, she awaited her husband with open arms. Ralph had not been very affectionate while they were courting, but Edith felt this would change now that they were married. And she was not to be disappointed.

Ralph had gone to the barn to do the milking. He had stirred up the fire in the living room stove, but had left the kitchen stove for Edith to get started. There had been a few coals left, so Edith had not had a problem, the kindling ignited immediately. She was not certain how long it would take Ralph to do the milking, she knew the rest of the chores would wait until after breakfast, so she didn't know how long she had to prepare breakfast.

She sliced some bacon and put that on to fry. She put some cold, boiled potatoes in a fry pan with a little grease and proceeded to chop them up so they would be warmed through and flavored with the bacon grease. The coffee was perking and would soon be done. She sliced some bread, and put jelly as well as butter on the table. She'd wait until Ralph came in the house before she put the eggs in to fry. They'd have time to cook while he washed up.

All went well, and when Ralph was ready to sit down at the table, his plate of food was placed in front of him. Edith sat across the kitchen table. She watched as he sat without moving, staring at his food as though it was some strange concoction, not a nutritious breakfast. What could be wrong?

Finally, he looked up and asked, "What kind of a breakfast is this?"

"What is wrong with it? It's a breakfast like most of the people I know eat." Although Edith was completely puzzled, she tried not to let her voice betray how much his criticism hurt.

"If this isn't suitable, what do you eat for breakfast?"

"I like two soft-boiled eggs, three minute ones, with two or three slices of fried bread. (French toast) I put my eggs in a glass so they can be stirred up," explained Ralph, very patiently, he thought.

"You eat soft-boiled eggs 365 days a year?" asked Edith. The tone of her voice was one of disbelief.

"Well, in the winter, I like pancakes with some sort of meat; oatmeal or cream of wheat once in a while is fine; I like fish if I have a chance to go fishing or spearing."

"You want fish for breakfast?" She found this difficult to accept.

"Sure. That's the only time to eat fish. Fried fish and fried bread. Can't beat that combination." He gave her a disarming grin.

"I'll try to do better for your breakfast tomorrow," she said with a slight touch of sarcasm which seemingly went unnoticed.

"Another thing. If you fry eggs, and I like fried eggs some of the time, especially with a piece of ham, break the yolk. None of this runny stuff for me." He poked at the yolk on one of the eggs and watched as it broke and ran over his plate.

"Here. I'll put them back in to cook longer." She rose from her chair, and reached for his plate.

"You needn't bother. I'll manage this time," he said as he proceeded to eat his breakfast as though nothing was really wrong.

Ralph had become especially fond of soft-boiled eggs while he worked at the restaurant in Ypsilanti. He had never complained to his mother about what she served for breakfast, but he felt that a wife could very well adjust to his likes.

Edith sat and watched him a moment before starting on her own serving. It seemed her appetite had disappeared, but she supposed she had better eat because it was a long time until dinner. What would Ralph find fault with at dinner time, she asked herself bitterly. She had never thought cooking would be a problem, her mother had taught her well, but she guessed her first breakfast was a complete flop, at least in her husband's eyes. Personally, she thought it had tasted good.

In a short time, Edith's hurt feelings turned to anger. Ralph's fried eggs had to be hard, but his boiled eggs had to be really soft. How inconsistent! She supposed she'd have to call Mother Setterington to ask how to fry bread or she'd undoubtedly do that wrong although she couldn't imagine how one could spoil fried bread.

The families she knew served meat, eggs, and potatoes for breakfast. Men doing a lot of manual labor needed a hearty breakfast. At least Ralph had managed to clean his plate with no trouble. Guess it wouldn't kill him either.

Who would have thought Ralph would be so finicky. He'd always seemed to enjoy the meals her mother served. Of course, in all fairness, Ralph had never eaten breakfast with her family. Pa and her brothers would have thought she had prepared a good breakfast. They had never complained when she got most of a meal if Ma was busy with something else.

Edith wondered if she should ask Ralph what he wanted for dinner and supper. Then, her German stubbornness took over, and she decided there was no way she would ask Ralph what would suit him. After all, she wasn't running a restaurant. He could eat what she cooked or go without. Although she had always enjoyed cooking, she might not continue to enjoy getting meals if her husband continued to criticize.

Ralph learned the horsehide robe from old Curly had been delivered at his parents' farm the day of his wedding. Edith thought it beautiful, Curly had been a sorrel and his winter coat was slightly wavy. The wool backing and the edging was a nice shade of green. However, Edith was to learn that the robe would always shed a little, but she had it for most of her married life.

After church on Sunday, Edith prepared to write thank you notes for their wedding gifts. She tried to talk Ralph into helping her, but he balked at the idea. He said that writing thank you notes was like the housework, garden, chickens, and washing. It was woman's work.

Edith finally prevailed upon him to write a note to Ivan Clark to thank him for the checkerboard the boy had given them. Ivan was about eleven or twelve, and Edith felt a thank you from Ralph would mean much more to the boy than a note from her.

The following Tuesday Ralph went to Elsie to meet with Dave Watson at the bank where they signed the lease that Mr. T.P. Steadman, the banker, had made out.

Ralph read the lease and felt it was accurate, fair, and complete.

The lease stated the eighty acres of land which Mr. Watson was leasing, was located in Clinton County, Duplain Township, in Section 17. The lease was in effect for one year from April 1, 1915. Of course, that wasn't exactly accurate since Ralph and Edith had put some of their possessions in the house a couple of days after the going away party for the Watsons. Ralph had brought the livestock over and, of course, they themselves had moved in on March 11, but all of that had been understood when Ralph had first accepted Mr. Watson's offer to lease the farm to him.

The rent of said premises was set at one-half the net product of the farm which was to include the income and increase from livestock and dairy. Each was to furnish half and take half. Ralph was to furnish work team and tools and do all the work and deliver all produce to market. Mr. Watson was to furnish 30 bushels of oats now and another 30 bushels of oats in the fall to be used to feed the work team. Mr. Watson owned the right to harvest the wheat now in the ground and also five acres of hay. Ralph was to do road work assessed against this land. In the event of loss of livestock, each was to stand half the loss.

Ralph was to keep the premises in good repair, and at the expiration of the lease, they were to be in like condition as when taken; reasonable use and wear thereof and damage by the elements excepted.

Since the lease was agreeable to both parties, Mr. Watson and Ralph affixed their signatures which were witnessed by T.P. Steadman and Hugh Watson, Dave's oldest son.

It was to be noted that no mention was made of chickens, or fowl of any kind. Usually, it was the woman who raised the chickens, ducks, or geese, and since she was the one responsible for them, none of the income from them was owed to the land owner. They were fed from the renter's share of whatever grain was raised on the farm.

Although Ralph was to lease this farm until the spring of 1920, this was the only time Mr. Watson felt the need for a written agreement. He and Ralph had a good relationship, and both had complete confidence in the honesty and integrity of the other.

Edith had never been one to have a great deal of confidence in her ability to do much of anything, and Ralph certainly had not helped her gain confidence. Whenever she served something different for a meal, she was fearful her husband wouldn't like what she had made. Although he had not complained since that first disastrous breakfast, each meal left her nervous. However, she tried her best not to let Ralph know of her concern. Then came the day when Edith opened a jar of the canned corn her mother had given her. She added a pat of butter and a little milk, then served the corn in side dishes as her mother always did.

Ralph took a spoonful of the corn, scowled slightly, then asked, "What's wrong with the corn? It doesn't taste quite right."

"There's nothing wrong with the corn. It tastes fine to me." Her heart sank because once again she felt she had failed.

Ralph made no further complaint, and he finished what was in his dish. At least he hadn't refused to eat it. She guessed she'd have to call her mother-in-law again. When she did, Edith learned that Miney always added a little sugar to her sweet corn. When Edith served the balance of the jar of corn, she added sugar and Ralph made no complaint.

Edith was rather excited because they were to have guests for Sunday dinner. She had talked it over with Ralph and they had invited Don Sherman and Thelma Turner, the ones who had stood up with them at their wedding.

Edith was in a quandary as to what to serve for the meal. She wondered if Don was as finicky as Ralph. She knew Thelma wasn't because over the years, she had had numerous meals at Aunt Frank's, Thelma's mother.

She finally settled on a beef roast, mashed potatoes and gravy, canned peaches, squash (Ma had given her the last one from their cellar a few days ago) and when she baked on Saturday, she'd make a cake but instead of bread, she'd make enough rolls for dinner.

All went well until they sat down to eat. Edith had stacked the plates in front of Ralph and placed the meat, potatoes, and squash within easy reach. Her father had always served when they had company, thus she assumed others did the same.

Ralph made some remark about Edith forgetting to put the plates in their proper place, then he proceeded to hand the empty plates first to Thelma, then to Don, then to his wife. He gave Edith an innocent grin.

To cover her embarrassment, Edith looked at Don and said, "And don't you dare laugh. I'm not responsible for Ralph's lack of good manners."

Don attempted to keep a straight face, but when he looked at Ralph, they both burst out laughing. Ralph was quick to pass the victuals, and everyone seemed to enjoy the meal. While Edith smoldered inside, she knew there was no need to bring up the subject after the guests left. Well, she'd know better next time. It was just like the older women always said, "You never know a man until you've lived with him." And she had felt she knew Ralph well.

Ralph sat on the back steps rubbing Bruno's ears. He felt a little sad as he noticed how gray the bulldog's muzzle was. Seemed as though Bruno had aged a lot in the past year. The dog's hearing was no longer acute, and Ralph thought his eyesight was much diminished. Of course, Bruno was fifteen which was really old for a dog. Still, Ralph hated to think his four-footed friend might not be with him much longer. He had been a good companion all those years.

Ralph realized Bruno had been somewhat confused since his master's marriage. The dog had always been especially fond of Millie, and the farm had been his first home; therefore, he often accompanied Ralph back to the farm. Usually, he followed Ralph and the team, but occasionally, he refused to leave when Ralph did. Sometimes, he came home across the fields, and sometimes, he followed the roads. However, he was always home by supper time.

Edith could tell that Ralph was reluctant to spend time plowing and fitting the garden spot. She hated to nag him, but a garden was very important to her. She wanted to have enough vegetables to eat fresh from the garden and yet have enough to can some for the winter months. A productive garden would save a lot on the grocery bill. If her expenses were less, she would then feel she was doing her share to help her husband be successful.

For some unexplained reason this year there was an over abundance of skunks. While skunks usually remained in the fields or woodlots, this year, it was common to see them around the buildings. Going to the toilet after dark was a dreaded experience since skunks are a nocturnal animal, and it was never certain there would not be a skunk or two in the vicinity of the outhouse. Rate had shot several much to Edith's relief.

Since moving on the Watson farm, Ralph had become friends with Georgie Walker who lived a short distance to the south. Georgie's father, Ed, was a brother of Jeff, who lived just down the road. While Georgie was a few years younger than Ralph, they got on well since Georgie was noted for his good sense of humor.

Ralph had stopped at his parent's on his way home from town. He couldn't believe his eyes when his father showed him his newest accuisition. It was a brand new Reo touring automobile. Ralph's inclination was to burst out laughing, but he knew this was not the time for levity.

"Gosh, Pa, when did you get this?"

"Day before yesterday. Spent a little time learning how to start the thing, which is really quite simple. It's the shifting that presents a problem. Think I've got that down pat now. I've been driving it around the driveway for practice. What do you think of it?"

"Mighty fine looking, Pa. Guess I'm just a little surprised in view of all the comments you've made against automobiles. How many times did you say they'd never catch on?"

"I know, I know. It's just that everyone seems to be getting one. I know Blanche thought we should have had one years ago. Of course, Blanche is always ready to try something new," he said with a chuckle.

The body was a shiny black; the wheels had wooden spokes and were nearly as large as those on a wagon. Fenders curved well above the hard rubber tires. Two large headlamps projected out from each side of the radiator. The windshield was high and could be folded down in the middle. The running board enabled a person to enter the automobile without difficulty. The steering wheel was made of solid wood about an inch in diameter. The seats were covered with black leather, held in place by leather-covered buttons placed so they made a diamond design. This made an attractive interior. The coated canvass top could be folded down; when up, the side curtains, to protect the passengers from the elements, were fastened in place by small catches which could be turned; this kept the side curtains snugly against the frame of the auto. A sturdy bumper projected several inches from the front and back of the automobile. Ralph chuckled to himself when he noted this. He figured Pa just might need that protection until he had more experience driving. Sure would be a lot different than driving a team, and Ralph wasn't certain his father was up to the challenge.

"Where are you going to keep it, Pa? It shouldn't set out in the weather all the time."

"Thought I'd build a garage on the north side of the granary. There's plenty of room betwixt the granary and the sheep shed."

"Seems a good idea," agreed Ralph.

On the way home, Ralph continued to chuckle because his father had actually purchased an automobile. Before he left, Millie had shown Ralph how easy it was to start the Reo (named for its builder, Ransome E. Olds) and had taken Ralph for a ride around the driveway. Millie wasn't as proficient at shifting gears as he would be with more practice he explained to his son. Ralph could hardly wait to hear what Blanche's reaction would be. He bet his sister would find the situation equally as humorous as he did.

The news from overseas worsened. Edith felt she did not fully understand all the ramifications, she only knew that her husband insisted that what went on in Europe was none of our business. Ralph still hoped the U.S. would maintain her neutrality.

Then came May 7. A German submarine sank the British steamer *Lusitania* off the Irish coast. This caused 1,198 persons to lose their lives including 128 Americans. While much of the nation was incensed because Germany had attacked a passenger ship, Ralph maintained that Germany had warned Americans they sailed on Allied ships at their own risk; therefore, they had no one to blame but themselves if they had been injured or had lost their life. Submarines were a real threat, and who knew what ships they would target? Ralph felt all governments were untrustworthy.

Ralph had just turned the cows out for the night when he heard someone enter the barn. It was Georgie Walker.

After a few moments of comments about the growing season, Georgie asked, "Hear about the fracas at our place a couple of nights ago?"

"Nope. Afraid not. What happened?"

"You know we've been having all kinds of trouble with skunks." Rate nodded his head. "Well, Pa's been watching for them about every night. Says he'd seen the same three skunks come into the yard from the tool shed, so he decided to wait and surprise them. He took his twelve gauge along with some extra shells. There's a sort of scaffold of only a few boards just inside the shed, so Pa climbed up there where he could see everything below. The moon was real bright and he'd left the doors open so he could see quite well. He didn't have long to wait before here came those skunks. Pa let them have it with both barrels. We heard the shot from the house. Then, we heard Pa yellin' and cussin', so I went out to see what was wrong. He got two of the skunks all right, but he also got the left front wheel of the buggy. Never knew a shotgun blast would tear something up that bad. Course Pa wasn't very far off when he shot. Believe me, he was fit to be tied. Kinda thought it was funny, but I sure didn't dare laugh."

"Was he cold sober?" Ralph knew that both Ed and his brother, Jeff, were heavy drinkers.

"Yeah. If he'd been lickered up, I could have understood how it happened. Guess he was concentrating so hard on the skunks, he just never saw anything else."

"Well, we've sure had more than our share of skunks this year. Still got 'em comin' around?"

"So far as I know. Pa hasn't exactly been pursuing them since his unfortunate shot. Guess he didn't feel the two skunks were worth a wrecked buggy wheel."

It was only a few days later when Georgie came to see Ralph again. He said that when he'd come home around midnight a couple of nights ago, he'd seen four skunks leaving from near the house. His mother was really upset. She was afraid to step out of the house after dark. No one wanted to get sprayed by a skunk.

Ralph and Georgie decided they would see what kind of luck they would have shooting a skunk or two.

A couple of nights later, Ralph and Georgie were in Ed's woodshed behind the house, peering out toward the house and the other farm buildings. They were quiet, not wanting to announce their presence should any skunks be wandering in the vicinity.

They had been there only a short time when Ralph tapped Georgie on his arm and pointed. A skunk had just come around the corner of the house. Right now, it was too far off for a good shot, so they waited. The animal moved slowly, stopping to smell of everything in its path. For a moment, the moon went under a cloud and the two men lost sight of the skunk. When the light returned, they noted the animal had turned and seemed to be retracing its steps. Both men shot at the same moment. Along with the report of the shotguns, there seemed to be a metallic sound.

"What was that?" asked Ralph.

"Don't know. We sure as heck must have got the skunk. Sounded like something hit tin, didn't it?"

Cautiously, they moved from their hiding place. No one came from the house since all knew Ralph and Georgie were looking for skunks. The body of the skunk lay near the downspout from the eaves trough which emptied into a cistern. Now, they knew what had caused the metallic sound. Apparently, both shots had hit the downspout in the same spot. The downspout was riddled with holes. In fact, part of it was torn away. They looked at each other in disbelief.

"Guess buggy wheels aren't the only thing the blast of a shotgun can ruin," observed Ralph.

"That's for sure," agreed Georgie as he looked disconsolately at the torn downspout.

"Is your pa going to be riled over this?"

"I'm not sure. Still, I think maybe Pa will be understanding since he had the problem with the buggy. At least I hope so. What a mess. Of course, Ma will be glad there's one less skunk around."

When haying time came, Ralph bought a hay loader. This was a machine that was pulled behind a wagon. The cut hay had to be raked into windrows, then as the wagon was driven straddle of the windrow, fingers on the hay loader picked up the hay where it was carried on slats to be dumped on the wagon. This not only saved a lot of time, it was much less work.

As usual, Millie felt the hay loader was a foolish investment. Ralph wondered why it was that his father was never in favor of anything that would make work easier for his son. Rate sometimes resented the fact that Millie thought him lazy.

Neighbors were not of the same opinion as Millie. Ralph was asked to rent the hay loader. They willingly paid him a dollar a day for the use of his machine. They paid more if Ralph worked with them. Ralph was quick to let his father know that the machine had been a good investment. Millie made no comment, but then, Ralph had expected none. Pa would never admit he just might be wrong about anything. Millie didn't suggest that Ralph use the hay loader to help him put up hay.

Edith had been well pleased with her garden. The weather had been good, and everything was growing well. She had anxiously watched for the first peas to be mature enough to have some for a meal. There was nothing better than fresh peas from the garden. The string beans were doing well and would soon be ready. They had already had lettuce. Although lettuce was not Ralph's favorite vegetable, surprisingly, he had made no complaint. Guess maybe she had put enough sugar on the leaves before she put on the watered-down vinegar. Seemed if food was sweet enough, Ralph was less likely to find fault.

Edith was having the first peas of the season for supper. She could hardly wait. Ralph had commented favourably when he noticed what she had in the side dishes. Except for preparing the garden, Ralph had done nothing to help with the planting, hoeing, or weeding, but Edith didn't care. She liked working in the garden.

Edith wasn't like her sister, Gladys, who never did a days work in her garden. Don, her husband, plowed, fitted, planted, hoed, and weeded. The most Gladys did was take care of the produce Don brought to the house. Of course, Don was a big eater, so Gladys did a lot of canning. However, Edith felt that Gladys was completely spoiled. Don took care of the chickens too although Gladys managed to gather eggs.

Ralph had finished washing up, and they sat down to eat. My those peas tasted good to Edith. There was just nothing better than the first garden-fresh peas.

Ralph looked up after taking a spoonful of peas.

"The peas don't taste just right, do they?"

"I thought they were exceptionally good. What do you think is wrong with them?"

"I don't know. They just taste different than Ma's."

Edith was becoming callous to Ralph's criticism. He was simply not a person who truly enjoyed eating. Actually, if something didn't taste right to him, it would not have bothered him to leave it uneaten. Well, thought Edith, I guess I better call Mother Setterington before I pick the next batch of peas.

Edith was to learn that Miney put sugar in peas the same as she did corn. Edith felt Ralph's mother certainly had a sweet tooth since she put sugar in vegetables. No one Edith knew did this. Maybe if she gradually began to put a little less sugar in the peas and corn, over a period of time she could wean Ralph from the sugar. It was worth a try.

It seemed to Edith that she had to contact her mother-in-law at least once a week to ask how she prepared something or get a recipe from her for something Ralph had mentioned that he liked.

Edith's father had given them a smoked ham, and when they had eaten the largest portion, Edith boiled the bone to remove the rest of the meat; she then cooked navy beans in the liquid. She sweetened the mixture with brown sugar. She served the ham and beans for supper.

Ralph was quick to note that Edith had a side dish of beans. Finally, he asked,

"How come you have a side dish of beans? You didn't take them from the serving bowl."

"I'm not accustomed to beans with sugar in them. I like them better without, so I took out some for me before I added sugar."

"Oh. How'd you know that I like mine sweet?"

"You like everything sweet. Actually, I checked with your mother. I wasn't surprised that she put sugar in the beans, she puts sugar in everything it seems."

"You must have put in the right amount because the ham and beans are real good." He gave her a disarming smile.

"Thank you. It's nice to know that I got something right the first time I made it."

Although the remark held a little sarcasm, Ralph ignored it as he helped himself to an unaccustomed second helping of beans and ham. Edith was glad she had talked with Miney before she served this dish. She was glad to see Ralph take seconds. Sometimes, she felt he didn't eat as much as he should for the amount of hard labor he did daily.

Ralph had stopped in at his parents to see how the work on the garage was coming. He figured it must be nearly done. While there, the horses had come up to the barnyard for a drink. Ralph noticed Nell and Monarch weren't with them.

"Pa, where's Nell and Monarch?"

"Sold both last week. Some fellow came by and offered me a really good price. It was just too good to turn down, so I sold them."

Ralph said nothing more. He had figured that after he paid off the note which was coming due, he would offer Pa a reasonable price for Monarch. Ralph liked to drive a matched team like grandfather had always done, so he thought Buster and Monarch would make a good looking team. He'd break Buster next year and Monarch would be ready to break the following year. Well, so much for those plans.

Pa had probably felt he could use the extra money since he was having to build a garage for his automobile. However, with a horse trader, it was difficult to tell what motivated them. Whatever the reason, Monarch was gone. Since farmers who had strawberry roans were few and far between, Ralph figured he'd never have a chance to get a horse to match Buster.

Toward the end of August, Nellie Holbrook stopped to talk with Edith and Ralph. Edith did not know her well, but since Nellie was keeping company with Edith's favorite cousin, Lee Brewbaker, she had met her on several occasions. Nellie had been hired to teach at the rural school south of the Watson farm. She needed a place to provide room and board, and she wondered if Edith and Ralph would be interested in letting her stay with them. Ralph thought the decision should be his wife's because whatever extra work would be involved would be Edith's, not his. Edith hated making a decision, but when the thought of the few extra dollars coming in, she decided Nellie could board with them. Besides, she felt that by accommodating Nellie, she was doing something for Lee.

Lee was her brother Carl's age, and Edith had always sort of looked after the boys. As Lee often said, she kept them out of trouble. When Lee decided to go to college, a lot of the relatives made fun of him behind his back, saying he only wanted to go to college because he was lazy, didn't want to work like most folks. He had begun classes at Michigan Agricultural College, but had had some sort of run-in with Dr. Kedzie, his chemistry prof. Lee had become so upset, he had transferred to the University of Michigan. Thus far, he was happy with the change. Edith felt that Lee's desire for an education was the business of no one other than Lee himself. Edith had always felt Lee was a very sensitive person, more interested in poetry and English literature than others she knew. Since Edith had always liked poetry, she felt she understood Lee better than others in the family.

Having Nellie with them during the week, Nellie often went home for the weekend was rather nice. Nellie often helped Edith with something she was doing unless there were a lot of papers for Nellie to correct in the evening. It hadn't taken Ralph long to discover Nellie was easily embarrassed. He often made some comment simply because he knew his words would make Nellie blush. She confided to Edith that she'd give anything to be able to hear Ralph's comments without her face and even her neck turning a fiery red. Edith was very sympathetic although she knew of no way to remedy the situation. Ralph would do as he pleased no matter what she said.

Bruno had not shown up at supper time. Ralph was more than a little concerned. It was not like the dog to be late getting home. Ralph had just about decided he should go look for Bruno when one of Jeff Walker's boys stopped in to tell Ralph he thought perhaps the dead dog a short distance north of the drive might be Bruno.

The boy was right. Bruno laid by the side of the road. Someone in an automobile had hit him. Ralph always thought whoever had hit the dog, had done it on purpose because Bruno always trotted at the edge of the road. He carried Bruno home, and after supper, buried his boyhood friend. There would be other dogs in his life, but none was loved as much as that brindle bulldog.

With fall, Edith had plenty of canning to do. She put up a few pints of string beans, carrots, and beets. She canned tomatoes and she and her sister, Gladys, made some sauerkraut. Edith hated having to buy jars, but she consoled herself with the thought that next year and many years thereafter there would not be this expense.

Since there was a grapevine, she made grape jelly which Miney had informed her was Ralph's favorite. There was a crab apple tree in the small orchard; therefore, she intended to make some apple jelly. Ma had given her some jelly glasses saying that since her family was getting so much smaller, she didn't need to make as much jam or jelly. Edith was glad she didn't have to spend money for jelly glasses.

Edith set the table for four instead of the usual three since Archie Carl had been helping Ralph and wouldn't be going home until after supper. Nellie had come home with such an armful of papers to correct, she had not taken time to change her clothes or help Edith with the meal. Edith had often told Nellie she didn't need to help get meals because Edith firmly believed Nellie was paying for this service.

Nellie had on a new white blouse. The material was a rather sheer dimity, and if one looked closely, the lace of her underskirt could faintly be seen. Edith thought Nellie looked really nice.

Soon after the meal began, Archie watched Nellie a moment, then asked, "Nellie, is that one of them see-more blouses?"

Nellie's face turned beet red. She kept her eyes on her plate. Edith knew she was trying to come up with an answer.

"Gosh, Nellie, I don't hear you answering Archie. Cat got your tongue?" Ralph's eyes danced, and he gave an irritating laugh.

"Ralph, don't you dare tease Nellie," interjected Edith.

"Me tease? Wouldn't think of it. I just thought Nellie was ignoring Archie, and I thought she should give him an answer." His eyes twinkled, and in spite of the serious expression on his face, both Nellie and Edith knew he was enjoying himself immensely.

"That's all right, Nellie. I really wasn't funnin' you. I ain't never seen no material like that afore. Really, you look mighty nice," Archie said sincerely.

"Thank you, Archie," she said giving him the brief hint of a smile. When she looked at Ralph, she glared. Somehow, she had to think of something to do to get even with Ralph for all the teasing.

A week later, Nellie came home from school, changed her clothes immediately, then joined Edith in the kitchen.

"Is Ralph still outside?"

"Yes. I don't believe he's up from the field yet." Ralph was doing some fall plowing.

"Why?"

"I didn't want him to hear me talking with you."

"Oh. You sound serious. Something wrong?"

"Nothing Is wrong, but I have an idea to play a joke on Ralph; however, I need your help to make it work."

"All right. He has asked for some sort of retaliation ever since you moved in."

"Well, some of the boys at school told me there is a little screech owl living in their toilet. No one seems to mind too much, but I think the owl should be removed. I'd not want to harm the poor little thing, I just want it to live elsewhere. Now, I think I can easily capture the owl. I thought, what if I brought it home and tied it up in one of the legs of Ralph's pajamas. What do you think?"

"Might be fun. Of course, Ralph would know whom to blame."

"I know, but it might disconcert him for a few moments."

The two women made their plans, and two nights later, when Nellie came home from school, she carried a mysterious package. With Edith's help, Nellie hastily transferred the sleepy little bird to Ralph's pajamas.

Then came the wait.

With supper finished, Nellie helped Edith do dishes and clean up the kitchen. The time was passing very slowly. She kept looking at the clock, but the hands seemed scarcely to move. Ralph had done the milking, and as was his custom, he sat to read for a while. Edith was doing some patching, while Nellie attempted to correct papers. She found it difficult to concentrate.

Nellie went to bed a little earlier than usual. From her room, she could hear the usual sounds as Edith and Ralph prepared for bed. Nellie didn't know exactly what she expected, but she was on pins and needles waiting for something. Not a sound. Then, she heard a door quietly open, and just as quietly, close. Must be Ralph had discovered the bird and had released it outside. What had he thought? She hadn't a clue. How disappointing.

The next morning at breakfast, Ralph greeted Nellie in his usual manner. Was that a glint in his eye that was not usually there? His demeanor seemed innocent enough but Nellie was wary. Somehow, he seemed too congenial, too pleasant, he must have something up his sleeve.

After breakfast, Ralph sat a few moments, then put on his light jacket to return to the barn to do chores. Just before he opened the door, he turned, and spoke to Nellie.

"Nellie, where did you find that screech owl?"

Poor Nellie. Her face turned red, and she made no answer to Ralph's back as he hurried out the door.

Ralph was quietly laughing to himself. He had known for several days that a screech owl had taken up residence in the boy's toilet. He had intended to offer his services to get rid of the small bird, but Nellie had taken care of that. He knew that any reference to the location of the bird would embarrass Nellie. Guess he'd sort of turned the tables. Sure gave him a good laugh and started his day on a high note. Ralph actually marvelled that timid Nellie had had enough spunk to enter the boy's toilet, forbidden territory in her opinion and capture the small bird.

"How'd he know?" Nellie asked Edith.

"He certainly knew where the owl had been living. I never mentioned the bird when Ralph was around."

"Oh, Nellie, I don't know where he gets his information, but somehow he knows everything that goes on in the neighborhood. I suppose he ran into some of the kids and they told him. I'm sorry he embarrassed you."

"It's not your fault. He just took me completely by surprise. Guess I really didn't get even, did I?"

Edith felt sorry for Nellie. She guessed she and Nellie were no match for Ralph.

Seemed a shame. Someone should be able to best him.

On the seventeenth of November, Ralph paid off a note to H.J. Taylor which he had taken out a year ago. Since he had not borrowed before and had no collateral at that time, Millie had signed with him. Edith had not known about the note until after they were married when Ralph admitted that he had borrowed $260.00 at 5% interest; therefore, he had to come up with $273.00 when the note was due.

At first, Edith had worried for fear they would be unable to pay that huge amount of money. Their share of the money from the Eureka Cheese Co. was not very large, sometimes only a few dollars for the entire month. Ralph had assured her that they would have at least two or three veal calves to sell when the cows freshened, and the checks from the Cheese Co.would be much better during the summer months. Besides, if he helped Pa some of the time, Pa had said he would pay him the same as he would any hired hand. He had told her that he intended to purchase a hay loader; there weren't any in the immediate neighborhood.

He was certain some of the neighbors would pay him for the use of the hay loader, and this had proved to be true. However, Edith had still been doubtful. This had been one more reason she had scrimped as much as she could on groceries, and the rent Nellie paid had been a big help. The garden had certainly paid off. They had eaten quite well during the summer months and the jars of canned goods would keep them eating well during the winter. Edith liked to think she had done her share in helping Ralph save the money needed.

She hated to be in debt, but she guessed they had really needed the money to buy machinery, cows, and the few chickens she had. Ralph had been saving toward the time when he would farm on his own, but he had lacked money for all of the really important items. At least they were out of debt now, and Edith felt as though a great weight had been lifted from her shoulders.

Next year, she would have more than a few eggs to sell to buy groceries and even perhaps material for Ralph's shirts or her aprons. She had set four hens and had had good luck raising the little chicks. They would eat the few roosters, but they had been lucky and the chicks had been predominantly pullets. They would have a garden again and she would not have to buy canning jars, and next year the wheat crop would be half theirs. They had had three heifer calves. Nothing there for next year, but the year after they'd have more cream to sell. She felt by being very frugal, they would make out all right. At least this was her fervent hope.

Millie asked Ralph to help tear down the log cabin on the forty. They had already salvaged some lumber, but Millie wanted the rest of the building out of the way. He told Ralph that for his help, he'd give him the logs and whatever else he could salvage for firewood. Ralph felt this was an excellent offer, because this year, he had not been able to cut wood for the stoves. Sure beat having to buy firewood. Except for chores, a farmer's work load was lightest during the winter months, so Ralph knew he'd have plenty of time to work on the project.

CHAPTER 9

It was past the middle of March when Ralph told Edith they were short of cash for the spring planting season. He didn't need much this time; he had given it a lot of thought and he figured sixty dollars would take care of their needs. He intended to ask for the money for only eight months. F.C. Coleman had said he'd loan Ralph the money without a co-signer, but he charged 6% interest; however, on such a small amount, at maturity, the interest would only be $2.40.

Edith hated to have Ralph borrow money again, but she felt that he understood these things far better than she did. Besides, they had managed to pay off a much larger amount last year, and all her worrying had been for naught. Besides, their income should be better this year. If everything continued to go well, perhaps they would not have to borrow next year.

The spring of 1916 turned out to be a wet one. This hindered farmers with their field work. About the only advantage was that the wet ground made it easier to build fence since the wooden fence posts were easier to drive into the ground when the ground was soft.

Mr. Watson agreed with Ralph that eighteen rods of an old rail fence needed to be replaced. Dave said that if Ralph would buy the fence posts and put up the fence, he could have the wood from the rails. Of course, Dave would furnish the woven wire fence. Ralph thought this sounded like a good proposition. There would be a lot of good firewood in those old hardwood rails.

The cost for cedar posts was seventeen cents a post. Since the posts for a woven wire fence were placed a rod apart, that meant seventeen posts would be sufficient because the fence would tie into already existing fences that had the larger, heavier, corner posts. Ralph paid Archie Carl a dollar to put in the posts and help him string the wire. The posts were pointed on one end, and a beetle ring was put on the topmost part which enabled the posts to be driven into the ground with a heavy wooden mallet without damaging the posts. The woven wire fence was pulled taut with wire stretchers, and it was then stapled to the posts.

Ralph had been over to Vern's, and when he returned he came into the house where Edith was cooking some navy beans with a ham bone. Ralph sniffed the air appreciatively. He was very fond of beans if they were sweet enough, and they were best when flavored with good, hickory smoked ham.

"You'll never guess what those two nephews of yours have done now."

"Something outlandish from your expression."

"They skinned their hobby horse."

"They what?" asked Edith, disbelief in her voice.

"They dragged their hobby horse out to the barn and proceeded to skin it. Vern didn't catch them until they were almost done. Blanche is ready to skin both of them. Vern is disgusted, but a little more understanding."

Beurmann's and Wilson's hobby horse had been covered with real horse hide. Vern had spent more on it than he should have spent, but it had looked so pretty, soft hearted Vern couldn't turn it down. This had been at least two or three years ago. Although Beurmann was getting to be too large for the toy, Wilson still rode it, and Wendell liked rocking on it if someone would pick him up and place him in the saddle.

"Those little demons. It was undoubtedly Beurmann's idea, and as usual, Wilson followed his lead. I wonder whatever possessed them to do such a thing?"

"I'd bet it was because they heard of someone who had a horse skinned and a robe made of the hide. But who knows? Those two have minds that work different than the average kid."

Edith could just imagine how Blanche felt. She wondered what Blanche had done to punish them. Vern wasn't likely to do anything but yell a little; it would be up to Blanche to come up with an appropriate punishment.

Ralph hadn't been feeling well of late. He was glad the cows were out on pasture at last because now there were no stables to clean. He had managed to get the corn field ready for planting, and had planted the corn.

A couple of days he had felt so rotten he hadn't argued when Edith said she was going to call Dr. Schweitzer. The doctor poked and prodded and asked a lot of questions, but could find nothing wrong. He simply told Ralph to make certain he was eating well, and to get his rest at night.

Ralph went with Edith to the wedding of Thelma Turner to Robert Schaar on the 28th of June. He hadn't felt like going, but he knew it was important to Edith; therefore, he had kept quiet about how poorly he felt. It seemed that some days he felt rotten all over, yet it was nothing he could specifically put his finger on. He simply knew he'd never felt like this before.

Ralph hired Archie Carl to cultivate the corn, but now, it was time to do the haying. Ralph worked three and a half days getting the haying done. When finished, he felt terrible, the worst he had felt yet. Edith called Dr. Schweitzer again with the same results. The doctor came again the next day only to find Ralph was no better. In fact he seemed to be worse. He said he felt terrible all over.

"Ralph, I believe if I was you, I'd see someone who could tell me what's wrong," said the kindly doctor. He looked completely baffled.

Edith called Dr. Hart. Upon examining Ralph, he announced in no uncertain terms that Ralph was suffering from appendicitis. It was certainly serious. He thought if Ralph stayed in bed a couple of days, his condition would improve enough so he could be transported to the hospital in St. Johns for surgery.

Trouble was, Ralph continued to get worse, not better. Dr. Hart decided it would be too dangerous to move him because he feared the appendix would rupture; however, if they didn't operate soon, the odds were great that the appendix would rupture anyway. A ruptured appendix would mean certain death. The only alternative was to perform the surgery at home, a rather radical decision; however, the doctor felt this would at least give Ralph a fighting chance.

Three doctors prepared Ralph for surgery: Dr. Gene Hart, Dr. Schweitzer, and Dr. Charles T. Foo. A table was brought in along with the other equipment needed. As asked, Edith had pans of water boiling on the stove. It was almost two o'clock in the afternoon before they had everything ready and put Ralph under. The lamps were lighted long before he came to.

Dr. Hart told Edith the operation had gone very well. Now, if no infection set in, Ralph would recuperate as expected. Edith, who was always a worrier, felt only somewhat relieved. Of course, since they had been forced to operate in the home, she worried about the possibility of infection. By the usual standards, her house was clean, but Edith felt it certainly didn't compare to a hospital. She had provided plenty of hot water, but she wondered if that was enough. She had waited for what seemed like an eternity for the surgery to be completed. It was a relief to have the operation safely over even if she felt she still had cause to worry.

The smell of ether permeated the air even though the doors and windows were open to the balmy summer air. Edith's stomach felt queasy. She didn't know if this was due to the remnants of ether or whether it was because she had been so nervous about the operation. The odor of ether clung to Ralph, but she felt she had to share his bed or she might not hear him when he awoke. She was very careful to slip into bed with no more movement than was absolutely necessary. She lay on her back on the very edge of the bed because she did not want to disturb her husband. Ralph slept although somewhat fitfully at times.

The first time Ralph awakened for a short period, Edith realized he was still pretty groggy. The doctors had told her it would take most of the night for the anesthetic to leave his system. Dr. Hart had left pain medication, but Ralph didn't seem to want it. He was thirsty, and would rouse up to ask Edith for a drink, then immediately go back to sleep. Edith was not as fortunate; it took her longer to fall asleep; consequently, she got very little rest that first night.

Ralph had thought he would feel much better after surgery, but he had not understood how sore he would be all around the incision. His entire abdomen was sore. Dr. Schweitzer came to change the dressing, and it was then Ralph discovered that he had a tube in his side. When he asked the doctor why it was there, Ralph didn't feel the answer explained the reason very well. The most he understood was that the tube was for drainage and would promote healing. How? He had no idea.

Ralph lay on his side for almost a week, and he became more discouraged with each passing day. When he tried to stand, he could not straighten up; worse still, he could not tolerate walking more than two or three steps at a time. Dr. Schweitzer came each day. He would pull some of the tube from the incision and snip off a piece. He seemed greatly pleased because there was no sign of infection. Instead of Ralph counting his blessings, his thoughts centered on what he considered a slow recovery. This was hardly what he had anticipated. He had felt he would be able to walk the day after surgery. How wrong he had been.

When Ralph could finally manage to walk without a lot of pain, he was told that he had to restrict his walking to inside the house. He was allowed to sit on the porch, but going down steps was strictly forbidden. Ralph began to wonder when he'd ever be able to do farm work.

Neighbors and relatives were particularly kind and helped as much as they could. He hadn't had to put out a lot of money--money he could ill afford to spend--to hire the work done. He was grateful to those who helped, but he wanted to be able to do his own work.

Although he wouldn't have admitted it to a soul, Ralph was concerned about how he'd feel for Blanche's wedding. She and George had finally set a date, the 27th of July. Blanche's wedding was important to him. He had been glad when George had given Blanche a ring, and they had announced their engagement. Even though Pa and Ma had always favored Blanche, he knew his sister had no control over the partiality shown. Ma had just naturally preferred girls, and as they got older, Pa had shown the same favoritism. He and Blanche had had their moments as most siblings do, but now, they enjoyed one another's company. Perhaps they still teased, but Ralph thought that was to be expected. Besides, he still owed his sister for taking his marriage license.

Ralph was like a work horse chomping at the bit. He was getting extremely impatient, and nothing Edith said seemed to help. When he was given permission to walk around the yard, he was amazed at how weak he was. He walked short distances several times a day to help get his strength back. He was not even content when he could resume doing the milking because he had to work slowly; however, he found he tired so quickly, he had no other choice.

Edith knew what it was like not to be able to do as one pleased. When she had been extremely ill in her early teens, it seemed as though it had taken her forever to have complete use of her arms and legs. The doctors had never known for certain what had caused her condition. Their best guess was that it had been infantile paralysis (polio), but not much was known of the disease. They had been relieved that there seemed to be no permanent disability. Her right arm was about an inch shorter than the other, and she still had to wear a thin lift on her right shoe, but that posed no great hardship. Ralph had never seemed to mind. In fact, she felt that the necessity of a lift was becoming less each year. Perhaps there would be a time when she would no longer need a lift to allow her to walk without limping. She hoped this would be true.

Edith found she was relieved to have her husband out of the house. He had been completely discouraged, and she had been truly sympathetic, still she had felt completely helpless. She knew the few times that Ralph had been short with her was because of his own frustrations. Her husband was not one to accept inactivity. Of course, she had worried far more than anyone, including her husband, had realized. Every day when Dr. Schweitzer changed the bandage and removed more of the tube, she had literally held her breath until the doctor had proclaimed all was well. She had been so fearful of infection, her worry had kept her from sleeping well. Her sister Gladys, told her she was beginning to look worn out. She hoped Ralph hadn't noticed. She wouldn't want him to be concerned about her welfare because he had enough worries of his own. Now that Ralph was healed, she felt certain she would rest better.

She had felt like crying when she found the finish on the library table ruined on one corner where one of the doctors had set a pan full of extremely hot water. She reminded herself that it was only a table, and the fact that Ralph was all right was what was important. She kept a scarf on the table to cover the spot so Ralph wouldn't notice and ask questions.

While Ralph rode the binder to cut wheat, he hired Archie Carl to shock it. His strength was near normal, but he still tired easily. At least he felt encouraged. It seemed as though he rested better nights and his appetite was steadily improving. He knew this made Edith feel better. Although she had tried not to show it, Ralph knew she had been terribly concerned. Some days he had eaten little although he knew this bothered his wife. With no physical activity, his appetite was completely lacking. Even when he was doing hard, physical labor, Ralph was never one to eat large amounts of anything. He seldom took seconds except for cake. Perhaps he had inherited his mother's sweet tooth because he certainly enjoyed cake, pies, and cookies.

By the end of the third week of July, Ralph felt he was finally back to normal. What a relief! There was plenty of farm work to keep him busy. The oats were cut and shocked, and it was now threshing time. Neighbors worked together at threshing time, and he felt that he could now carry his share of the load. It was a good feeling.

Blanche came home to prepare for her wedding. George would arrive the first of the week. They'd go to St. Johns to get the marriage license, and they would be married on Thursday.

Blanche made a beautiful bride. Her gown was not nearly as plain as her usual attire. It was white and sheer, and had a ruffle at the neckline and a ruffle at the cuffs of the long sleeves. There was a ruffle just above the sash at the waist. Deep ruffles formed the generous skirt. Her only adornment was a gold necklace.

Ralph and Edith went with Millie and Miney to see the newlyweds off at the train station. The couple was taking a cruise for a honeymoon. They were assured by the ticket master that the train would be arriving on time, thus they had only a few minutes to wait.

Ralph looked like the cat that had eaten the canary. He chuckled to himself.

Then, he asked, "George, are you going to be like Christ and walk on water?"

"What do you mean?" asked George with a perplexed look.

Blanche gave her brother a withering look. She didn't wait for him to give George an answer. She looked at her husband and asked, "George Ryan, where did you leave the steamer tickets?"

"In my suitcase, where else?" he replied innocently.

"You poor fool, you," she said, shaking her head in disbelief.

"Why? What's wrong?

"Ask my brother. Just ask him where the tickets are."

"You mean they aren't in my suitcase?"

"No. I'm sure they are not. All right, Ralph, you've had your fun. What did you do with the tickets?"

"Why, sister dear, what makes you think I'd take something from George's suitcase? If they're not there, they undoubtedly simply fell out on the floor. Sometimes, things have the darndest way of falling from where they belong." He gave her a laugh that he knew would irritate.

"And I suppose you happened to see them on the floor, and out of the goodness of your heart, you picked them up knowing they must be important."

"I'm so glad you understand."

"I understand all right. Do you expect me to beg?"

Ralph could tell that his sister was losing her patience. The prank had gone far enough. He had no intention of making her truly angry. After all, she knew she was being repaid for filching his marriage license from his pocket. He simply wanted to worry her a little. He had no intention of spoiling her wedding day.

"Not you." Ralph gave his sister a look of complete innocence. "Here, George, I guess you're just lucky I found these and brought them along." Ralph took the tickets out of his inner pocket and held them out to George who took them somewhat gingerly and examined them as though to be assured they were really the proper tickets, the ones he had left in his suitcase.

"Thank you. Although I'm not certain thanks is in order. In fact, I'm not completely sure just what went on between you and your sister." He looked from one to the other with a puzzled frown on his face.

"Don't worry about it. Blanche knows, don't you, Blanche?"

"I guess we're even, if that's what you mean" She glared at him a moment, then laughed. "As Pa always says 'One good turn deserves another.' It seems you agree. I think I hear the train whistle. Guess they were right, and for a change it is on time."

Edith had been quiet through all of this exchange. She had no idea when Ralph had acquired the steamer tickets. From the expressions on the faces of her father-in-law and mother-in-law, they had been completely unaware of any such shenanigans too. George had seemed bewildered, as though he didn't completely understand the situation. But now his Irish wit returned as he and Blanche boarded the train. Edith was relieved that all had ended well. Sometimes, she thought Ralph's teasing got a little out of hand, especially where his sister was concerned.

Edith had liked George's sister, Frances. While Frances was as accomplished as Blanche, she had much of her brother's wit; therefore, Frances had not seemed like a stranger from the moment they had been introduced. Frances had mentioned that she had some vacation time coming. She also mentioned how much she enjoyed being in the country. She said the country was much more restful than the city, and it seemed that just lately her job had been very stressful. Without really knowing why, Edith asked her if she would like to spend a few days on the farm with her and Ralph. Frances said she'd be delighted if she wouldn't be too much trouble. She knew Ralph had had a rather slow recuperation after his appendectomy. Edith assured her that Ralph was doing well and would have no objection to having her visit.

Frances spent a few days with Ralph and Edith. Edith hadn't known quite what to expect since she really didn't know Frances, but she was pleasantly surprised. Frances was quick to help Edith with the household chores, and when she knew how much feed to give the chickens, she insisted on feeding them and gathering the eggs. Frances also was willing to help Edith in the garden. She said this type of work was actually restful.

Threshing was done for the year and the second cutting of hay was in the barn. There would be a slight lull before it would be time to plant wheat. Actually, farmers didn't get many days when there was no field work to be done during the growing season.

Supper was over, Edith had finished the dishes, and Ralph had just come in from doing the milking. The cows had been turned out to pasture for the night.

Edith sat with her chair drawn up near the lamp on the table doing some patching. After washing up, Ralph sat down in a rocker but didn't pick up the book he had been reading. He watched his wife a moment before he spoke.

"How would you like to go away for the weekend?"

"What do you mean, go away?"

"Just what I said."

"How can we go any place when we have livestock that needs dally care?"

"Supposing I had someone willing to do the milking and feed the chickens? The horses will be on pasture and need no care as long as the tank is kept filled with water."

"I guess that would be all right. Where did you intend to go?" Edith sounded completely puzzled. Obviously, Ralph had been giving this much thought.

"Well, Pa and Ma are going to Detroit to visit Blanche. I thought maybe we could go along."

"Does Blanche have room to put up four extra people?"

"I guess so. Ma said Blanche asked if she thought we'd be able to come. Ma said Blanche would like to have us visit."

"You mean she's forgiven you for taking their steamer tickets?"

"Of course. No one got hurt, and Blanche doesn't hold a grudge. At least she never has. No, if she told Ma she'd like for us to come with them, she means it."

"When would we go?"

"We'd leave this Friday afternoon and come back Sunday afternoon."

"Who will do the chores and can we afford to go?" Edith was thinking of the promissory note due the 29th of November.

"Vern said he could take care of things and Carl will give him some help, so we'd not have to hire anyone. Train fare won't be much. Yes, we can afford it. You know we've sold a couple of veal calves and we got top dollar even if we only had half the money. I have most of the money for the note, if that is what is bothering you."

"Well, if you think we can afford it, and the livestock won't suffer, I guess I'd enjoy going to Detroit. I've never been there you know. Are you sure we won't be imposing? I don't want to put Blanche out."

"Don't worry about my sister. She can handle any situation."

Thus it was that Edith and Ralph accompanied Miney and Millie to Detroit. Both Blanche and George met them at the train station. If Edith had had any misgivings, they soon dissipated. Blanche seemed truly glad to have them there, and George was his usual laughable self. Somehow, George always made Edith laugh and she forgot to be self-conscious.

George and Blanche had decided they would entertain their guests on Saturday by taking them to the Riverview Amusement Park. Edith had never seen anything like this. She had heard Ralph talk about such places because, of course, he had not only been to Detroit many times, but he had been to Chicago. While she wasn't enthused about the rides, she enjoyed some of the other attractions. Ralph and George talked her into going on the Ferris wheel and another rather quiet ride. The two men went by themselves on the more exciting rides.

When they came to the roller coaster, all except Ralph and George looked at it rather skeptically. Miney announced firmly that if anyone had any idea of getting her on such a contraption, they needed their heads examined. George cajoled and teased to get at least some of them on the coaster. Finally, he convinced Millie that riding a roller coaster was really fun.

George bought the tickets and settled Millie in the front seat of the first car. He sat with his father-in-law while Ralph took a seat directly behind. Millie looked around with interest as the roller coaster inched its way up the first high incline. George knew when the cars were no longer being propelled. Seconds later, the car plunged down the first drop. Millie said nothing, but George noticed that Millie was hanging on as though his very life depended on how tightly he held onto the bar in front of him, and with each drop, Millie's tense body was raised inches out of his seat. His knuckles showed white. His face lost its color. George had at first thought it funny, but now he became worried. He hadn't expected such a severe reaction to something he viewed as being exhilarating. Perhaps this hadn't been such a good Idea.

When the ride was finished, the men moved to join the women. When asked how he liked the ride, Millie said it was just fine. The whiteness of his face belied his answer. Both Blanche and Ralph knew their father would never admit to a soul that he had actually been afraid. It was several minutes before the color returned to Millie's face. George felt much better when his father-in-law was back to normal.

Lee Brewbaker and Nellie Holbrook visited Ralph and Edith before Nellie had to return to teaching and Lee to classes at UM. Lee and Ralph spent the time discussing the situation in Europe, mainly with Germany. Both felt that the clouds of war were getting darker day by day. Although Germany had agreed to President Wilson's demand for reparations for the loss of American Lives on the *Lusitania,* Lee voiced the belief that we would never see one penny of the promised payment. He felt it was simply a ruse to pacify the U.S. for a time.

Even though Germany's submarines had been quiet for several months, Lee still did not feel comfortable about the situation. He said there was nothing the Allies could do to guarantee the world that shipping was safe from Germany's submarines.

Ralph was in favor of restricting American travel to Europe. Both he and Lee felt the Germans and the Central Powers could not be trusted. Of course, Ralph did not have a lot of confidence in the word of the Allies either. Lee was a little concerned because the National Defense Act called for an additional 200,000 men for the regular army. It was to be enacted over five years, but Lee felt the Act was a harbinger of war. Since he was enrolled in Michigan's R.O.T.C. (Reserve Officers Training Corps) he knew he would be called to active service.

Long after Lee and Nellie left, Edith mulled over the conversation about war. If war came, would Ralph be called to go? If so, whatever would she do? The farm was rented a year at a time, and Mr. Watson could not have her living here if there were no crops. What would she do with their livestock? She could hardly ask Pa to take care of her. He had enough responsibilities of his own. She told herself she would just have to trust in the Lord. As it was, no one, not even the politicians, seemed to know from one day to the next what was going to happen.

Lee felt that only single men would be asked to serve their country, but Edith knew there were many determining factors which were difficult to control. Carl was still single, and he'd be the right age. Luckily, Vern and Art were married. It seemed as though there was always something to cause worry. She could say nothing to Ralph about her fears because he would only laugh at her and tell her not to borrow trouble.

Ralph and Edith had been visiting at a neighbor. As they walked home, Edith told Ralph that her period had not begun as it should have that morning. She was always regular. When they got home, Edith soaked her feet in a pan of hot water thinking that might start her menses. It didn't. After a few days, she decided that she was in the family way. Both she and Ralph were pleased. Of course, Ralph teased her because soaking her feet had done no good.

Edith was especially pleased to know they would have a child next May. Her brother, Art, had been married in January, and he and his wife, Ethel, were expecting in November. Of course, Edith reminded herself, she had not wanted a child until she and Ralph had been married for at least two years. It seems they were getting her wish. Still, she felt Art was fortunate that Ethel was in the family way because Art was past thirty; therefore, it was time for him to become a father.

The first part of September, Edith had a post card from Frances Ryan. Frances had changed jobs, and while she had been extremely busy, she said she "liked the new place just fine." She also told Edith that the time she had spent on the farm had done her a world of good because she felt "just dandy." She even asked about Ralph's health which Edith felt was very considerate.

Since Ralph had spent most of the spring barely able to do the chores and a little field work, he had done nothing about breaking Buster to drive. The colt was well behaved in the barn, but it had not always been so. Last winter, Buster had reached down and bitten Ralph. Luckily the colt had bit Ralph on the heavy rubber boots he wore. While the bite had not caused Ralph pain, he knew the colt had to be punished or there would be a repeat performance and the next time, Ralph might not be so lucky. Ralph had picked up a length of chain and had hit the colt several times on his rump. Buster never bit Ralph again, or for that matter he never offered to bite any person he knew; however, he was never completely trustworthy around strangers. He did not like many people, and he especially did not like those he didn't really know.

Buster had developed well. His body girth was good, his chest broad, his legs slender but sturdy. He had a long, narrow head topped by dainty ears, and his eyes held an intelligent but wary look. If angry, the ears flattened back, and he looked dangerous. He had never been a kicker. Of course, he was also obstinate--the last one to return to his stall, the one who was always looking for a gate left open. His strawberry roan hide was sleek and shiny during the summer months. Ralph was mighty glad Pa had given him the colt.

Sure would have been nice if Pa hadn't sold Monarch. Golly, Buster and Monarch would have made a spiffy looking team. Oh well, as Pa always said, "No use to cry over spilt milk."

Some young horses present no problem when it came time to break them. They were simply hitched in with an older, steady horse, and they worked well. Buster was different. For one thing, he was smarter than most colts, and he was far more stubborn than most. If Ralph called "Whoa!" Buster wanted to take three or four more steps. Ralph said "Com'ere" when he wanted a team to move forward. Buster always hung back and waited for his companion to start forward, then he stayed a step behind. After trying to break Buster of this habit, Ralph simply outwitted the horse. He fastened Buster's tugs shorter than he did the other horses; therefore, Buster was actually doing his share of the work even though he lagged behind. That way, both Ralph and Buster were satisfied.

Ralph spent the better part of a year breaking and training the three-year-old to be a trustworthy draft horse. Because the colt wanted to do as he pleased, Ralph was forced to put a jerk rope on him, the bit in his mouth was not sufficient. The jerk rope went under the tender upper lip, then over the head, back to the person driving the team. When jerked, it was very uncomfortable, and tended to convince the horse he should obey commands. After a time, Ralph put the jerk rope on Buster, but simply hung the coiled rope on Buster's hame. Since Buster didn't know Ralph couldn't use the rope, he behaved. Ralph always insisted that he had to be especially alert to outsmart this horse, and with age, Buster became even smarter. Ralph viewed Buster as a challenge, and he dearly loved that horse.

Ralph had just finished his nightly chores. He had turned the cows back out to pasture thinking that it wouldn't be long before he'd have to keep them in for the night. Although there had been ample rain, pasture was getting short and the nights would soon be cold. Milk production would be better if the cows had plenty of feed, and the quality of hay was good this year. Rate had been lucky not to have any of his hay get wet even if he had had a rough time putting up first cutting.

He hesitated on his way out of the barn. Yes, he had definitely heard the sound of an automobile as it came in the drive. It was a little unusual because most of his neighbors still drove buggies. He reached the stable door just in time to see Millie getting out of his Reo. It appeared his father was alone. At least Ralph didn't see his mother going to the house.

It was unusual for Millie to be away from home this late at night unless he had been to a Grange meeting. Ralph had a premonition that something might be wrong. After the initial greeting, Rate waited for his father to open the conversation.

"Won't be turning your cows out much longer, will you?" Millie commented as he watched the cattle moving out of the barnyard down the lane.

"No. Pasture's getting short and the nights are getting cold."

Millie nodded his head in agreement. Then, he turned to look at his son.

"Ralph, your grandparents are coming from California on Thursday. Their telegram said the train would get in at 3:30 that afternoon. I want you to meet the train." Millie didn't ask Ralph if he could or would meet the train. It never occurred to him that his son might not be available.

"And where am I supposed to take them? Are you letting them stay at the farm?" Ralph asked rather bluntly.

"Don't figure I can send them elsewhere. But I darn well don't have to meet the train and act like I'm glad to see them."

"They could stay here," offered Ralph.

"No. I'll be the dutiful son in spite of what Pa has done. I talked with John and he said Pa and Ma expect to spend a couple of days with him. He didn't sound any too thrilled with the prospects, but we both decided we'd have to put them up because of Ma. I've given it a lot of thought and I don't believe Ma had anything to do with Pa for not giving me the eighty. Shouldn't punish her for what the old man has done."

"All right, Pa. I'll meet their train. How long are they staying?"

"Not long. I think they'll go to John's on Sunday. Have no idee how long they will be in Michigan before going back home. Can't be soon enough for me. Let them go back to Mac and Ruby. They are the reason Ma just had to move to Californey."

Ralph could tell his father was still bitter, and perhaps he had a right to be; however, nothing could be done to change what was past. Better to move on.

Rate met his grandparents at the train station as expected. If either Grandmother or Grandfather thought it strange that their son hadn't picked them up, neither mentioned it. Both seemed genuinely pleased to see Ralph. Grandmother even gave him a hug. Ralph thought both of them looked well. It didn't seem as though Grandfather had aged much in the last ten years. At least now that he was older,

Ralph no longer feared his grandparents. He simply had a lot of respect for them.

When Rate arrived at the farm with his grandparents, Millie had not yet come in from the barn. Ralph knew that at this time of day, this move was intentional. Ma had seemed a little ill at ease, and he wondered just what his grandparents were feeling. It was certainly obvious from the behavior of the two women, that relations were somewhat strained. However, Horatio, true to form, seemed perfectly at ease, accepting Millie's absence as perfectly normal.

Ralph left before Millie came to the house. He had absolutely no desire to witness a reunion between father and son. Of course, if Pa followed Grandfather's suit, both men would behave as though nothing was amiss. Being a Setterington meant your deepest feelings were kept inside so no one else knew what you were thinking.

Rate convinced Edith that they should have his grandparents over for supper. Edith, worrier that she was, felt any modest meal she could provide would seem extremely ordinary to someone who was as wealthy as everyone said Horatio Setterington was. Still, she wanted to please her husband. She had not understood why Ralph had met their train instead of Father Setterington. Sometimes, she didn't understand why the Setteringtons were so close-mouthed. She knew what was happening now had its genesis several years ago, that period of time when Rate had simply indicated his father and grandfather had had a falling out.

Edith discovered that her worrying, as was often the case, was completely unwarranted. Miney had led her to believe that Lovina was a dictatorial ogre, but Edith felt the woman had been very congenial. Both Horatio and Lavina told them about California, and Edith found this very interesting. Imagine travelling all that distance to our west coast. Then, as soon as the meal was finished, Lavina helped Edith clear the table and insisted they get the dishes done before they joined Horatio and Ralph. Who would have expected her to do this?

My Horatio was certainly a dignified looking man. His hair had thinned to almost nothing, but that which was left was steel gray as was his neatly trimmed Vandyke. He was taller than Ralph, and he stood perfectly straight, shoulders square, even though he was almost 74 years old. Edith found it difficult to believe Horatio and Lavina were wealthy. At least they were considered so by the people she knew. They seemed very common, and Edith discovered she liked both of them. Having them in her home had not been the ordeal she had anticipated. She was actually glad Ralph had wanted to ask them for supper. She had been brought up to respect her elders, thus she felt it was good for Ralph to spend precious time with his grandparents.

As expected, Millie said nothing to his son about his parents visit. He still seldom mentioned either of them. Rate wondered why his father couldn't let bygones be bygones instead of holding a grudge that benefited no one.

Blanche and George came for the weekend a couple of weeks later. When they came to spend some time with Edith and Ralph, Blanche told them that Horatio and Lavina had spent three days with them.

Naturally, Grandmother had been quick to bring them up to date on Lois' various activities. Horatio stated that at his age, he left most of his business in the hands of Mac who had even invested money in a silver mine in Mexico. According to Mac, it seemed like a sound idea. (In fact, the mine actually went broke.) Mac was also investing heavily in real estate. Horatio had said that perhaps Mac was spreading them too thin, but he was sure Mac knew what he was doing. George was of the opinion that Horatio had placed too much trust in his son-in-law's business acumen. George felt that ten years ago, Horatio would never have let Mac control all their business interests. Blanche agreed wholeheartedly. She had always felt Mac was incompetent when it came to sound business decisions. All he ever seemed to do was aimed at making a fast buck.

Blanche said she was at least relieved that Grandmother no longer tried to tell her how she should live her life. In fact, Grandmother seemed to approve of her marriage. Blanche felt George had rather charmed her.

Although Grandmother said she enjoyed living in California mostly because she was near her daughter and the weather was nice. Blanche thought she sometimes seemed a little sad. In fact, as they were doing dishes, Grandmother had said, "Blanche, I've had very few friends in this world. People always misunderstood me." This had reminded Blanche of the way Hattie Sickels had described Grandmother. Hattie had said that Grandmother was like a cow giving a full pail of milk and then sticking her foot in the pail.

Both Ralph and Edith found this assessment laughable. Yet, all of them found Lavina's admission rather sad. Blanche thought the fact that Grandmother had lived so many different places following Grandfather wherever his business took him probably had not helped. Perhaps that was one reason she had never made any strong friendships. Of course, her dictatorial manner certainly hadn't helped. Grandmother had never seemed to be able to meet strangers with the ease Horatio had. She had always been quick to give to anyone in dire need, but somehow, this had never helped her to gain friends.

Alice Brewbaker decided it was time to make apple butter. Her three daughters as well as her two daughters-in-law would help; consequently, they would make plenty and everyone would share.

There were plenty of apples this year since the season had been a particularly good one. The tart cooking apples made the best apple butter. The copper kettle was large, it would keep the women busy for some time to peel and core the amount of apples needed. Wilson had had some cider made a few days ago, so there would be whatever quantity they needed. Don had made a corn husk broom for Gladys to use to keep the thinly sliced apples and the cider stirred to keep it from burning.

The men built a fire under the kettle, but it was up to the women to keep it fueled. Because the heat near the kettle was uncomfortable, the women took turns stirring the mixture. After the apples had cooked sufficiently, sugar and spices were added; the fire was allowed to die down somewhat, but the mixture had to be watched closely and stirred almost constantly until the mixture was of the proper consistency. No one wanted to ruin the product after all this work had been put into it.

The apple butter was finished in plenty of time for the women to return to their own homes to get supper for their husbands. Edith liked working with her mother and sisters, and now she had two sisters-in-law to help. She knew Blanche much better than she knew Ethel. She had the feeling that she and Ethel would never be as close as she and Blanche, but she had been glad to have the whole group together. Making apple butter was a slow and tedious chore, but so many hands had made it seem much less tiresome. They had not asked Ethel to stand on her feet to stir the contents of the kettle since her child was due next month. However, Ethel had done her share of peeling and had quickly learned how to use the apple corer.

Art and Ethel's daughter was born the 17th of November. They named her Rita Onalee. Edith chuckled to herself when she visited because Art was such a proud papa. One would think no one else had ever had such a beautiful daughter. Art had always liked children, but Edith had not realized how proud Art would be of a child of his own.

On the 29th of November, Ralph paid off the promissory note, and Edith felt much better. Once again she had worried for nothing. It just proved that Ralph understood money matters far better than she did. Hopefully, they would not need a loan next year.

CHAPTER 10

When George and Blanche came home for Christmas, Ralph and Edith joined them at Millie's for dinner. Edith had a good laugh listening to Blanche describe her efforts to learn how to make a plum pudding. It seemed that George's mother had no written recipe to follow, and some ingredients were dumped until it looked like the right amount. Blanche asked Miney if she remembered that she had had to write a recipe for Blanche's favorite things since Miney had baked much the same way. Of course, Miney remembered. She couldn't understand why Blanche thought it odd that George's mother had no recipe to follow. Plum pudding sounded pretty much like the steamed suet pudding she often made in the winter months. Miney couldn't remember if she had ever written down a recipe for Blanche for suet pudding. If she had, Blanche could follow that, and Miney was certain no one would know the difference.

Edith was glad her mother had always had written recipes for whatever she baked. At least that had made it much easier for Edith and her sisters to learn to bake.

Edith had learned that at special family meals, Millie was quite likely to tell some stories about when he was growing up. This seemed odd to her since her father had never been very talkative at meal time. She had always noted that Millie was a hearty eater more than her father. Of course, he was a much larger man than her father, so she supposed he simply required a lot more food. Pa was short, but Millie was the tallest person she knew and his shoulders were exceptionally broad. Even Ralph, who was taller than Elzie and Art, the tallest of her brothers looked small beside his father, and Ralph was six foot one.

Even though he and Horatio were at odds, Millie seemed willing to speak of the time when he lived with his parents. Ralph felt his father had modified his resentment and anger since Horatio and Lavina had visited. Ralph hoped the relationship would continue to improve. A rift in the family made no sense to him. Of course, Pa would never admit his attitude towards his parents had changed.

Millie gave a little chuckle as he began speaking. "No matter what business Pa was in, John and I always had chores of some kind. Believe me, Pa never left us with no work to do. I usually tried to do mine to the best of my ability, but John was forever slacking on his work and was always getting punished. Pa used the buggy whip quite regularly on John. I got it once in a while. I'd try to work in closer to Pa because the heavier part of the whip didn't sting as much. Pa would say, 'Stand out there, boy, and take your licking.' I never saw a time when I would have sassed my dad. Sometimes, it was John's mouth that got him in trouble. He never seemed to learn that Pa wouldn't accept any back talk from him. Mostly, John asked for what he got."

Edith understood this. While her father had never whipped any of the girls, he had been known to use the buggy whip on the boys. She guessed this was the way of fathers who demanded obedience.

Millie quit speaking as he helped himself to the second piece of pie. He took a bite then continued speaking.

"Pa owned a furniture store and funeral parlor when I was about fourteen. Back in those days, a furniture store was the usual place to have a funeral parlor. This was before the time when bodies were embalmed. We had a piece of plate glass that fit over the opening on the caskets to keep the flies off the body. No matter how one tried to keep the door closed and the flies swatted, they sure seemed to congregate. Trying to keep the fly population down was one of my jobs.

"There was this one funeral that stands out in my mind more than all the rest. It was for a little girl who was about six years old. She had blonde hair and was the prettiest little girl I had ever seen. I thought it was such a shame that this young, beautiful child had died.

"Shortly after I had cleaned the glass and placed it on the casket, I noticed that moisture had collected on the underside. I thought this was strange because it had never happened before. I cleaned the glass, but in a short time, moisture had collected once more. It reminded me of how you can cloud a mirror by breathing on it.

"I felt that the little girl must be alive. What else would explain the build-up of moisture? Yet, I could detect no other sign of life except the moisture that kept collecting on the glass. No one else seemed to notice. Of course, kid like, I didn't say anything to anyone, just kept cleaning the glass.

"Some years later, I read an article about sleeping sickness. I have always felt that we buried that little girl while she was still alive and she was somehow suffering from sleeping sickness. I could think of no other explanation."

Tears filled Millie's eyes as he finished speaking. Those at the table were very quiet, each engrossed with his own thoughts. Edith was thinking what a terrible thing had occurred.

Ralph asked, "Pa, is there any cure for sleeping sickness?"

"Not that the article said. They didn't seem to know too much about it back then, only that there was such a thing. I guess there was nothing that could have been done for the little girl. Still, it was a horrible thought that she had been buried alive."

The topic of conversation changed, but Edith was to learn that for several days, she would think about what Millie had said. How horrible to think that child had quite likely been buried alive. The thought sent chills down her spine. She wondered if the child had suffered. She also felt compassion for the little girl's parents. Had there been other children? She was accustomed to learn of children who died of pneumonia or diphtheria, but she had never heard of sleeping sickness. Where had the disease come from? Goodness, one just never knew for certain if you had children if they would live to be an adult. Ma had lost little Wilson and Aunt Frank had lost Maitland. My, she hoped she and Ralph would not have such a heartache.

With the first of the year, the weather turned extremely cold. There had been more snow than usual, and the wind often drove the small white flakes with a ferocity which made being outside highly disagreeable for man and beast. Huge drifts were everywhere. Ralph kept paths shoveled to all the buildings and he helped neighbors clear the drifts from the road to allow travel. A couple of times the milk hauler had failed to pick up their milk because of the huge drifts. In this cold weather, the milk was still good the next day, but Ralph did not have extra cans to be able to skip more than one day.

The stoves had an insatiable appetite; therefore, the wood Ralph had corded in late fall, he had thought the amount would see them through the winter was disappearing at a rapid rate. The strong winds hadn't helped because they found every crack to penetrate the house, and often an especially strong gust made the windows rattle. Even with a roaring fire, the rooms were often quite chilly.

Ralph decided it was high time he cut some more fire wood. He hired Harry Johnson to help him since it took two men to use a crosscut saw. Although the sun shone brightly, the snow in the woods was deep and this made the work much more difficult. Both men were warmly dressed and Ralph had on a new pair of rubbers which came above the ankle like a work shoe. The long heavy wool socks he wore came clear to his knees. At least his feet stayed warm and since there was no wind, Ralph didn't mind the cold even though the temperature hovered in the teens.

Just as Ralph struck with the freshly-honed, double edged axe to cut a small limb from the trunk of the tree they had felled, he slipped. The axe glanced off the tree branch, came through the snow, and sliced into his rubber on the right foot. A closer inspection revealed the sharp axe had even cut through his heavy sock. Ralph felt very fortunate because the axe had missed his toe. He certainly had no time to be laid up with an injured foot. Besides, Edith would have a conniption over the ruined rubber boot let alone what she'd have done if he had been hurt. Edith was a born worrier. Now that she was in the family way, Ralph wanted to spare her any emotional upset because he felt the child might suffer.

Actually, Edith's pregnancy was going well. She had morning sickness for a few weeks, but other than that, she felt fine. She truly enjoyed making flannel diapers, crocheting baby sweaters, bonnets and booties. She made dresses, underskirts and undershirts. Whether the baby was a boy or girl, dresses were appropriate for the first few months. She would be pleased to have a boy because she felt that every man desired a son, but all she really cared about was that they be blessed with a healthy baby.

Ralph seemed to be as pleased as she was; however, there were times when he hurt her feelings. Edith was excited when she first felt the baby move. One night, she had been cuddled up to Ralph when the baby gave a vigorous kick. Ralph had quickly moved so they were no longer touching. When she asked what was wrong, why had he moved away, he explained that he couldn't stand the feeling of the child moving. He said that it felt weird, and it was unsettling.

Edith could not understand why the child moving should bother him. After all, she sometimes couldn't sleep because the child was so active. She'd remember to stay on her side of the bed from now on. For a time, she felt bitter, but the feeling didn't last since she was so pleased they were to have a baby. Children were what made a marriage complete. She certainly hoped they would have more than one child. She didn't want to be like her sister, Gladys. She often felt sorry for Gordon because he was an only child. Without siblings, she felt a child had a lonely life. Besides, she shouldn't complain. Ralph still asked her to sit on his lap. She suspected her corset kept him from feeling the baby's movements. Sometimes, when her back ached, it was particularly nice to be held and cuddled.

Now that Edith was beginning to show, Ralph often teased. Vern and Blanche had come over in the evening. When the talk turned to Edith's pregnancy, Blanche made some remark to Ralph about his pending fatherhood.

With a most serious expression, Ralph said, "I'm not sure I'm going to be a father. Many times I come in the back door just as Jeff Walker is sneaking out the front door." The implication was obvious.

"Ralph Setterington! Whatever made you tell such an outlandish lie?" Edith was irate. She looked at her brother and sister-in-law and said, "You know what he says isn't true."

"You're saying Ralph is wrong?" asked Vern with a chuckle. "Jeff Walker? Gosh, Sis, he'd certainly not be my choice."

"Vern Brewbaker, don't you dare side with Ralph. You know he's making all of this up," said Blanche with a wicked glance at Ralph.

"Besides, Ralph, if you were coming in the back door, how could you possibly see who was going out the front door? You couldn't, so that just proves you are lying." Edith's demeanor showed she thought none of this was the least bit funny, and Ralph could tell that she was losing her temper.

"Perhaps I was mistaken. Could have swore that I saw Jeff sneaking away. More than once too," he added, supposedly as an afterthought.

He gave Edith an innocent grin. He knew Vern thought the whole thing humorous, but Blanche was another matter. For some reason, both women gave him a scathing look. He guessed he'd better change the subject before he really got in hot water. After all, he really hadn't intended to make Edith angry, he just wanted to tease.

Sometimes Edith felt like wringing Ralph's neck and this was one of those times. She certainly hoped she had heard the last of any such accusations. Jeff Walker of all people! If Ralph was going to lie, he could have thought of someone more appropriate than Jeff. Of course, she realized, that was exactly why he chose Jeff. Ralph knew she disapproved of the man in every way.

* * * * * * * * *

On January 31, Germany warned the Allies that she was renewing her submarine warfare on all shipping; therefore, on February 3, President Wilson broke off diplomatic relations with Germany. Between February 3 and March 21, Germany sank six American ships.

Ralph hated hearing this news because he felt we had reached a point where war was inevitable. He had given little thought to being called into the service. He was a farmer, he was married, and he was about to become a father. He believed those were three good reasons why he would not be drafted if there came a time when civilians were drafted into the armed services.

Ralph had gone to a farm sale without any intention of buying anything stock or tools. However, as he looked over the draft horses, he was completely surprised when he recognized Monarch. Rate thought he looked a trifle thin, and the colt was definitely a little smaller than Buster. Still, with his strawberry roan coat, there was no doubt about who the colt was. He would be three come May. As Ralph rubbed Monarch's nose, he made up his mind to stay around and bid on the colt. He hoped there weren't many others who were interested because his finances were extremely limited.

When Ralph went home, he had Monarch with him. Ralph wondered if Monarch would be as stubborn as Buster when the time came to break him. My, what a good looking team they'd make.

On April 2, 1917, President Wilson spoke before a special session of Congress and called for a crusade to make the world safe for democracy. On April 4, the Senate voted for war, and on April 6, the House followed suit. America was now at war.

Everywhere one went, the topic of war came up. Some felt it was about time the United States helped England and France while others thought we should not send troops to Europe. After all, our shores were not about to be invaded.

Ralph had taken grain to the mill to have a grist ground for the cows. Anton Karber worked there, but because he had been born in Germany and had only been in the United States for a few years everyone referred to him as "the Old Dutchman." Ralph didn't think he was all that old, but he supposed because the man spoke with an accent, some just thought of him as being older.

Anton was helping Ralph dump the grain to be ground.

Ralph asked, "Do you hear from any of your family in Germany?"

Anton stopped what he was doing. He gave Ralph an intense look, then seemingly decided Ralph was truly interested. Some people blamed him for what Germany did and treated him accordingly, but Ralph didn't seem to be in that category.

"Not for long time. Mail is never certain now," he explained.

"I suppose not with all the submarine activity. I was hoping we'd stay out of the war."

"You will go?"

"I don't think so. Since I'm a farmer, married, and with a child on the way, I don't think I'll be drafted.

"If you have to go, is not so bad as for me. If I go, I have to fight me own bruder."

Ralph said nothing, simply nodded sympathetically. Anton resumed work. Ralph mulled over the man's words. Yes, it would not be pleasant to have to fight your own brother and undoubtedly other relatives. He wondered if Anton still felt some loyalty to Germany.

May 18, saw the Selective Service Act which called for the registration of all men aged 21 to 30.

Edith and Ralph said little about this latest turn of events. Ralph knew his wife was deeply concerned, but he didn't want her to worry. The baby was due in just over a week. He felt certain the birth would go better if Edith was free of worry.

Edith awoke about four in the morning on Tuesday, May 22. She had a twinge across her abdomen almost like sometimes happened before she had a bowel movement. She thought nothing of it, and dropped back to sleep. She and Ralph usually arose around 6:00 A.M. Occasionally, they got up earlier if Ralph wanted to be in the field earlier than usual. However, he insisted cows did better if their milking time was regular day after day.

While preparing breakfast, Edith experienced several more twinges followed by the baby's hearty kicks. She then wondered if there was any correlation, but decided it didn't seem likely. She felt certain the baby wouldn't arrive until the 30th; therefore, she failed to consider the fact that she might be experiencing the first contractions of labor. Gladys had given her version of how excruciatingly painful labor was, but Edith had taken all of that with a grain of salt. The whole family knew Gladys had been spoiled first by her father and then by her husband. Her tolerance for pain was extremely low.

Edith said nothing to Ralph until evening. The pains had become more severe and more regular, but they were still far apart; however, she now wondered if they were the beginning of labor. She decided to wait until morning, and if the pains were more intense and more frequent, she would have Ralph call the doctor.

Morning came. She didn't feel rested because the intermittent pains had prevented her from having a good night's sleep. The pains were still far apart and irregular, but they were definitely more intense. Ralph decided to give Dr. Hart a call.

The doctor verified that Edith was in labor even though the pains were far apart. His examination revealed the baby had not progressed down the birth canal; therefore, he felt the birth was a number of hours away. He left after telling

Ralph to call him immediately if the pains lasted longer with more severity or if they became regular and more frequent.

Edith wondered why this seemed to be taking so long. The hours dragged by slowly. She managed to do some of her housework with the periods when she rested becoming longer each time. Ralph showed his concern by getting the meals which Edith truly appreciated. She was uncomfortable standing on her feet. Edith timed the pains, but they didn't seem to be getting more frequent although she thought they were more severe. Perhaps this was just her imagination.

About mid-morning Thursday, Ralph decided to call the doctor. Edith's pains had been increasing in severity although they had not settled into a specific rhythm. When Dr. Hart arrived, he examined Edith, but made no comment except to say that it would be a few more hours before birth. Ralph thought the doctor looked worried, and he wondered if something was wrong. When he asked the doctor, all he was told was that it appeared it was going to be a difficult delivery.

Edith had eaten very little yesterday and today she told Ralph she could not think of food because her stomach felt queasy. He had never thought having a baby would be such an ordeal.

In early afternoon, Dr. Schweitzer stopped in. Ralph correctly assumed Dr. Hart had asked him to come. Both doctors disappeared into the bedroom where Edith lay. When they came back to the living room, both doctors looked exceptionally serious. Ralph looked from one to the other expectantly. Finally, Dr. Hart spoke.

"Ralph, there are complications. Dr. Schweitzer corroborated what I surmised. The baby is coming breech."

"What does that mean?'

"In a normal delivery, the baby comes head first. This baby is doubled up, head by the feet and the buttocks are coming down the birth canal. A breech birth is always difficult, but it is even more difficult when it occurs in the woman's first pregnancy."

"What is going to happen?" asked Ralph.

"I wish I knew. We're not sure. Your wife is worn out, but she tries to do as we ask. What we're concerned about is whether she will dilate sufficiently to allow the child to be born. The trouble is, if it takes too long for the child to be born, it will likely be born dead. All of this is very debilitating for your wife. I'm sorry to have to tell you this. Dr. Schweitzer and I will do our best to save both your wife and the baby."

Ralph had a sinking feeling. He had never realized a pregnancy could have such dire possibilities. Edith had felt well all those months, and they had both wanted the child badly. And now these doctors seemed to be preparing him for the possibility that his child might be born dead and that his wife might die as well. He felt completely helpless.

Ralph had never given consideration to the fact that his wife could die in childbirth. Yet, he had known that Aunt Ettie had died in childbirth, and he also knew his mother had never forgiven Uncle Doc for his wife's demise. Would his mother blame him if Edith died? He now realized what his mother had meant when she said Blanche was doubled together in other words, a breech birth. His mother had survived the ordeal. He fervently hoped Edith would as well. If not, would it be his fault? No. This condition could not have been foreseen, and Edith was certainly healthy. This was just one of those quirks of fate which no one, not even the doctors could explain. Still, his mother's words about Uncle Doc being responsible for Aunt Ettie's death continued to nag. If Ralph had been one who believed in prayer, he certainly would have made an appeal to God to spare the life of his wife and child.

Edith was so worn out she was scarcely aware of what was happening. She only knew the pain was severe and it seemed as though one spasm had no more than passed when another one began. The doctors kept telling her to push, then one would say relax. How could one relax when the pain was almost constant?

She heard Dr. Hart say, "I always save the mother first, don't you?"

"I want my baby. I want my baby," she moaned.

"Yes, yes. Just do as we say. Now, push, push. That's it."

The procedure was taking too long. Something had to be done. Dr. Schweitzer climbed onto the bed with Edith, and when the next contraction came, he placed his knee on Edith's abdomen just above the baby and pushed. At the same time, Dr. Hart used instruments to assist the baby. There! The baby was expelled!

However, all was not well. The baby did not cry.

"My baby?" moaned Edith.

"Your baby is a girl. Dr. Hart took her to the kitchen to wash her and get her clothed." Dr. Schweitzer spoke placatingly and with much more assurance than he felt.

What he didn't say was that he felt the baby might not make it. Her breathing was rapid and shallow which did not bode well for the small girl.

Dr. Hart suctioned mucus from her throat, but this did nothing to improve her condition. She had made a couple of mewling cries, but what he wanted to hear was a hearty, lusty cry.

At Dr. Hart's request, Ralph had put cold water in a small tub. There was already a tub of warm water on the table. Dr. Hart then dipped the baby first in one tub, then in the other.

Ralph stood at his side and kept asking, "Will she be all right?"

To each question, the doctor kept replying, "I don't know."

After several minutes, the baby gave a weak cry. Then, as if that had been only a test, she began to cry in earnest.

"Ralph, that is a mighty sweet sound. I might not want to hear it all night, but for now, it sounds wonderful. Your little girl will be all right."

The doctor handed the baby to Edith's mother who quickly and expertly dried, diapered, and dressed her grandchild. Alice had been there for the past hour or so, but had sat quietly out of everyone's way. She was glad the ordeal was over, and she could see the relief on Ralph's face. From what little had been said, she thought Edith had been in labor for at least 36 hours. No wonder her daughter had looked wan and completely worn out.

Alice wrapped the baby in a receiving blanket and took her to the bedroom to place the now quiet babe in Edith's arms. The look of joy on Edith's face brought tears to Alice's eyes.

Edith was content now that she could hold her baby who seemed to be all right. Several days passed before Ralph admitted to Edith how close they had come to losing the baby. They had named her Helen Rhea. The "Rhea" was after Edith's best friend, Rhea Coverdale. Edith didn't dwell on the "what might have been" because she was so pleased to have her first child. Her abdomen was mighty sore, but she knew each day would bring improvement. She would be glad when she would once again be allowed out of bed.

Millie and Miney had come to see their first grandchild the day after her birth. Of course, Miney was ecstatic because the child was a girl. Edith had a few misgivings because she felt her in-laws would do their best to spoil Helen. Edith was determined to keep this from happening, and she hoped Ralph would support her efforts.

Edith's sister, Edna, had been there to help while Edith was confined to bed. Edna was a good cook, and she was also handy with Helen. Edith thought it was nice to have family around at a time like this. There had been others who had stopped by, including sister, Gladys. Edith had been amazed when Don had immediately picked up Helen. His hands were huge, but he handled the baby with as much expertise as any woman. Watching him, Edith wondered if Don wished he and Gladys would have another child or whether he was content with only Gordon who was now four.

On the 5th of June, Ralph went to the Selective Service Board in St. Johns and registered as was required. He was almost certain he would not be drafted because farmers were needed on the home front. He did his best to convince Edith he would not be called because he hated to have her worry.

Ralph had been over to his parents' farm. He had left right after dinner and it was now supper time. Millie had asked him if he could spare the time to help pick up stones from the field north of the barn. Ralph knew how much his father hated this job. Because the weather had been so cooperative, Ralph was actually ahead with his field work so he had been glad to give his father a hand.

One look at Rate as he entered the kitchen for supper and Edith was certain something had happened which he found humorous. He had that little half smile which he so often had just before he related some incident to her which he found truly laughable.

"Pa's a little disgruntled," he said as he pulled out his chair to sit at the table.

Edith had just finished putting the victuals in place.

"Over what? Didn't you get the stones picked up?"

"Oh, yeah. We finished hauling them to the stone pile back down the lane. I even helped him bring up a load of firewood. No, he's upset because he got a notification from the state that his automobile has to have a license if he's going to drive it on the road. That maybe wouldn't be so bad, but he has to go clear to Lansing to get the license. He asked me if I'd go with him next week. I told him I would."

"Why do you have to go to Lansing?"

"There's no local office that sells these licenses. Guess the state didn't give any consideration to having easy availability for those who needed to get a license. Anyway, Pa figured we'd take the interurban from St. Johns. We have to go to the Capitol. Although he'd never admit it, I think Pa is afraid to go to Lansing on his own. Don't think he's ever been to the Capitol. Of course, he thinks having to have a license is a tom-fool idea."

"Wonder why the state decided autos should have a license? Are there really that many autos now?"

"Guess so. I think the state needs money to improve roads since we will be getting more automobiles all the time. You know these machines need better roads than a horse and buggy. Suppose the state has to get the money from somewhere."

"I guess that makes sense. The ones that own automobiles should be the ones to pay for improving the roads. Will there be a time when the farmers can't be responsible for grading the roads?"

"In time. Sooner or later the county is going to be forced to take care of the roads as more people buy autos. Can't expect farmers to be responsible for all the road work especially when most of the automobiles will be owned by people living in town. And they are the ones who are going to insist on better roads."

Edith mulled this over. She supposed Rate was right. Goodness these automobiles were certainly making many changes. She supposed the correct term was progress. She wondered if she and Ralph would be able to afford an auto in a few years. She was certain that for now it was out of the question.

By the time Edith was fully recovered from the ordeal of giving birth, Millie and Miney began coming over each evening after Millie was done with chores. They were so taken with this first grandchild, they felt they just had to see her every day.

At first, it really didn't matter because Helen slept a good share of the time, and her grandparents were content to sit and watch her sleep. However, Edith felt their presence left she and Ralph very little time to themselves in the evening, and she resented the nightly intrusion. Still, she made no complaint to Ralph and she tried to be gracious to her in-laws. However, it bothered her that there was never a time when her family could visit without her in-laws being present. She felt that some evenings she would liked to have some quality time with some members of her own family.

When Helen began to be awake for longer periods of time, both Millie and Miney were quick to suggest to Edith that she could quite likely keep the baby awake until after their visit. Edith felt obliged to comply with their request.

Actually, Helen did not respond well to being kept awake until nearly 8:00. Edith nursed her just before she and Ralph had their supper at 6:00 and Helen was ready to go to sleep shortly after. She would wake again about 10:00 for another feeding. Trying to keep her awake until her grandparents arrived was a problem, and it upset the baby's whole schedule. Edith put up with this for several weeks, but then, one night when Helen was particularly fussy, Edith put the child to bed and Helen immediately fell asleep.

When Millie and Miney arrived to see their granddaughter, they were keenly disappointed because she was sleeping. Edith explained the situation and Miney told her they had never realized they were upsetting Helen's schedule. Edith felt Miney had simply been so absorbed with her granddaughter, she had given little or no thought regarding the time when the child was tired and wanted to sleep. Miney truly wanted whatever was best for her granddaughter.

From that time on, Miney would call to ask if they could come over, and ask if Helen would be awake. Edith was much more satisfied with this arrangement.

She tried to be accommodating now that Millie and Miney were more considerate. Actually, in Edith's opinion, Miney had been rather demanding, very similar to how she had always described Lavina. Edith laughed to herself when she considered how Miney would feel if she knew that someone thought she had a characteristic like her mother in-law. At least when she knew they were bothering Helen, Miney had changed quickly. Edith felt Grandmother Setterington would have been equally considerate. In spite of what Miney had to say about Lavina, Edith had liked her. Perhaps Lavina had mellowed with age. She reminded herself that it was easy to see that both grandparents doted on their first grandchild.

Ralph enjoyed watching his baby daughter, but as yet he showed no inclination to hold her. Edith thought this strange, but then, she reminded herself that Ralph had no younger siblings and he had never been around babies. She chuckled as she recalled the first time she had asked him to hold Helen. Edith had been hurrying to finish supper, and Helen would not stop crying. Edith had changed her, but that made no difference. Helen still wailed.

"Ralph, can't you hold her while I finish getting supper?" she implored. "She'll be quiet if you hold her."

"All right." He had sat down in a rocker and Edith had given him the baby. He had held her lengthwise on his lap, her feet resting on his stomach while his hands had been cupped under her head.

"She won't break, you know," Edith had said with a chuckle.

Ralph had ignored the remark, but as Edith moved back to the stove, she had heard him say, "My gosh but your dad will be glad when you're a little bigger."

Edith had found the situation rather humorous. Her father had always been quick to pick up a baby to rock if the child had been restless while her mother was in the midst of some chore. Ralph had looked extremely uncomfortable. She wondered how old Helen would be before he felt at ease holding her.

Ralph came in the kitchen door ready to wash up for supper. Edith was just finishing the meal. She always had his meals on time, and he really appreciated her promptness. However, tonight he gave her a second look, then asked, "What's wrong?"

"Nothing."

"Don't tell me that. You've been crying. Is Helen all right?" "She's fine. She's playing in her crib."

"Then why were you crying?" he persisted.

"Lee was here earlier. He has his orders to report to camp. He was only here a short time, but said he'd stop back to see both of us before he left."

"You knew this would happen. Lee received his commission when he finished his R.O.T.C. program at the end of the semester. He's a 2nd Lieutenant now."

"I know all that. It's just that I don't want anything to happen to him. He was in uniform, and he did look handsome."

"They always say a uniform turns a woman's head," Ralph teased.

"Lee may not even go overseas. They are certainly going to need plenty of personnel to train these raw recruits, and someone certainly has to be responsible for sending food and ordnance with the troops that we do send overseas. Lee will be fine. At least he is an officer. Most of the ones I know that will be going in the Army will be merely Privates. I'd say Lee has an advantage."

"I suppose you are right, and I know it does no good to worry. Our family was too young or too old for the Spanish American War, so this is the first time I've had someone I love be called to serve our country. I also think Carl will be drafted before this is over."

"We can't do anything about that, so you must not worry. Neither Lee nor Carl would want you to be fearful for them."

"I know." She gave Ralph a brief smile. Sometimes it was so difficult not to worry even if she could not change the way events were unfolding. She'd just have to trust that God would take care of Lee wherever he was sent. As of now, Carl was still home, so she really had no worry there.

Edna had come to spend a few days with them. She had not stayed with them since Edith had been able to be up and about to do her own work. It was truly hot July weather. At mid-morning, she wanted to know if she should take a drink to Ralph. He was in a back field cultivating corn. Edith agreed that Ralph would quite likely be thirsty and would appreciate a drink. Neither of the women had observed the weather. If they had, they might have concluded it was going to rain most any time.

Ralph had had his eyes on the weather. He was just about to unhitch the team and start for the house when he noticed Edna trudging down the lane. He sat down on the cultivator and laughed to himself as he watched her come. He felt certain it would start raining about the time she reached the field. How right he was. Edna had no more than reached him when the first few raindrops came down. Ralph unhitched the team, and turned each horse loose knowing they would head for the barn. He and Edna started to run for the house.

As they ran, Edna, now thoroughly soaked dress kept riding up her legs. Of course, Ralph was quick to notice, and he said, "Edna, pull your dress down." He behaved as though she should be ashamed because so much of her legs were showing. Edna was completely humiliated. She struggled to get her dress back in place, but they had gone only a short distance when Ralph admonished her again. "Edna, I thought I told you to pull your dress down. Showing off your legs like that is rather unseemly."

Edna didn't realize Ralph had intentionally waited for her even though he was pretty certain they'd be caught in the rain. She didn't know he thought teasing her more than made up for getting soaked. After all, it was a warm rain. He'd been out in far worse.

Edna was glad to get to the house, and was particularly relieved that Ralph had to stop at the barn to take care of the team. His absence would give her time to collect herself so she wouldn't be embarrassed when Ralph came to the house. See if she ever offered to take him a drink again. He could die of thirst for all she cared.

Ralph had taken oats and corn to the mill to be ground into a grist. He had left the bags there while he went into Elsie to pick up some rivets so he could make some harness repairs. When he returned home, he took care of the team but left the chore of carrying the bags of ground feed into the barn for later.

He entered by the kitchen door. Edith was checking a roast. Ralph savoured the odor of the cooking meat a moment before he spoke.

"Learned today that they have begun calling up draftees. Seems that Aubrey Sheldon was one of the first ones Uncle Sam called. Talk around town is that Aubrey is so scared to go, Sheldons will pay anyone $500 to take his place."

"Isn't that illegal?"

"I should think so. However, Sheldons don't seem to care as long as their precious Aubrey can stay home. Let some other sucker put his life on the line."

"Have they found anyone yet?"

"Not so far, but I'll bet it won't be long before someone takes them up on their offer. $500 is a lot of money."

A couple of weeks later, Ralph was once again in Elsie. Don Huffman sat on a bench in front of the dry goods store. He looked mighty pleased with himself. Ralph stopped to pass the time of day. Don told Ralph that he had taken Aubrey Sheldon up on his offer and he was now $500 richer.

"Yes, sir, Rate, thirty per and Uncle Sam pays the freight," he said proudly. "Can't ask for better than that. Might get to see some of the country. Heck, I might even get to see gay Pairee."

Ralph thought Don sounded extremely satisfied with his arrangement. Thirty dollars a month must have seemed like a substantial amount, and of course, there was the $500 bonus. Ralph wished him well.

Ralph wondered how Don's parents felt about him going off to war. Their eldest son, Lona, had fought in the Spanish American War. He had returned from the war, but had been in very poor health because of food poisoning contracted shortly before the armistice. He had died in January of 1901, lacking four months of his twenty-first birthday.

A few weeks later, Ralph learned that when it came time to fill out the insurance papers, Don had quickly had a change of heart. If he died, Don reasoned he certainly did not want the insurance money going to Sheldons; therefore, he admitted he was not Aubrey Sheldon, but was in reality Donald Huffman. His enlistment went through without another hitch, so he was in the Army at least he was under his own name.

It was only a few days after this disclosure that the authorities came to Elsie and took Aubrey away. His plan had failed, and he now found himself in the Army. All of this was the talk of the town, and many people felt Aubrey got what he deserved.

CHAPTER 11

Ralph wondered what It would be like to break Monarch. Just as he watched the colt around the barn, his temperament was much different than Buster's. When he first began to get Monarch accustomed to having a bit in his mouth and the feel of a harness on his back, all went even better than Rate expected. Nothing seemed to bother Monarch. When Ralph hitched him in with one of his older work horses, the colt worked willingly just as though he'd been doing it for years. Other than color, he and Buster didn't have much in common. Of course, Ralph felt some of this was because Buster was the more intelligent of the two.

It would be some time before he hitched the two colts together. After all, he didn't want Buster to corrupt Monarch. Rate really looked forward to the time when he could drive the two strawberry roans as a team. Even though Monarch was a trifle smaller, they'd make a striking pair.

Ralph had been over to Vern's. He had taken a detour coming back from Elsie. Somehow, he usually found something to laugh at while visiting his brother-in-law. Beurmann and Wilson were always glad to see him, and while Wendell wasn't always with the older boys since he was so much younger, it was obvious he liked his Uncle Ralph too. Besides, Rate also enjoyed teasing Blanche because she never seemed to know when he was simply teasing; therefore, he often made her angry. He truly enjoyed the situation when Blanche sputtered at him for some remark he had made. Of course, Vern was always ready to laugh at any exchange between Ralph and Blanche even though he was careful not to let his wife know how he felt.

Today had been a little different. When Ralph drove into the south driveway, he noticed that Blanche had both of the older boys standing by the back steps in front of her and was obviously berating them for something. Vern was just coming from the barn, so Ralph continued on the drive past the house to pull up by him.

"What's got Blanche so hot under the collar?"

"Oh, she had some clothes hanging on the line. The boys forgot to lock the gate to the goat's pen. He can open it if he wants to unless it is locked. He wandered out and pulled some of the clothes off the line. Blanche says he even tore some of them before anyone noticed what he was doing. According to Blanche, the goat was trying to eat the clothes. I rather doubt that, but I will admit he sure made a mess of things, At least she's right about that. If they aren't torn, they are dirtier than they were before she washed them." Vern shrugged his shoulders to indicate this was nothing he could help since the damage was already done.

"No wonder she's mad. She never really approved of you getting the goat in the first place, did she?"

"She was always against having a goat. Guess she believed all those stories about how goats will eat anything, even tin cans. She never took into consideration how much fun the boys have had driving him on that title green wagon. Even Wendell likes having the goat pull him around. Honestly, Rate, one couldn't expect the goat to drive any better than he does. He likes the kids, and they really like the goat. I'll be able to smooth this over, but if he vexes Blanche another time, I'll have to get rid of him to keep peace in the family."

When Rate related the story to Edith, he added, "I think Vern is quite right that if the goat does one more thing to irritate Blanche, Vern will have to get rid of him. Her patience won't last forever."

"Can't say as I blame her if the goat ruined any of the clothes. After all, they never have much spare money, and clothes are expensive. This doesn't even take into consideration the amount of time it will take her to repair what the goat did this time, and the fact that whatever he pulled down will have to be washed again. Doing a washing isn't much fun. It's hard work. I can certainly sympathize with her. Of course, those two scalawags quite likely thought the whole thing was extremely funny. They are much more likely to share Vern's cavalier attitude. No wonder Blanche was upset."

The war news continued to bother Edith. Now that Lee had left, she wondered who would be next. Thankfully, brothers Harley and Garth were too young, but Carl was the right age. Still, there were others she knew who had already been drafted, and Ralph knew some who had been sent overseas as soon as they had finished basic training. Of course, some had enlisted instead of waiting for the draft.

Ralph had learned a short time ago that Vere Brown had been called up. He and Vere had gone to school together at Stafford. Rate was told Vere was in the cavalry. Rate had told Edith that this seemed an odd place to put a man who was tone deaf. Vere couldn't even recognize The Star Spangled Banner when it was played. He said he often had his hat knocked off because of this. From all Rate had read, one had to be able to follow commands which were given by the bugler. How, he wondered, would Vere ever manage. (After the war, Vere told Ralph that while he didn't know one bugle call from another, his horse knew all of them. He then explained that they were told if they became unseated during a charge, they were to remain prone on the ground and the horses would manage not to step on them. If they tried to stand, the horses would knock them down.) Ralph figured whoever was responsible for assigning inductees their place in the Army, had sure blundered with Vere even if it had worked out in the long run.

It was the latter part of August when Don Sherman came to visit Ralph. Since the milking was done, the cows turned out, the two men sat on the side porch. There was a gentle breeze from the south, which felt really good after the heat of the day.

"Just came to let you know that I've enlisted in the Navy. Figured It was a helluva lot better than having to go in the Army."

"You want to tangle with German submarines?" asked Rate, a note of disbelief in his voice.

"Aw before I'm trained, the war will likely be over. At least the news seems to indicate the fighting is going better for us now. Besides, I've always felt swimming was a helluva lot better than walking. You know that."

"Sure. But did you ever consider swimming in the ocean is a lot different than swimming in Maple River or some small lake. Drowning sure doesn't appeal to me." Ralph remembered how worried he had been when he had cramps while swimming in the Huron River at Ypsilanti.

"You're not being very encouraging. Stop and think, Rate. I'll quite likely get to see parts of the world that we've only read about. I've heard that the Navy is real good about shore leave when in a foreign port."

"With your sense of direction, you'd likely end up lost and not ever make it back to your ship."

"Funny, funny. After all, I won't be alone. I'm sure I'll be able to find my way around. You're just jealous because you have responsibilities and can't go with me. An old married man like you is better off at home. Us single men who are foot loose and fancy free is what the Navy needs." Don gave a laugh, then continued, "Hell, I might even drop you a line now and then to let you know how much fun I'm having." Don gave his friend a grin knowing full well they would miss each other. Their relationship had been special all these years. Even though Rate was married, they still saw each other often, and Don had always felt welcome in their home. Edith was a very likable person, and she had always been good natured and put up with his teasing.

"When do you leave?"

"A week from today. Go to boot camp in Chicago. Hard to tell where I'll go from there. Should get assigned to some ship, I guess. They didn't tell us a whole lot when I signed up."

"You know I wish you the best." Both were silent a moment, then Rate said, "They always say a sailor has a girl in every port. That gonna be you?"

"Can't never tell. Guess it depends on where we go. Too bad I don't know a couple of other languages."

"If I know you, you'll make out all right anyway. I can't see anything like not speaking the same language being a barrier for you," said Rate with a chuckle.

"Don't know what makes you arrive at that conclusion."

"Well, I've never known you to lack for a girl to squire around. True?"

"Guess you're right there. It's never been a problem. I've just been smart enough never to let one catch me." Don gave Ralph an impudent grin."Maybe that will change after I've seen something of the world," he added more seriously.

After Don left, Rate and Edith discussed his imminent departure. Edith sensed that Rate hated to see Don leave almost as much as she had disliked having to bid goodbye to Lee. Well, she guessed that was understandable since she figured Don was the brother Ralph had never had. If only this war would end. Why, oh why, did there have to be wars? She felt that if some of the leaders of the countries involved had to go to the front lines to fight, they would be far more hesitant to declare war.

Ralph and Edith splurged and bought Helen a high chair which could also be folded down to become a child's rocking chair. It was a sturdy piece of furniture, and they knew it would last to be used by other children they might have. Neither of them wanted Helen to be an only child. Both of them had always felt sorry for their nephew, Gordon, because he was an only child. Edith had always felt that her sister, Gladys, was the one who wanted no more children just because she had had a difficult time after Gordon's birth. However, Edith felt Ralph would certainly like to have a son even though he had seemed content to have his first born a daughter. She truly hoped that In another year or two,

God would see fit to give them a son. She gave little thought to the long labor she had had for Helen. Her mother assured her that another birth would quite likely be much easier and Edith felt that after giving birth to ten children, her mother should know.

Edith noticed that since Helen was now six months old, Ralph was more likely to pay attention to her. He even picked her up occasionally for short periods of time. It was easy to see that he truly loved his daughter and the bigger she became, the more he was at ease with her. Edith felt Rate would truly like it when Helen began to talk. She bet he'd be thrilled when Helen could first say, "Daddy."

When Helen got her first tooth, Edith felt it was only natural. However, Miney and Millie behaved as though Helen was the smartest baby in the world because she now had one tooth. Edith thought the situation was hilarious. Her parents had simply accepted the event as a sign Helen was maturing on schedule. Of course, they also had more grandchildren.

While Miney often expected to hold Helen, which Edith quite understood, she was surprised the first time she had seen Millie pick the baby up and literally smother her with kisses. She had never expected her father-in-law to be so demonstrative. His actions certainly indicated that he dearly loved babies. Edith's father was quick to hold a child, but she never remembered her father showering a baby with kisses. Millie had always seemed to hide whatever emotions he felt, but now, Edith thought that underneath all that Setterington reserve, he was truly a caring person.

Ralph kept informed on the war, reading whatever he could. Sometimes, he resented that American troops had to cross the ocean to help France and England with their war with Germany. It had seemed that the Allies were making better progress since General Pershing had arrived in France in June with what was known as the American Expeditionary Force. However, Ralph wasn't certain what bearing the Bolshevik Revolution in Russia in November would have on the war effort. If what he read was true, it was surmised that Lenin had made some sort of treaty with Germany, so now the Kaiser could expend all his military might pushing further into France. Although German casualties were extremely heavy, it was evident the Kaiser was determined to sacrifice as many of his youth as necessary to reach his objective. Ralph correctly assumed this would mean more American soldiers would be sent to France to offset Germany's new offensive.

Still, Ralph was not worried about being drafted. So far as he knew, draft boards had been able to fill their quota with single men who were not actively engaged in farming. He figured Carl would be called up even though Carl intended to plant some small acreage to corn. Rate didn't think that amount would benefit him with the draft board. Rate knew Edith worried about Carl being called, but there was no way he could assuage her fears.

Both Ralph and Edith felt Christmas this year was extra special since it was Helen's first. Of course, Millie and Miney had been looking forward to Christmas since the Thanksgiving holiday. It was easy to see they idolized their first grandchild. Sometimes, Edith worried about whether she would have trouble with her in-laws after Helen learned to walk, the time when the child would undoubtedly need to be disciplined at times. She hoped not. Even if she had to assert herself, Edith was determined that Helen would be taught acceptable behavior.

Shortly after the first of the year, Edith thought Helen was old enough to begin giving her small amounts of solid food. She very carefully give her mashed fruits, eggs, and vegetables. She gave her chicken broth, gravy on mashed potatoes, as well as puddings and Jello. Helen seemed to take to solid food exceptionally well. Although Edith didn't realize it at the time, her milk supply was not really adequate, and Helen was actually hungry; therefore, she seemed eager to eat whatever Edith provided.

Millie had been over to the farm to help Ralph build another calf pen in the barn; therefore, he was there for dinner. Although Edith had fed Helen before the adults sat down, she was surprised to see Millie pick up his granddaughter to hold her on his lap while he ate. Helen seemed engrossed with what Millie had on his plate. After all, she normally sat in her high chair at meal time, so being on Millie's lap was a novelty. Edith was aghast when she observed Millie chewing some food, then bending his head to Helen to place the food in the child's mouth. Edith had heard of this being done, but she had never actually seen it done before. She was so taken aback, she didn't know what to say. Millie did this several more times. Helen appeared to like what he gave her. Ralph was engrossed with his meal and didn't seem to notice what his father was doing. Edith resolved that the next time Millie was there for a meal, she'd have Helen where this would not happen again. At this time, she wasn't certain how she'd manage, but manage she would. Pa always said, "Where there's a will, there's a way."

It was the seventh of February when Miney's brother-in-law, Norm Duncan, called her to that her sister, Lorin, had passed away in her sleep early that morning. The news made Miney feel weak in her knees. She knew Lorin hadn't been feeling well lately, but she had not expected this. Of course, Lorin had turned 70 last December. Miney had never been one to dwell on the fact that her half-sister was nineteen years older than she, and the age difference had never seemed that great. Now that Lorin was gone, Miney was the only one left in her family, and it made her particularly sad. Now, there was no one to share memories of when she was a child. First Ettie, then Mary, and now Lorin. It made Miney feel very much alone. Then, she reminded herself that she still had a husband, Blanche and Ralph and a beautiful, precious granddaughter. She was truly blessed.

Of course, Miney had never felt close to Norm because he was known to drink, and Pa had brought them up to see the evil in drink. Then, she had never felt close to Georgie, Lorin's only child. He was kind of an odd sort, but Lorin had been odd in many ways, so she guessed it was understandable.

Miney knew she should call Ralph as well as Blanche. Norm had thought the funeral would be Saturday, but Miney doubted if Blanche would come from Detroit to attend. Blanche had never been overly fond of Lorin, and, of course, Lorin had always seemed to be partial to Ralph, she thought a little resentfully. It had been Mary who Blanche idolized which was understandable since Mary had been so much like Ma. She was certain Ralph and Edith would attend, so she wouldn't be alone. Blanche could make her own decision.

Millie and Miney were going to Detroit for a week to visit Blanche. Millie figured he had better take the time for a visit before the spring planting season arrived. Of course, Miney was willing to go any time to visit her daughter.

Millie had made arrangements for someone to take care of the cows and do the milking; however, he asked Ralph if he would see to taking care of the hogs and the horses. While the cows had to be milked twice daily, the hogs and horses would do all right if Ralph took care of them once a day. Ralph assured his father that he would.

The second day, Ralph arrived to feed, water, and bed down the hogs and horses, he decided there was a book in his old room that he would pick up. He went to the house, entered by the kitchen door as usual, and after slipping out of his boots, made his way up the stairs. When he opened the door to his old bedroom, he nearly gasped with surprise. The room was nearly full of one hundred pound sacks of sugar. It seemed as though all the available space around the furniture was filled with the large sacks. Ralph counted them. There were twelve bags.

Where had all this sugar come from? Sugar had been rationed for quite some time, and he knew Edith sometimes found it difficult to get along with their ration. Of course, they had a little more since they had Helen, but his parents only had an amount for two. Besides, they could not have bought in such quantity at any grocery store. Something was certainly amiss.

Finally, it dawned on Rate where his father had come by this twelve hundred pounds of sugar. There was an old bachelor living on the Frank Sherman farm, and he raised sugar beets the only one in the neighborhood who did. Of course, for anyone who grew sugar beets, there was no rationing. They could keep as much as they wanted from what they raised. Supposedly, they then received no ration coupons.

Rate knew that his father sometimes helped the man with field work, and apparently, Millie had been amply paid in sugar. Rate was strongly tempted to steal a bag, but he quickly put aside such feelings. Maybe Pa would offer to give him a bag when he and Ma returned from Detroit to sort of pay Ralph for doing chores. Millie never made the offer, and every time Ralph thought of all that hoarded sugar, he felt more than a little resentful. He never mentioned the incident to Edith. He knew she did the best she could with the meager amount of sugar they were allotted. He realized that with his mother's penchant for putting sugar in everything, she had undoubtedly been having a rough time getting along on their ration of sugar.

Spring had finally arrived, and Ralph was busy plowing a field for corn. He noted with satisfaction that the field of wheat looked really good, and the pasture and hay fields were greening up nicely. He had already sowed clover seed in the wheat field, and the oats were showing nicely where there had been corn last year. Thus far, the weather had been most cooperative and Ralph was satisfied that his work was going well, perhaps even a little ahead of schedule.

It was a cloudy day, and without the sun, Ralph depended on his grandfather's watch to know when it was quitting time. He kept the gold watch on a leather thong fastened to his overalls where the watch easily slipped into a pocket on the overall bib. He was giving the team a breather, so he reached for the watch to check the time. The leather thong was there, but when he pulled on it, there was no watch on the other end. My gosh! What had happened? He knew he had stopped halfway across the field to make an adjustment on the whippletree. Had the watch fallen out then? He tied the team and retraced his steps, looking for that bright gold case. No luck. He finally decided that the watch had somehow become unfastened and had obviously fallen out and been plowed under. There was no way he could find it. It would be like looking for a needle in a haystack like the old adage said. Sine the watch had belonged to Horatio, it had meant a lot to Ralph. It was one discouraged man who came up from the field that night.

Edith sensed that something was wrong when Ralph came in for supper. He sat at the table, then explained the situation to her.

"Are you certain you had the watch back in the field?"

"Yes. I had checked the time earlier. Somehow, I must not have put it back in the pocket like it should have been. I just don't know how it got loose," he said morosely. It was easy to see that he felt he had been careless.

"Will it show up when you disc and drag?" Edith asked hopefully.

"I doubt it. It's probably at the bottom of a furrow. Guess I shouldn't have carried the watch except for when I was going to town."

Ralph looked completely dejected, but Edith didn't quite know what to say. She realized her husband was extremely upset, yet she did not know how to comfort him. The watch was gone, and nothing she could say would bring it back. She felt like crying. What a shame to have lost a family heirloom.

(In later years, Edith's sister, Edna, and her husband, Louis Hehrer, lived on that farm. About 1934, they came over to Ralph's all excited because they had the watch. It seems Lou had plowed it up, and knowing the story, they had immediately brought it to Ralph. The case was fine, but the works were rusted. The case had been slightly sprung when a cow had jammed Ralph up against the barn wall. Ralph's sister, Blanche, took the watch with only Edith knowing she had it, and had new works put in it. Ralph was like a little boy when he got his watch back with the same case, only different works. He was taken completely by surprise, but he was forever grateful to his sister for her thoughtfulness.)

Edith's sister, Gladys, wanted to go shopping in St. Johns, and since she didn't want to go alone, she asked Edith to go with her. She told Edith she had already spoken to their sister, Edna, about taking care of Gordon and Helen while they were gone. Gladys knew their mother would be glad to have the children around, and with Edna to see to their needs, it would not be tiring for their mother.

Edith was glad of the opportunity to go to St. Johns because Helen was growing so fast, she needed to make her daughter some new clothes. She felt the choices for material at a reasonable price were better in St. Johns than in Elsie.

She was a little surprised that Gladys had volunteered to drive because Gladys often went no place unless her husband could drive her. Edith felt there were times when Don would have been in the field working if Gladys hadn't insisted she be taken some place. Gladys never seemed to fully understand that Don's farm work was their livelihood and had to be done on time.

On the designated day, Gladys and Edith left right after dinner and expected to be back in time to get supper for their husbands. Since St. Johns was almost twelve miles away, Gladys kept the horse at a fast walk. There were times when the horse would gladly have trotted, but Gladys was not all that daring.

As usual, Gladys was busy finding fault with Don. This never failed to irritate Edith because she thought Don catered to Gladys, and that her sister really didn't make a very good farmer's wife. She was so concerned with a clean house, she couldn't even feed her chickens like other farm women.

"Don plowed and fitted the garden over a week ago, but what good does that do if he doesn't get it planted?"

Edith knew it would do no good to suggest that Gladys plant her own garden like their mother had always done. Edith would have been delighted If Ralph had already plowed and fitted their garden. She knew Ralph would do nothing with the garden spot until he had the corn planted, and it would make no difference if she did repeatedly ask him about it. Besides, she did not want to be like Gladys and hound her husband when she felt he did the best he could.

"I think Don is busy trying to get his corn in. Ralph said Don told him he was somewhat behind," Edith explained.

"Well, if he'd go out after chores now that it is still light by then, he could do a little at a time in the garden. After all, it doesn't have to be planted all on the same day." Her somewhat strident tone irritated Edith even more.

"Did you ever consider he's quite likely too tired? Plowing and fitting a field is hard work even for a man as large as Don." Don was as tall as Ralph, but he was a lot heavier. Because of the nature of his work, he carried little fat, only muscle.

"Oh, I suppose you are right. I just am anxious because I only have a few jars of vegetables left, and I'm looking forward to having fresh vegetables from the garden."

And you'll expect Don to bring the produce to the house instead of you going to the garden to harvest anything, thought Edith, although she made no further comment. If a garden was so important, then why couldn't Gladys do the work instead of leaving it all up to Don? Guess she would never fully understand her sister. Of course, Gladys' house was always spotless, and she ironed everything she washed, even Don's denim overalls. It was just that any work outside the house didn't seem to be on her agenda.

They were coming into St. Johns from the north along what was the town's main street. About a block before the business district, the railroad crossed the street. It was equipped with gates to prevent people from going on the tracks when a train drew near. A man in the watch tower controlled the gates.

Since this was such familiar territory, and the horse was moving at a slow walk, Gladys was busy talking, not paying attention to her driving.

"Gladys! Stop! The gate in front of us just came down. And now, the one in back is down. Whatever shall we do?"

Neither Edith nor Gladys was noted for keeping a cool head in the time of crisis. There was room to turn the horse and buggy sideways along the track, but it would take a steady hand to keep the frightened horse in this position while a train rumbled by.

Gladys stopped the horse. "Edith, I don't know what to do. Major can hear the train whistle even though it's a long way off yet. I won't be able to manage him" Fear was evident in the tone of Gladys' voice.

"What about the watchman in the tower? Can't the man see what he's done? Maybe if we both scream, he'd hear us and realize something is wrong. I don't see anyone else around to help get that man's attention."

Just then, Edith noticed that the man in the tower was looking at them, obviously laughing at their predicament. The train whistle sounded again, and she realized the train was much closer although it was still out of sight. The horse realized the train was nearer too. He began to prance and dance, obviously afraid.

Edith shook her fist at that laughing man. Apparently, he found this even more humorous. Oh, what Edith would have said to him given the chance. Then, the front gate rose, and with no urging, the horse bounded across the tracks seemingly as relieved as the two women were to be safely away when the freight came roaring through.

''Edith, I feel weak all over," said Gladys as she pulled the horse up to a hitching post. "I don't feel like shopping, but there are some things I have to get now that we are here. How are you?"

"Mad. Mad clear through. That man trapped us on purpose. Oh, I'd like to give him a piece of my mind. But you're right. Let's get our shopping done and get back home. I've had enough of St. Johns for one day."

Edith did not mention the incident to Ralph. She was certain her husband would not have found the situation as frightening as she and Gladys had. Besides, it was over and done with, and she'd just as soon forget the whole episode.

Ralph had told Edith that Carl had planted about twenty acres of corn on rented land. However, Ralph told her he was almost certain this would not be enough to keep him from being drafted, but perhaps the war would end before Carl would be fully trained.

Edith knew that she was pregnant once again. My, she did hope they would have a boy. The old timers said you should "fill up your beds as you go", but she knew she'd be keenly disappointed if they had another girl. Helen was a sweet child, and had always been easy to care for. She had never been demanding and was usually good natured. Although Rate had said nothing, Edith felt he would certainly like a son. Besides, they needed a male to carry the Setterington name to another generation.

It was a pleasant Sunday afternoon, sunny and warm. Ralph was reading, and Edith had just finished the dinner dishes. It was almost time for Helen's afternoon nap. As it was, Helen was hanging onto a chair and walking cautiously around It. She had begun doing this just before her first birthday, but thus far, she had not been brave enough to take steps without having something to hang onto. Edith had tried to get Helen to take a few steps on her own by holding out her arms to entice the child. Helen's remedy was to drop down on all fours and creep the short distance to her mother.

Edith hadn't heard anyone drive in, but the side door opened and Carl called out, "Anyone home?"

"Of course. Come on in. I didn't hear a buggy," said Edith as Carl dropped into the nearest rocker.

"That's because there wasn't one. I walked. Figured I'd better get accustomed to walking since Uncle Sam wants me to report to Camp Custer in three weeks."

"You've been drafted?" asked Edith not certain that Carl wasn't simply teasing even though he looked completely serious. Like Art and Vern, Carl loved to tease, especially his sisters.

"That's right. Now, Lee won't be the only one to wear a uniform. Gosh, Sis, think how handsome I'll look. I heard you thought Lee looked mighty fine in his uniform."

"Spoke of it for days," volunteered Ralph. "Seems those uniforms sure do impress a woman."

"Just wait until you see me in mine. All those lovely young women will be chasing after me."

"What a dreamer," said Edith, laughing in spite of herself.

"When did you get the notice?" asked Ralph.

"A couple of days ago. When I told the draft board about my corn, they said it wasn't enough to make a difference. Of course, they didn't give me any idea of when I might be drafted, but I've been expecting it, and now I know for certain. No more wondering each day. Those of us who are in our early twenties will certainly make better soldiers than the older ones. Don't you agree, Sis?" Carl gave her an irritating grin.

"Oh sure. You think you want to go because Lee has already left. You never could stand having him do something you couldn't do You've been that way since you were about eight. Where did it ever get you?"

"Well, there's one thing I can't change. Lee is a Lieutenant and I'll be just a buck Private. Then, too, Lee had been away from home before, and I never have. Sure will be different. Guess I'll quite likely miss everyone, even you, my dear Sis."

"You'll probably be kept too busy to be lonesome," said Ralph. "I saw Don Huffman when he was home on furlough just before he was sent overseas, and he says they really work the recruits. They don't have much free time."

"I had a chance to talk to Lee before he left, and he said the same thing. I guess there will be a lot to learn. After Pershing got over there, things sure went better, so I was hopeful peace wouldn't be that far off. Now, I guess the Russians have botched everything, so we will have to send more Americans to get things done. After all, England and France don't seem to do too well on their own, do they?"

"Germany isn't going to give up easily even if we do send more troops." cautioned Ralph. "Don't suppose you have any idea what kind of an outfit you'll be assigned to. Don Huffman is with a machine gun company with the infantry. Now that Don is in France, I wonder how that makes his folks feel. Lona was never the same after he got back from the Spanish American War. If anything happens to Don, all they will have left is Hazel."

"I had heard that Don had left. Well, he wanted to go, so I guess it's all right. At least Aubrey didn't get out of going even if he is still in the States. Lee told me he wasn't certain how they determine where us raw recruits are going to be placed. Guess there is some sort of testing. Lee said the artillery is a good place to be better than the infantry anyway. Don't suppose I'll have a choice, just be put where they need men the most."

Carl played with Helen and seemed to enjoy how his niece would laugh aloud when he blew in her neck. He tried his best to coax her to take steps to get to him, but Helen could not be enticed. Edith noted that Carl certainly did like children. If he ever had any of his own, he'd be one proud father, maybe even more so than Art. Edith just hoped his stint in the Army would turn out all right. If only the war would end before he and Lee were sent overseas.

Ralph had registered with the Clinton County draft board on June 5, 1917 as had been required. However, he had been told that only single men were being called and there had been a great many volunteers, so the County had easily met their quota. Ralph still maintained that because he was a farmer he would be exempt from military service, but Edith had worried anyway. Then, in June of this year, Ralph had been classified IV, so Edith knew all her worry had been for nothing.

Edith had also been concerned about her brother-in-law, George Ryan. She hated to think George would be drafted. He and Blanche seemed so happy together, Edith felt they should not be separated. However, Ralph had told her that since George no longer worked on the streetcars, but worked for Ford, he wouldn't be called. It seems Ford made something for the military, so his work was indispensable. She guessed making the job change had been a good idea. Of course, when she thought of George's explanation, she had to laugh. George had said that Blanche had fallen for the uniform he wore while working on the streetcars, but he had thrown the uniform away and all she got was him. George could always put something in a humorous light. Edith guessed that was why she never felt intimidated by him. His Irish wit usually made her laugh even if what they were discussing was of a serious nature.

Edna came often to visit. She was accustomed to Ralph's teasing, and it seldom bothered her. She liked him anyway and usually tried to do something to retaliate which Ralph found hilarious. More often than not, he was the one who won out in any battle of words or deeds. Edna was always glad to take care of Helen while Edith was busy. She knew Edith was in the family way again, and she felt happy for her sister. She knew Edith felt children were the blessings of being married.

It was a Sunday afternoon. Edith and Ralph had decided that since the weather was so nice, warm but not as hot as July can get, they would go to the river by the Colony for a picnic. Edna had spent Saturday night with them, so she was included in the plans.

On the east side of the bridge over the river, on the south river bank, the land was level and the drop-off to the river was not great. At this time of the year, the river was actually too low for swimming. The women didn't care, but Ralph would have enjoyed a good swim. As it was, Ralph finally talked Edna into taking off her shoes and stockings so she could go wading with him. She was a little hesitant, not completely sure this was what she wanted to do. However, once she was in the shallow water, she discovered she enjoyed feeling the water, although it was less than halfway to her knees, and the sandy bottom actually felt good on her feet.

Ralph had moved off a short distance when he heard a splash. Good heavens! Edna had somehow managed to fall flat on her face. Since the water was so shallow, Ralph expected her to get up immediately. She didn't. He moved quickly to her side, grabbed her arm, and pulled her up. She was gasping for air. It was apparent she had not only swallowed some water, but had got it up her nose as well. After a few moments of coughing, she was all right although a mite shaken.

"My gosh, Edna, why did you just lay there?" asked Ralph, a puzzled expression on his face. "You could easily have pushed yourself out of the water."

"I-I-don't know. I was terrified. I just knew I was going to drown."

"In eight inches of water? I guess if I hadn't been here to pull you up, you would have laid there and drowned. I'll know better than to take you wading again. At least you've taught me something. I thought a person had to be in water over his head to drown, but you've shown me a person could drown in as little as six inches of water." Ralph was beginning to see the humor of the situation. Edna was soaked, and she did look bedraggled. So much for her once clean dress.

"Don't make fun of her," put in Edith. "Guess we had better be getting home so Edna can get out of those wet clothes."

"Good thing it's warm, isn't it, Edna?" Ralph gave her an irritating grin.

"Oh, just hush up. I don't know how I happened to fall. You probably pushed me." She gave Ralph an accusing look.

Ralph laughed at this idea. At least he was glad Edna's sense of humor was returning, a sure sign she was all right.

Of course, for weeks, Ralph often teased his sister-in-law about how he had saved her life. Edna took the teasing good naturedly, but she never forgot the panic she had felt when she was face down in the water. She really didn't expect a strong swimmer like Ralph to fully understand.

The whole episode had bothered Edith more than she let on, mostly because she was afraid of the water. She knew Ralph had enjoyed swimming since he was a young boy, but no one in her family had learned to swim. She actually had thought Edna was quite adventuresome to wade in the shallows of the river. Thank goodness Ralph had had the presence of mind to help Edna so quickly. Bet Edna would think twice about going in the water again.

The time came for Carl to leave for Camp Custer. Edith tried unsuccessfully to hold back the tears when Carl gave her a hug and a kiss as he said his final goodbye. Perhaps when the holidays came, he would be able to get a furlough. He told Edith to keep that thought in mind, and he assured her he would write soon. After all, wasn't she his favorite sister? This made Edith laugh as Carl had known it would. He hated having Edith worry about him. He assured her he would be fine.

Actually, Edith wondered if Carl would keep his word and write to her shortly after he arrived at Camp Custer. She certainly hoped so. Lee had not been all that good about writing, but she supposed he was busy and what free time he had, he wrote to Nellie and his parents. At least as yet, Carl had no particular girl friend to write to.

It was noon and Ralph came in for dinner.

"You look exceptionally pleased over something," he observed.

"I am. We got a letter from Carl. He wrote it on Sunday. That's pretty good since he only left Thursday. Actually, he sounded as though he's enjoying himself." The tone of Edith's voice seemed to indicate she found it unlikely that anyone would enjoy being in the Army away from home. "He says he's with a great group of fellows."

"Did you want him to be depressed?"

"No. Of course not. I was just worried, that's all. They've already begun testing them, but Carl didn't explain what the testing covered. Guess they must feed them pretty good. For Sunday dinner he said they had roast beef, potatoes, sweet corn, lemon pie, coffee and ice cream. Sounded pretty good to me. If they eat like that every day, he sure won't starve. Bet some of the draftees are eating better than when they were home."

"I don't doubt that. However, I'll bet Army food isn't half as tasty as what your mother cooks. Of course, if they work them hard, they need good meals."

Ralph had been to St. Johns with Vern. When he came in the house, Edith knew something had happened which he obviously found humorous. There was that tell-tale glint in his eyes.

"You and Vern have a good time?"

"It was fine. As usual, Vern's always good for a few laughs. He got the material to patch up that old harness which is, in my opinion, hardly worth saving. I guess there is no way he can afford a new harness. However, I believe if he went to some of these auctions, he could get a used harness in pretty good condition fairly cheap. But you know how Vern is. He always thinks he knows best.

"We met someone he knew from St. Johns. I found what the man had to say rather comical. You know how they raise peppermint on both sides of the road on that muck land just north of St. Johns. Well, it seems that this year there was an exceptionally good crop. Guess the weather was just right. It seems they have to take the oil to Lansing to sell it since there is no market for it locally. Sometimes, I'm told, they even hire men to go along with the shipment to protect it since it is worth so much money. Well, it seems this one owner, forget his name was bragging that he had at least $1500 worth of oil in each of two jugs. Imagine, $3000. Well, as he was expounding on how good his crop had been, trying to impress the men he was talking to, he was swinging a jug in each hand. Guess he was so busy bragging, he didn't realize how far he was swinging the jugs. The jugs hit together, broke, and there went his $3000 worth of oil all over the ground. Guess the other farmers had a good laugh over that. I doubt if any of them really felt any sympathy for him since the result was because of his own carelessness."

"He lost $3000 just like that?"

"That's what the man told Vern. Guess it doesn't pay to lord it over your neighbors. If the man hadn't been such a braggart, he'd still have his peppermint oil."

"I can't really imagine what it would be like to have all that money at one time. It must have been a bitter blow to lose it."

"I have no idea how well off the man is, but I'll wager he will be more careful in the future. I doubt if the ones in his audience will soon let him forget what happened."

Carl continued to write quite regularly and Edith sent him a letter at least once a week. He said they had begun to get a series of shots. He didn't exactly say what the shots were for only that some of them made him feel sick for a day or two and his arm was mighty sore. Most of the fellows had the same problem.

Then, he had been worried about his corn, first wondering if anyone from the family had cultivated it, then worried because there had been a lack of rain. He had facetiously suggested Edith carry water and water his corn, all twenty acres. This made her laugh. She guessed Army life wasn't changing her brother. He could still joke and tease as he had always done.

Carl came home on furlough the middle of August. While the time was short, Saturday night and all day Sunday, Edith felt the time was well spent. It was obvious Carl had missed everyone. He said they were usually pretty tired after a day of drilling, and there were times when he was more than happy when the time came for lights out. He seemed especially glad to see Helen, and this time she would walk to him. Even she seemed intrigued with his uniform, the buttons were the main attraction. Carl told Edith that he thought of Helen several times a day. He said she was the sweetest child he knew. Edith felt proud because Carl had never made such a fuss over Art's Rita.

Carl told Ralph that from the reports they got at Camp, everyone expected the war would soon be over. Ralph hoped Carl's officers were telling the men the truth. Even when Carl said an officer from the French Army spoke to them, and his message was that the Germans were daily losing, Ralph remained rather skeptical. He hoped he was wrong partly because he hated having Edith worried. Although her pregnancy seemed to be going well, he felt it would be much better if she was not concerned about Lee and Carl.

Ralph had been to Elsie to have grain ground for a grist. When he came home, he took care of the team, but instead of unloading the sacks of ground feed, he went directly to the house.

Edith looked up from the patching she was doing when Ralph came in the door. "What's wrong? Are you all right?" she asked anxiously.

"I'm all right. It's just that I heard some bad news while I was at the mill. It seems that a few days ago, Huffman's received word that Don had been killed the sixth of October. He was somewhere in France. Sure must have been a blow for them. First Lona, now Don. Guess it really is a good thing that they have Hazel, not that she can make up for the loss of their son, but at least they aren't childless. Sure am glad he enlisted under his own name and that Sheldons won't be the ones to collect his insurance."

"How terrible this must be for the family. Oh, I hope Carl is right, and that the war will soon be over."

"I'm not always sure the news we get of the fighting is accurate. From all accounts, it doesn't seem as though Germany can last much longer."

Although it took several days for the news to reach this country, an armistice was signed 11 November 1918. The whole country celebrated. After all, this had been a war to end all wars.

Edith was anxious for Carl to be sent home. She knew it would be at least six months after the armistice before Lee would be discharged, but she expected Carl was no longer needed. They had had a letter from him dated December 2 in which he wrote that his Sgt. Major said that in two weeks his division (78th Inf.) would be a thing of the past. However, he didn't seem to think he'd be home for Christmas. Certainly he would be mustered out shortly after the first of the year. How good it would be to have him home.

CHAPTER 12

O n the 26th of January, Edith gave birth to a son. Although he was a rather large baby, she had had no problem with the delivery. Ralph was much relieved that everything had gone so well. He was surprised that Edith had not been concerned about this pregnancy. It was as though she had forgotten what an ordeal Helen's birth had been. They named their son Keith Horatio, which made him the fourth Setterington to bear the name Horatio.

While Millie seemed pleased that the grandson had been given Horatio for a middle name, it was easy to see that Helen was still the favorite. Edith consoled herself by thinking this was probably because Helen was at such a cute age. Perhaps when Keith was older, the grandparents would enjoy him more.

Edith had realized that she had not had a sufficient supply of milk for Helen, so she and the doctor decided that since Keith was such a large baby, she should not try to nurse him. The doctor was certain her milk supply would be insufficient for such a large baby; therefore, Keith was given Horlicks Malted Milk and thrived.

Miney, of course, had been hoping for another girl. However, since both Ralph and Edith seemed so pleased to have a son, she admitted that she was happy for them. She did like the fact that the baby's middle name was Horatio. She felt continuing a family name was important, so she decided God had given Edith and Ralph a son for this very reason.

Edith truly enjoyed her children. Helen was interested in everything that had to be done for her baby brother. Both Edith and Ralph tried to give her a lot of attention so she wouldn't be jealous of Keith. Of course, Ralph was no more inclined to hold his son than he had been his daughter. Instead of being annoyed,

Edith found the situation humorous and she sometimes teased Ralph by saying, "Don't you want to hold your son?" He often said, "I'll pass." He'd give her a knowing look as though he realized she really didn't expect him to take the baby.

Helen had begun to say words quite early and now she was talking in short sentences. Edith thought this perfectly normal, but Ralph's parents seemed to think this meant Helen was far more Intelligent than most children. No one could make them believe Helen was simply developing normally.

It was a Sunday, so Ralph was in his favorite rocking chair reading when Helen came up to him, crying a little.

Between sobs, she said, "Heiney hurt your Heiney."

Ralph looked at her a moment before he answered. Her admonition had startled him.

"How did she do that?" he asked.

Before Helen could sob out an answer, Edith came from the kitchen and spoke to her husband.

"You are supposed to ask where it hurts."

Ralph did this and Helen tearfully pointed to her left elbow.

Ralph looked at his wife expectantly, waiting for further instructions.

"Now, you kiss the hurt to make it all better."

As soon as Ralph kissed the spot where Helen pointed, she stopped crying and moved off as though nothing unusual had happened.

Edith laughed at the confused look on Ralph's face. "Isn't it miraculous what relief a kiss can bring?"

"How long has she been doing this?"

"I don't know. I guess a couple of weeks or so."

"What gave you the idea to make the hurt go away by kissing the spot?"

"That's what my mother always did. Kisses heal many bruises, those imagined and those that are truly real."

Ralph digested this last remark before returning to his reading. Guess he had a lot to learn about kids.

A few days later when Ralph came in from morning chores, Edith told him he had a letter postmarked Newport News, Virginia, so she supposed it was from his best friend, Don Sherman.

Edith was correct, and Ralph chuckled often as he read the missive, then he shared parts with Edith.

"He's on the U.S.S. New Jersey and he wrote it February 3. He said that he had a letter from home saying 'there was another (little thing) around your place.' He goes on to say, 'Mother said it was a boy this time. Well, you see which you like best then I will know what to order, How do you get them? C.O.D. or pay in advance?'"

Both Edith and Ralph laughed at this. The Navy certainly hadn't changed Don's wit.

"He went on to say they had been to the Azores Islands where they could buy all the oranges they wanted. This had seemed good to have the fresh fruit. Said he didn't think much of France. While the harbor at Brest was one of the best he'd seen, the rest of France in his words 'was all wrong.' Bet he'll be glad to get home."

Edith figured Ralph would be glad to have his friend safely home once again. Although he had never voiced his opinion, she felt her husband had truly missed Don. There had been a time when the two were almost inseparable.

Millie and Miney continued to visit Ralph and Edith often. However, Edith noticed they seldom paid attention to Keith although Miney usually asked how he was doing. Edith began to harbour the suspicion that her -in-laws would always place Helen first, and this rankled. Her own parents showed no preference for either child which, in Edith's opinion, was as it should be. Of course, Pa had had a lot of experience handling a baby, so he was completely comfortable with either child. Whereas Millie had often held Helen, he didn't seem inclined to hold Keith.

Helen was becoming very adept at feeding herself and seldom spilled anything. Both Ralph and Edith had noticed that when given a piece of bread, she studied the butter on the buttered side a moment, then deliberately turned the bread over so the buttered side was down. Only then did she eat the bread.

Millie had been quick to notice this procedure and found it laughable; therefore, one day when he was there to eat with the family, he was quick to offer Helen a quarter slice of bread. As usual, she closely examined the piece, then promptly turned it over. However, since Millie had buttered both sides, she still could see butter. She turned the bread again with a puzzled expression as she beheld more butter. She turned the bread several times in the attempt to understand why no side came up without butter. She finally gave up and slowly ate the bread. Of course, Millie had found her reaction extremely humorous as did Ralph. Edith and Miney laughed, but each still felt a little sorry for the child. As was often the case, Edith wondered about her husband and father-in-law's sense of humor.

Ralph had finally begun hitching Buster and Monarch as a team. What a good looking pair they made! He had driven them to Elsie on the sleighs a few times, and they had behaved well. Actually, they both made Ralph laugh and feel great pride in owning such a nicely matched pair. It seems they could be plodding along, seemingly showing no interest in where they were until they reached the village limit. Then, both horses would perk up, trotting easily, head held higher than usual on arched necks. They raised their tails a little which made the long hair cascade in a pleasing manner. It was as though they were saying, "Look at us. Aren't we handsome?" As long as they were being driven in town, they showed off this way. As soon as the village was left behind, they once again lost interest and simply pulled as was expected. Ralph felt Buster was the leader and that Monarch simply followed his lead.

Ralph had been up town, and when he got home he spoke to Edith. "Heard Don Sherman was discharged from the Navy the latter part of February. Guess he's been too busy to come see us. Talk is that he has a girl friend in Carson City. If that's so, he probably spends any free time he has going to see her."

Edith felt Ralph's feelings were hurt because Don had not called or been to visit. "Well, you know he was gone at least a year and a half. Besides, I've felt he wants to settle down with a wife. I think he'd like to have children. Give him time. I'm sure he will come to visit an old married couple just so he can tease."

"I guess you're right. I wonder if he had started dating this woman before he enlisted. He sure never mentioned her to me."

"Of course not. He might not have wanted to be teased and you know that's what you'd have done."

"You're right, but it's no different than he was with me."

As Edith had expected, Don Sherman dropped in just after the middle of March. Ralph accused him of neglect since he had been home over three weeks. Don merely said that he'd been frightfully busy. He seemed surprised when Ralph commented that trips to Carson City certainly were time consuming.

"How in heck do you know?"

"You should remember how word gets around. Let's see, her name is Mildred Barrett. Seems she's a very lovely young woman, so what does she see in the likes of you?"

"Must be my charming ways," replied Don with a smug laugh. "Seriously, Rate, we're getting married April 26. After all, I can't wait around. You are already way ahead of me. I'll have to hurry to catch up. Should I order a boy first?"

"I don't care what you order, you'll take what you get."

Both laughed at that, then they talked of other things. Don told Ralph of some of the places he'd been.

"Rate, I rather enjoyed being in the Navy once I got my sea legs, but I'm darned glad to be home. I didn't see any other place where I'd want to live.

Actually, even other states don't appeal to me. As far as I'm concerned, Michigan is the place for me."

Edith knew Ralph felt much better since he had seen his friend. They discussed Don's impending marriage. Ralph knew he wouldn't see much of Don now, but he understood this likelihood was inevitable. He was just glad his friend was home safely and he certainly hoped Don would be happy. They sure had plenty of good memories which Ralph found very satisfying.

The last of March, Edith's brother and wife had their second child. Art and Ethel named their son Arlington. Edith was glad to have another nephew. Now, both she and Art had a first-born daughter and then a son. Her family was expanding. She felt it wouldn't be long before Carl would settle down with some nice girl and raise a family.

Winter held on longer than usual, and Ralph became anxious. There was always so much to do in the spring. He was always glad when the cattle could be put out on pasture during the day. This made the job of cleaning stables easier and the time spent much shorter. However, Ralph liked to get his oats planted early since this usually meant a better crop.

The weather finally began cooperating and it seemed as though one day it was still winter and the next day, spring was well on its way. Edith was always thankful for good farming weather. She had long ago discovered that her husband was forever a pessimist. However, she realized that in spite of Ralph's dire predictions, they often had better crops than some of the neighbors.

When Ralph came home from taking a grist to Elsie, he merely stopped the team in the drive by the house. As he came in the kitchen door, Edith looked at him in surprise.

"A pup. You've got a collie pup."

Ralph put the pup, a sable and white, on the linoleum floor.

"Yup. She's about three months old. I felt like it was time I had another dog in my life. Besides, the man who was selling the pups in town said both her parents were good cattle dogs. The roof of her mouth is black and that usually indicates high intelligence. Sure would be a help sometimes to have a good dog to work with the livestock. Certainly could save me a lot of steps. "Have you thought of a name for her yet?"

"Think I'll call her Fleet. You don't care that I bought her do you?"

"Heavens no. I've always liked dogs. Helen will take to her now, and I'll bet Keith will like her when he can walk around. You've missed Bruno, so it's good that you have another pup."

When it came time to put in the garden, Edith found it a little more difficult to find the time now that she had the responsibility of two children. She tried to do the work when both Keith and Helen were taking their afternoon naps. However, it seemed that on some days Helen didn't sleep very long. Even as a baby, Helen had not seemed to require as much sleep as Edith expected. Less sleep never seemed to make Helen cross, so Edith simply tried to adjust her work accordingly. It wouldn't be long before Keith would be sitting alone, and Edith felt she could then put him in the buggy to go with her to the garden spot. He was such a contented baby, she was certain he would watch her work without crying for attention. Helen usually had a kitten from the barn to play with, and Keith often showed an interest in the small animal.

Ralph's farm work was progressing well. The oats had been planted on time and he had the corn field plowed and fitted ready to plant corn. Vern had been over lamenting the fact that while he had finally got his oats planted, he had only just begun to plow the field for corn. As usual, Ralph could not understand why Vern was always behind with his farm work. He simply was not cut out to be a farmer.

"Since I have my field ready for planting, I could come over tomorrow afternoon and help you with the plowing," offered Ralph.

"No, no. It's all right, Rate. I'll get it done somehow." From the tone of his voice, he gave the impression that he was completely discouraged.

"Don't argue. I'll be there right after dinner to give you a hand."

Vern finally agreed although Ralph had a sneaken suspicion that Vern had definitely wanted him to offer to help. Sometimes Vern could be manipulative, and Ralph figured this was one of those times. He really didn't care and was glad to lend a hand to help his brother-in-law.

Edith decided she would take the kids and go visit her sister-in-law. She and Blanche didn't see as much of one another as they had in the past. Besides, Edith knew her nephews would be glad to see her. Of course, both Beurmann and Wilson would be in school, but Wilson would be home early since he was only eight.

While Ralph finished plowing Vern's field, Vern had begun going over the plowed furrows with the disc. Ralph wondered how many days it would be before Vern would plant. Ralph intended to put his corn in the next day.

It was after supper when Ralph asked Edith if she had enjoyed spending time with Blanche.

Edith laughed and said, "It seemed good. Blanche was complaining about how Vern takes a nap after dinner, sitting upright in his rocker, mouth wide open, snoring like a buzz saw. He used to do that at home too, so I told her I had the perfect remedy. She was all gung ho until she found out what the remedy was."

"What did you do to your brother?" Ralph asked.

"Nothing much. I just cut off a good chunk of raw salt pork and dropped it in his mouth. He chewed on it, stopped, then chewed a couple more times, before it woke him up. Was he ever mad! Of course, everyone knew what I had done, and we all laughed at him. At least he quit his snoring when taking a nap after dinner. Blanche asked wasn't I afraid he'd choke. Told her the piece was too large for that, but she still didn't think it a good Idea."

"I can imagine Vern losing his temper. Bet that raw meat didn't taste the best."

"Don't suppose it did, but Vern is always ready to tease someone, so it was just tit for tat. I figured he'd do something to get even with me, but he never did."

"Probably figured it was just better to forget the whole thing. You know, they always say to let sleeping dogs lie," Ralph said with a laugh.

Sometimes his wife amazed him. In some ways she sure could hold her own, but in some areas, she was anything but confident in her own ability and needed someone to look out for her best interests. He guessed maybe that was why he had wanted to marry her. He wanted always to be able to look after her.

Ralph had been over to his folks. When he came in for supper, he spoke to his wife as he sat down to eat.

"Ma and Pa had a letter from Glen Curtis today. You know, he's my Aunt Ettie's son. Aunt Ettie was always a strange one and Glen is even more so. Seems he's always In need of money. Pa usually sends him a few dollars. He has always lived from hand to mouth. He'd get into a town broke, but he could always earn a little money by repainting signs for merchants. Seems he always carries his brushes with him. Guess he does have a talent, but he is anything but a responsible person. Of course, he left home early when he was only sixteen or seventeen. Guess it was Aunt Ettie that kind of kept him in line."

"I've really never heard you talk about him. I just know they lived up north."

"Well, I only saw him a few times. Pa says one time he was bragging that he'd get on a train with no money and no ticket. Of course, the conductor came around between stations to collect tickets. Since Glen had none and couldn't buy one, he'd be put off at the next station. He'd simply wait for the next train, and pull the same stunt until he got where he wanted to go."

"Certainly wasn't being very honest, was he?"

"Nope. Think the only reason he wrote to Ma and Pa now was to ask them for some money. They didn't exactly say, but he never seems to get in touch except when he needs money. I sure don't understand that mentality."

Edith agreed. She could not understand why someone would be willing to take money from an aunt and uncle. At least Aunt Lorin's Georgie had never been in that category even if he was rather odd and never seemed to visit his aunt. Ralph's relatives were certainly different from hers.

It had been a good year. The crops were doing nicely. Wheat harvest had been better than usual, and the oats had done well. Since there had been an adequate amount of rain, the clover for hay had done exceptionally well. Ralph knew there was no way he'd run short of feed for the livestock. Of course, he had corn to harvest yet, but it was maturing on schedule and Ralph expected a bumper crop. Although he was usually a pessimist and truly believed in the old saying, "Never count your chickens until they're hatched," he felt certain he'd have no problem getting the corn in even if the weather did turn bad.

Ralph often helped his father with some work. Millie usually had a hired man, but on occasion, he worked alone. Although Millie never expressed his gratitude for his son's help, Ralph was certain his father appreciated him. Still, it would have been nice if just once Pa would have told him so.

Millie hated having to repair something, but work was needed on the sheep shed before winter set in. Ralph had decided he'd better give him a hand if the work was to get done. Although Pa thought everyone should never put off until tomorrow what could be done today, he never seemed to apply that to something he hated doing.

The two had been working without conversation. Then, Millie stopped to rest a moment.

"John was here last weekend. He's decided to give up farming and horse trading. That's the best decision he's ever made. We all know John was no farmer, and I don't think he ever made a dime trading horses. More likely he lost money there. He sure didn't have any of Pa's sense when it came to horses."

"What's he going to do?"

"Seems he's moving to Flint. Says he's got a job lined up. He's to be a policeman. Now, that I can understand. John's size would intimidate a lot of men. Seems the police usually have to contend with barroom or pool room brawls and such. No, I think John might finally have found his proper niche in this world."

Ralph digested this piece of information. Uncle John at six foot four and a half inches often stood a head taller than other men. Of his 280 pounds, none of it was flab, just plain muscle. Ralph felt his Uncle John was the strongest man he knew, stronger than Pa, and Pa was no slouch when it came to strength. Yep, he was sure Uncle John could hold his own in any free-for-all. He'd sure have no trouble with the average man.

It was only a few weeks later when an acquaintance from Elsie had been in Flint at a pool hall. He related his story to Ralph, chuckling as he did so.

Seems three patrons got in a fight. This was just about the time John was making his rounds. He told Ralph, "Before you could bat an eye, John had two of the rowdies handcuffed together, and he literally grabbed the third fellow, lifted him off his feet, when he explained that he expected no trouble from him. John then took all three to the station. They sure looked completely cowed. Of course, John was almost a head taller than the tallest one of the three. Things were really quiet for a while. I'm tellin' you, John sure impressed the other patrons. No one raised their voice in any argument. I thought the whole episode quite funny. I didn't say anything about knowin' John, but I just listened to the talk after he left. Believe me, John sure impressed that bunch, and the owner was pleased no damage had been done."

When Ralph told Millie what he'd learned, Millie had a good chuckle. Guess John was doing right well for himself. Well, it was about time. Millie felt John had spent most of his life doing exactly what he knew would bring Horatio's disapproval. Maybe now that Horatio was in California, John could finally become a responsible individual.

Ralph had been correct about Fleet. She was a natural born cattle dog. Ralph was patient teaching her just what he wanted done. Ralph had always talked to Bruno like he was a human, and he saw no need to change this now. He truly had a knack with dogs, and they usually idolized him. Fleet was no different. Now at six months, she knew when Ralph was going to the barn to do the milking, and she worked quietly behind the cows in the pasture to bring them to the barnyard just as Ralph opened the stable door. No more waiting for the cows to come up from the pasture or maybe having to go out to chase a stubborn cow into the barn. Fleet was living up to all of Ralph's expectations.

At this time, many men hunted rabbits with a ferret. It was perfectly legal. The ferret would go down a rabbit hole and chase the rabbit out where the hunter could shoot the animal. Vern had a ferret that was more of a pet than most. The ferret had been pretty young when Vern got him, and Ralph had found it laughable how Vern had spent time with the small animal. Vern had never been one to have a dog, but he sure liked having the ferret for a pet. When loose, it would follow Vern wherever he went. The small animal avoided the boys, and they seemed to leave the ferret alone. Ralph wasn't sure how good the ferret would be when it came to hunting since it seemed to want to be at Vern's side whenever it was out of its cage.

Edith had been over to visit her sister, Gladys. Gordon was excited because this was the year he was to begin school, and school would begin in less than a week. He had about a mile to walk. It was almost half a mile from his house to the corner, then another half mile or so to the school. This was considered close in the farming community because some of the students walked over three miles to attend a small, one room school. Edith thought Gordon's enthusiasm was a good thing. However, she felt the only reason Gladys wanted him in school was because he'd be gone most of the day. Somehow, Gladys had not enjoyed being a mother. She looked upon motherhood as a lot of extra work.

Edith wondered if Don would expect Gordon to haul the firewood even though his time to do chores would be much shorter. Ralph had often expressed his opinion that Don made Gordon work too hard for his age. Gordon was sort of a skinny kid and didn't look to be very strong. Ralph felt the lad should not be expected to handle heavy chunks of wood. There were times when Ralph felt sorry for the young boy. Ralph vowed he'd never expect Keith to work that hard at such an early age. On a farm, each family member was expected to contribute to their well being, but Ralph felt the work expected should be tailored to a person's ability.

Ralph and Edith had just sat down for supper. Keith was in the high chair contentedly chewing on a piece of bread. Helen sat in her usual place, perched on two catalogs on the chair which were needed to make her high enough at the table. Edith had fixed Helen's plate, fed Keith some mashed potatoes and some peas which she had mashed with her fork. One thing about Keith, he ate with relish everything she gave him. Helen was sometimes more particular and even at this age, showed a distaste for some foods.

Edith studied her husband a moment as he silently ate his meal. Then, she said "You're being mighty quiet tonight."

"Guess I've got things on my mind."

Ralph offered no further explanation and Edith didn't pursue the matter. She thought her husband looked exceptionally serious. Well, as she had learned long ago, getting Ralph to talk when he didn't want to was like pulling teeth from a chicken. Impossible.

After the dishes and chores were done, and the children tucked in bed, Ralph finally looked up from the book he was reading and spoke to his wife.

"You knew I was going to stop in at Pa's on my way home from town." Edith nodded her head, so Ralph continued. "Well, Pa wants me to take over the farm. Says he's tired of the constant work and he'd like it best if I came home to run the farm. He intends to buy a house in Elsie. He says he'd lend me a hand some of the time, and we'd share everything 50-50. He also indicated that I should be interested in the place because some day it quite likely will be mine. I think that was what he considered to be an added incentive to get me to agree with his proposal. I told him I'd think about it and get back to him next week."

"What do you want to do?"

"I don't honestly know. That farm where I was born and raised is important to me. I'd hate to see someone else living there. It's a good farm. The 50-50 deal is fair. Of course, like now, any chickens, ducks or geese would be yours, while Pa would have a share in the rest of the livestock. Guess I'd never thought of Pa leaving farming. He will only be 55 years old. Most men go longer than that. What do you think I should do?"

"It has to be your decision. I like it here, but there is always the possibility Dave will sell the farm. Then where would we go? Whatever you decide will be all right with me."

"Some help you are."

"Isn't a wife supposed to leave such decisions up to her husband? If you'd like to take your father's offer, I'm all for it. Having the children grow up in your old home would be kind of nice."

"Well, I'll tell Pa next week I'll accept his offer. Then, I'll have to tell Dave I'll be leaving next March so he can line up someone else to rent the property unless he decides to sell. It will be good to work land that Pa and Grandfather put under cultivation. There is still one field that is virgin ground, never having been plowed, just used for pasture. Of course, Pa has worked at burning out the stumps for years."

"The barn is much larger now and if I know Pa, he will expect me to keep more cows than he ever did. He has both sheep and hogs, but from what he said, I'd share in any sale there even if I don't have either sheep or hogs to contribute. I guess he's willing to make some concessions because he knows I can match him on cattle and young stock. Now, with Buster and Monarch, I've also got two teams of horses. I guess it would all even out."

Edith thought Ralph seemed pleased with his decision. If he was happy, that was all that counted. Edith knew there was a nice orchard with five or six different kinds of apples plus a pear tree, some grape vines south of the house, and a good fenced in spot for a garden with a few raspberry bushes. The brooder house was small but adequate, and the chicken coop was a nice size. She could have more chickens which meant more eggs and more roosters to sell. That way she could contribute more for groceries and items she needed around the house instead of being dependent on Ralph for everything. Since her father-in-law had added onto the kitchen a few years back, it was a nice size, and the large stone cellar was certainly a good place to store vegetables and canned food. Yes, the house was all a woman could ask for. The pump for drinking water was just outside the kitchen door which wasn't always the case, and the pump in the kitchen pumped water from a cistern that was kept supplied with rain water from the eaves whenever there was a rain. Of course, this water was only for washing up, but it was right handy.

A few days later when Ralph came into the house for supper, he noticed Edith looked upset. The kids seemed to be all right, and she was busy placing the food on the table, right on time just like always. Still, he could see something was certainly bothering her. Edith was always one to enjoy her food, but tonight she had taken very small portions and her mind seemed elsewhere as she fed Keith. Of late, Ralph had taken over the job of preparing Helen's plate since Keith always seemed to be in a hurry to be fed.

Halfway through the meal, Ralph asked, "What's wrong?"

"What makes you think something is wrong?" she countered.

"It's easy enough to see. You've hardly spoken, and you seem miles away."

"Well, yes, I am thoroughly upset. Gladys was here for a short time and she said Gordon hates school. He has even refused to go a few times and she says she switches him all the way to the corner. Once he turns toward the school, he will go on his own. She thinks that is because other children can see him then."

"Why doesn't he like school? He's smart enough. He should do well."

"I asked Gladys the same question. She finally admitted what was wrong. As you know, Gordon is left-handed just like Elzie. Well, it seems the teacher maintains using the left hand to write is unnatural and unacceptable. She explained this to Gordon, but when she caught him using his left hand to make his letters, she tied his left hand behind him, forcing him to use his right hand. Now, every day she ties Gordon's left hand behind him except for recess and noon hour. I asked Gladys what she intended to do about It. She made some excuse that she couldn't do anything, so she simply whips Gordon to make him go to school. She's just plain cruel."

"Has she talked to the teacher?"

"Not meek, spoiled, little Gladys. She became upset with me when I told her that any decent mother would inform the teacher there was nothing wrong with Gordon being left-handed. I asked her if she thought Elzie was weird, and of course, she said no. Honestly, she makes me furious. Poor Gordon. He doesn't deserve such treatment. Believe me, I cannot understand a teacher who is so narrow minded."

Ralph could understand why Edith was upset. Gladys was certainly an enigma. Ralph had read somewhere that forcing a child to use their right hand when their natural inclination was to use their left, sometimes gave them other problems. If Gordon was his kid, he'd certainly tell the teacher to let nature take its course.

Ralph's corn crop exceeded his expectations, so he was completely satisfied. He didn't relish having to move his share come spring, but half of the crop was rightfully his as well as a portion of the oats and wheat. He didn't know just what they would do about the hay. Pa might have enough to tide them over until the livestock could be put out on pasture. He and Dave would divide the livestock when the time came. It seems there was plenty to be worked out before he left the Watson farm.

Blanche and George had come home for the weekend. Miney had asked Ralph, Edith, and the children to have Sunday dinner with them. Edith noticed that Ralph had made an effort to talk with his sister away from the others. When they were back to their place, Edith brought up the subject.

"What were you and Blanche discussing?"

"I just wanted to know if Pa had said anything to her about asking me to take over the farm."

"Had he?"

"No. Not that I had expected him to tell her. I told her he'd asked me to do, the farming, and that Pa was going to buy property in town. I asked her If she thought it was a good idea. She said she thought I'd really like being back on the homestead. Told me to be aware that Pa and I didn't always see eye to eye, but she still felt it a good move."

Ralph thought a moment, then continued, "I know Pa and I will disagree on any number of things, but he knows that I'm a good farmer although there are times when I feel he hates to admit it. I'm just not certain I can change his mind when it comes to something new. Pa was never one to want progress."

"Well, look how he always spoke about automobiles, and yet he bought one."

"That was because too many of his friends had autos. Anyway, Blanche thinks Pa and I can have a good working relationship. She did say she was surprised that Pa wanted to leave the farm. She seems to think that if I didn't come home, he'd farm for a few more years. Suppose that is possible. I have the feeling that he will be at the farm often to lend a hand, and probably tell me I'm doing something wrong. It is just that he no longer wants the total responsibility of all the work seven days a week."

Edith realized that his sister's approval was important to Ralph. Of course, he'd be the last to admit it. Still, while he and Blanche never showed affection for one another, she felt they had a normal brother-sister bond. She thought Ralph felt better about his decision now that he had spoken with his sister, and that she had given her approval.

CHAPTER 13

Edith had been working at packing some of her dishes in boxes, making sure they were well cushioned with old newspapers. She certainly didn't want anything to get broken. She hated the act of moving, but she thought Ralph seemed eager to get back to the farm where he had grown up. Once they were settled in, she was certain she would like living there. She'd be no further from her folks, and she'd be much closer to Vern, Blanche, and the boys, and that was certainly a plus. She did love her nephews, and although loathe to admit it, Wilson was definitely her favorite.

Ralph had left shortly after morning chores to help his father move some of the heavier furniture. Ralph wasn't certain if Millie had bought the house in town, or whether he was renting until he found something he really wanted. The house was located on the north side of Pine Street. The side street from Main to Pine formed a T corner in front of the house. It was only a stone's throw from the house Grandma Smith had owned. The front porch was vine covered on the east and west, and the yard was rather small in Ralph's opinion. He wondered if Millie would be content there after having so much room on the farm.

When Ralph came home for dinner, Edith asked if they had moved all the furniture.

"All but their bedroom furniture, kitchen furniture and a couple of rocking chairs. Ma was right there to supervise since she says men folk are just not as careful as they ought to be. Guess she remembers that when we moved into town when I was ten, the glass on the secretary got cracked. She informed us she didn't want it completely broken out." Ralph gave a chuckle. "Don't think Ma's quite forgiven Pa for that glass getting cracked in the first place."

"I suppose if it was actually broken out, she'd have to have it replaced," said Edith.

"If I know Ma, she'd hate having to spend money for a new glass. After all, she's put up with that glass cracked all these years. However, we got it there in the same condition, so Ma's got nothing to complain about."

Edith was glad all had gone well for her mother-in-law. It was a shame to have anything damaged. She hoped nothing happened to any of her furniture, not that they had much, but she'd certainly hate to have any of it marred. Golly, this moving could be quite an ordeal.

It was past the middle of March when Millie and Miney left the farm and moved into Elsie. Within a few days, Ralph, Edith, and the children moved into the house on the Setterington farm. The livestock and Ralph's share of the wheat, oats, and corn had been moved earlier. He and Dave had had no problem dividing everything to the satisfaction of all concerned.

Edith had wondered if Helen would hate leaving the only home she had known, but the child had been intrigued with all the activity brought on by moving. Edith had been a little upset when Helen pushed her hand through a layer of newspaper into a crock filled with apple butter. She felt she had been remiss and had not watched Helen as closely as she should have. Ralph pooh-poohed the idea and said no harm was done.

Edith had also worried about Fleet. She had asked Ralph if the dog was likely to go back to the Watson farm. Ralph had told her there was no way the dog would leave him. Fleet was smart enough to know that the horses were the ones she was accustomed to, and she knew which cows were theirs. She just accepted the fact that those strangers seemed to belong to them too. Ralph understood dogs. Fleet was always content to be wherever Ralph was, ready to do his bidding. She turned out to be the best cattle dog he ever had.

Even though they had moved to Elsie, Millie came to the farm each night to get a small pail of milk. (The pail had once held lard, and probably held almost a quart and a half of milk.) Sometimes, Miney came with him and sometimes not. Ralph felt Millie wanted to come each night so he could see for himself what work his son had done during the day.

As of now, not all the stanchions in the cow stable were filled. Although Millie hadn't exactly said as much, Ralph felt his father wanted all the stanchions filled with milch cows, and the remaining heavy duty stanchion would be occupied by a bull. This would mean Ralph would have seventeen cows to milk. Quite an increase from the twelve they were now milking. Not only would the milking take longer, but cleaning the stables would be much more time consuming.

They were still sending cream to the creamery in Eureka, so more milk meant it would take longer to put the milk through the separator. Of course, the hogs would appreciate the extra milk.

They had four young heifers coming up to be bred, and when they freshened, they would almost fill out the herd for next year. Ralph hoped his father would be content with that. Ralph did not want to buy any cows because he felt, at least with his own, he had been improving his herd, and felt they were much better milk producers than the cows of most of his neighbors. He knew they were better than some of Pa's.

It was a busy time to get the large field ready to plow for corn. It had been a hay field the last couple of years. Before being plowed, the manure piles in the barnyard had to be spread on the field. The manure was the only fertilizer Millie used although Ralph would have liked to use some commercial fertilizer as well. In another year or so, he felt he would bring up the idea, but he was almost certain he knew what Pa would say. "Rotate the crops and spread manure. That's all the fertilizer any crop needs." Even though Pa had invested in a manure spreader a couple of years ago. Ralph felt this was mostly because Will Fizzell had one, Pa was usually against trying anything new.

Millie seemed satisfied that Ralph had been able to plow last years corn field early and had the oats planted on time. Of course, he failed to tell Ralph that he was pleased with his son's efforts. Still, when Ralph began plowing the field where they were to put corn, Millie came out and began going over the field with the disc.

Ralph was thankful for the help. They needed a good corn crop to put field corn in the crib and have enough of the corn they grew for silage (silage corn had white ears, not yellow like field corn) to fill both silos. With the increase in the number of cattle, it was going to take more feed if they were to produce well. Of course, on this he and his father failed to see eye to eye. Millie had grained his cows, but he had given each cow a like amount no matter what her milk production was. Ralph grained his differently. As long as a cow's milk production increased, she received more grain. Some cow's production stayed the same on less grain and increasing the amount of grain did not increase her production. Ralph pushed each cow to reach her maximum. Pa had maybe voiced skepticism at this process, but he hadn't told Ralph he had a fool notion. Perhaps he had already observed they were getting more production from those that had been "his" cows, and even though he would never have admitted the extra grain might be making the difference, he was glad to be getting more money from their monthly checks from the creamery.

Field corn was always planted first since it had to completely mature. The corn on the cobs had to be hard or the kernels would shrivel and not keep well, and shriveled kernels do not make particularly good feed--too much cob for the amount of corn. The silage corn was cut to fill silos when the ears were still in the milk stage; therefore, it could be planted a little later and still make good silage.

It was during the summer that Ralph noticed the pump had to work longer to pump enough water to fill the stock tank. He knew the well was only 18 feet deep, and Pa had put down a new point only a couple of years ago. He began to wonder if they would need a new, deeper well to meet their demands. When he spoke about his concern to Millie, he was told the well was fine and not to worry.

Millie had Harry McQuistion shear the sheep. Ralph felt they were lucky because Harry was completely sober. He had heard from others that Harry sometimes showed up after he had been drinking, but drunk or sober, the man was a whiz at shearing sheep. Millie took the bundles of wool to Elsie to sell.

It was now time to dock the lambs' tails. Lambs are born with long tails, and if not docked at a very early age, they simply load up with burdock burrs and other dirt. Millie used the tool which was really designed for dehorning cattle. It had two levers that when pulled apart, raised a knife in a frame that resembled a guillotine. The lambs' tail was placed in position, the handles brought together, bringing the sharp knife down, severing the tail neatly. There was never much blood, and the lambs never seemed to be in pain afterward. They continued to nurse and play as they had always done.

Shortly after this, Millie and Ralph had taken the flock of sheep and some young cattle to the forty for summer pasture. Ralph had taken Fleet along so the dog would know where they were taking the animals. He felt that when they brought them home, Fleet would understand where they had to turn a corner, and he would not have to get ahead of them to turn them, the dog would do that. Sure would save him a lot of foot work. While most of the flock would follow the bell weather, there was always one or two that would follow some of the young cattle who were often intent on going the wrong way.

Having the livestock pasturing on the forty meant that Ralph had to go there once a day, it was a drive of about two and a half miles to check on the livestock and make sure they had a sufficient supply of water. There was a pump with a gasoline engine to pump the water needed. The sheep could only reach the water in the large stock tank when it was full, so there were a couple of iron kettles for them. Ralph often went there after the evening milking was done. Sure made for a long day.

Blanche and George had been home for Decoration Day. While spending time at the farm quite often bothered Blanche's asthma, she was no doubt happy that her parents now lived in town. However, she and George had been quick to visit to see how well Ralph was doing. Blanche managed to get her brother aside long enough for him to assure her all was going well and he was glad to be back on the homestead. He laughed when he told her that he and Pa had had no big disagreement as of now. Blanche chuckled and told him it was early yet, but he was to farm like he wanted even if Pa did disagree. Blanche realized their father was adverse to new ideas.

About a week later, Miney confided to Edith that Blanche was in the family way. The baby was due the last of November. Edith was pleased for them. George had often indicated he wanted children, but Blanche had never disclosed how she felt. Blanche had always been quick to talk to Helen and she gave Keith attention since he was now walking around and saying a few words. Edith felt Blanche would make a very good mother.

Edith had asked Ralph if his father had told him about Blanche.

"What makes you think Pa would tell me anything like that?"

"I don't know. I just thought he might. Mother Setterington Is really worried although she says Blanche says she feels fine."

"Oh, Ma would worry about Blanche if she had a hang nail. I thought Blanche looked well, and she certainly seemed herself."

"That's what I thought. I think it is rather amusing because your mother keeps referring to the baby as "she." I reminded her that the baby just might be a boy. She informed me that Blanche was certain to have a girl."

"I know. How could anyone as perfect as Blanche disappoint her mother by having a boy?" Ralph gave a chuckle before he continued. "I don't think Blanche would have a preference. She'd just be glad to have a healthy baby, and I'll bet George would like a son. Poor Ma. I'll bet she's praying every night not only for Blanche's health, but for a granddaughter. It's hard for her to accept that she has no control over this. Of course, whether Blanche has a boy or a girl, Ma will think the child is wonderful."

"She's also worried because she says Blanche will have too much to do when the baby comes."

"Ma always hated to admit that Blanche can cope with anything. I guess that is partly because when Blanche was young, Pa used to tease her if she strongly voiced an opinion by saying, 'Grandmother.' Ma hates to think that Blanche has any of the same qualities as Grandmother. In some ways perhaps Blanche is like Grandmother. She's never let anyone push her around, and Ma could never understand how Blanche could be so able to take care of herself. Blanche is completely competent, and she will manage a baby just fine."

Any horse that was driven regularly on the road was kept shod. However, once a month the shoes had to be pulled, the horses hoofs trimmed and the shoes put back on. Ralph had decided he wasn't going to need the team on the road for a spell, he decided to pull their shoes before he turned them out to pasture.

As was often the case, Buster was not as cooperative as he should have been. Ralph had already done his front feet, but when he came to do his hind feet, Buster wouldn't let Ralph pick up his foot. Ralph lost his patience rather quickly because he knew Buster was just being ornery. A short length of chain was nearby, so Ralph picked it up and began to hit Buster on the rump.

At this moment, Miney came into the stable. "Ralph! Why are you striking that poor horse?"

Ralph explained that Buster wouldn't let him lift his foot.

"Well, there should be some other way to get his cooperation. I don't think his actions warrant you beating him with that chain. Think how much you are hurting him. Poor horse."

Ralph could tell that his mother was truly upset.

"Seems like I remember you switching my legs when I was young. That didn't bother you. Well, using a chain on a horse's rump doesn't hurt them any more than a switch did me. Besides, he knows what it's for."

He laid the chain aside, stepped up to Buster and said, "Buster, give me your foot." Without Ralph even touching his fetlock, Buster picked his foot up for Ralph to remove the shoe. "See, Ma, he just has to learn who's boss."

Miney half-heartedly admitted Ralph was no doubt right. Still, striking the horse with a chain seemed like a drastic measure. She knew Ralph was right when he said that she had switched his legs numerous times, and she had felt that punishment was well deserved. She guessed she just didn't understand animals all that well.

The year of 1920 saw two major fires in the village of Elsie. One was the Hasty Stave Mill, and the other was the Ann Arbor depot. Since the depot fire had not damaged the rail tracks, the trains continued to run. Out of necessity, the railroad brought in an old box car to serve as a depot while the new brick structure was being built. The box car was not very handy, but it did serve the purpose.

Ralph felt a certain degree of nostalgia when he learned that the Silver Family Circus would not be coming to Elsie this year. In fact, the story was that it was disbanding. Two brothers had been the owners. Now, one brother was being tried for murdering his brother. Apparently, the man had felt his brother was paying too much attention to his wife, so in a fit of rage, he had killed his brother. So, with one brother dead, and the other being sent to the penitentiary for life, the circus had been dissolved. Of course, it had been a small affair, nothing like the large Ringling Bros. or Barnum & Bailey circuses that only came to the larger towns. Still, the youngsters as well as adults had always looked forward to having the circus in town.

For Ralph's first year back on the homestead, it seemed that all went well. The weather had been most cooperative, which was not always the case. Wheat and oat harvest had been ample, the corn had been more than knee high by the Fourth of July, and looked really good. Ample rain had kept the pasture growing well, so there had been no need to supplement the feed for the cows to keep their production up.

They had had four veal calves to sell (These were male calves that were sold when only a few days old, shortly after their mother's milk was good) and were raising another three heifers. The cows Ralph had contributed were due to freshen (give birth) later in the fall. As Ralph had learned in Ag class, a cow's overall production was better if she freshened in the fall instead of in the spring. Many of the old timers thought spring was a good time since the cow would be on pasture shortly after she calved, and that fresh, green grass helped her to produce well. Ralph knew that a cow's production was always good right after she freshened, so when this happened in the fall, production was good and just as she started to drop off, she would be on pasture which always gave her production a boost. Besides, since a cow went dry (no longer gave milk) a couple of months before she calved, that meant she was dry when pasture began to get short. Ralph wasn't certain he could ever change his father's way of thinking.

The closer the time came for Blanche to have her baby, the more worried Miney became. She even told Edith of her fears.

"Blanche says she feels fine, but I don't think she'd tell me if she didn't. She wouldn't want me to worry."

"I think you are worrying for nothing. We had a letter from Blanche, and she said she's doing well. She will be all right."

"But Edith, both times I gave birth, it was so difficult. Blanche came doubled together, and Ralph came feet first. What if she takes after me? Are such things hereditary?"

"I don't know for certain, Mother, but I don't think so. I'm sure Blanche is taking good care of herself."

Edith remembered what an ordeal Helen's birth had been, and she hoped Blanche would have a perfectly normal birth. She wished there was something she could do to ease her mother-in-law's mind. But as Ralph had said, Miney would worry about Blanche whether she had just cause or not.

Ralph continued to worry about the well, but he fully realized there was nothing to be gained by talking to his father. The livestock wouldn't drink as much during the cold winter months as they did in the heat of summer. Ralph sure hoped nothing went wrong during the coming winter.

One night at supper, Ralph told his wife that he had stopped to see his parents while he was in Elsie.

"Pa says that after Blanche's baby is born, he thinks they will stay with she and George for a spell. Ma just can't be convinced that Blanche is perfectly capable of taking care of a baby without Ma's help. Pa says that since all the fall field work will be done, I'd get along all right without his help. We intend to fill silo next week, and then have the corn husker in for the field corn, so he is right about the fall work being finished. I might do some fall plowing, but that has nothing to do with Pa."

"Did he expect to be back in the spring?"

"Of course. Pa wouldn't think I could put in the crops without him here to give me his opinion. Pa will never admit that I know as much about farming as he does."

"I wonder what Blanche thinks of the idea."

"That doesn't matter. Ma got her mind made up and where Blanche is concerned, she can be awfully stubborn."

It was a good fall, and Ralph decided to plow where they would put oats in the spring. This usually meant the oats could be planted earlier because plowed ground dries out faster and the field can be worked sooner. The walking plow only made about a fourteen inch furrow, so plowing a field was slow, arduous work.

When plowing, there had to be enough room between the beginning of a furrow and the fence to allow the team to make the turn without coming too close to the fence. This portion of land was called the headland.

First, Ralph began by making what was called a back furrow. When plowing, the earth was rolled over to the right of the plow. After the first time across a field, in the next pass back across the field, the plow was positioned so the earth was rolled over to meet the earth rolled over from the first trip. This was the back furrow. While doing this, both horses walked on level ground. Now, on the second round, the horse on the left walked on the land side and the other horse walked in the furrow.

After a few rounds, as Ralph came to the headland, he simply tipped the plow over on its left side and picked it up again in time to settle it for the next furrow. The lines from the horses were tied around his waist because he needed both hands to manipulate the plow. It was an easy matter to use one hand to give a tug on that line to guide the horses where they should go.

Ralph now discovered Buster had found one more way to aggravate him. Buster was the horse on the land side while Monarch walked in the furrow. For a few rounds, Buster had worked as he should. But then, just as Ralph should have been ready to pick the plow back up, Buster would swing against the tug just hard enough to throw the plow out of line; therefore, Ralph would have to stop the team, make them back up a few steps while he pulled the plow backwards to get the plow into proper position. Ralph realized Buster knew exactly what he was doing, but Ralph never was able to figure out how to break the horse of that habit. Sometimes, when they first got to the field, Buster behaved well. However, as it got near dinner time, Buster became cantankerous on every round. It was the same just before quitting time at night. Ralph felt Buster simply was tired of his boring job, and the horse knew when it was almost quitting time. He was almost as good as a watch.

Edith began to notice how her mother-in-law showed so much partiality between Helen and Keith. She was always quick to hold Helen on her lap. Keith didn't talk much yet, but he would back up to his grandmother, and anyone could tell that he wanted to be picked up too.

After a time, Miney would say, "Oh, Keith, did you want Grandma to hold you? Why, Grandma didn't know what you wanted."

Edith felt that Miney had known all along. It was just that she cared so much more for Helen. Edith began to hope Blanche would have a boy. Miney would love any child Blanche had, but she never failed to let it be known that she expected Blanche to have a girl.

At first, if the wind was not strong enough to run the windmill to pump water for the livestock, the water had to be pumped by hand. Millie had already replaced the old, wooden windmill with a new metal one which was a little taller and seemed to need less of a breeze to run it. However, Millie had become tired of sometimes having to pump water by hand so he had invested in a gasoline engine.

The engine was mounted on a wooden framework where it could be used to run the pump jack to pump water or with the wide belt reversed, it could run a buzz saw on the back of the carriage. A sizable log could be placed on the table which would tilt forward to bring the log in contact with the saw. This was much easier than having two men pull a crosscut saw back and forth to cut the log in pieces small enough to fit in the dining room stove or be chopped into kindling for the kitchen stove.

Ralph bought Edith a washing machine that could be run from this gasoline engine. The washer had a wooden tub, and the agitator was located on the hinged lid of the washer. The agitator looked like four pieces of a broom handle set at a slight angle which were about eight inches or so in length. The wringer could be swung to allow clothes to go from the washer to a tub of rinse water, then to another rinse water, then, finally, to a basket. The wheel which ran the washer was just over three inches in width. Rate would shift the framework which held the engine so the engine faced the washer instead of the pump. He had a long belt that came from the flywheel of the engine to the drive wheel on the washer. Ralph always had to get this set up for Edith since there was no way she could move the engine much less crank it to get it started. When not in use, the washer stood in the southeast corner of the north porch.

During the summer, doing the weekly wash on this north porch was really quite handy. The clothesline was just across the drive, and when it came time to empty the wash water, it could be poured by the edge of the porch where it soaked into the ground. If the season was extremely dry, Edith might carry some of the water to put on the flower beds nearest the house. There was a huge elm tree by the drive and Edith felt that in the hot summer months, the tree needed the extra water. The ground was kind of gravelly and no grass grew between the porch and the tree. Ralph knew that every Monday he had to set up the washer because Edith washed on Monday no matter what the weather. If it rained, clothes could be hung on a temporary line on the south porch, or even on the porch to the east.

The time came when Millie and Miney went to be with Blanche. Then, on Thursday, the 28th of November, a healthy Dale Emerson was born. While Miney was sadly disappointed because Blanche had a boy, she was thankful both Blanche and the baby were doing well. Although she had felt Blanche would have a girl, she guessed God had a different plan. Well, so be it. She already loved this baby boy.

Snow settled on the land, so Ralph used sleighs to carry oats and corn to the grist mill to be ground into feed for the cows. On one such day, he had to go on into the village before he went home. He tied Buster and Monarch at a hitching rail on the south side of Main Street, across from the pool room. Ralph often stopped in there as he said "to shoot the breeze" with some of the old timers from town. Ralph always enjoyed speaking with the men his father's age.

Ralph happened to look out the window and noticed that a retired minister, whom everyone called old man Brass, was talking to someone just in front of Buster and Monarch. The elderly gentleman always waved his arms when he talked and today was no exception. Ralph could tell that Buster was not too receptive of the man's actions. Buster stood with his ears laid back, watching the man's every move. Ralph had just made up his mind he should go across the street and calm Buster when Rev. Brass backed up to sit on the hitching rail where Buster and Monarch were tied. Buster had had all he was going to take from this stranger. In an instant he had picked Rev. Brass up by the seat of his pants, shook him, and then released him.

Rev. Brass was not injured, but he was full of rage. He ranted and raved and asked everyone he saw who owned the team. Ralph knew that almost everyone in town knew the team was his, but no one would admit to Rev. Brass who the owner was. The man hung around for quite a spell, and just about the time Ralph felt he was going to have to confront the man because he needed to get home, the man gave up and left. Of course, there were any number of people who thought the episode was extremely funny.

That was the last time Ralph ever tied Buster on the street. Buster didn't like strangers and Ralph was afraid he might actually hurt someone..

CHAPTER 14

Both Blanche and Miney had written to Ralph and Edith since Dale's birth. Blanche's letter had been rather matter-of-fact, simply stating that both she and the baby were doing well. She did mention the fact that Miney felt she should be the one to change the baby, pick him up at his first whimper, and give him his bath. She also said that George was really proud to have a son.

Miney's letters were filled with words of praise about her grandson. Even though she had been keenly disappointed because Blanche had had a boy, it was evident she truly loved the little fellow, and in her eyes he was indeed perfect. In her letters, she usually said to tell Helen that her grandmother missed her. Almost as an afterthought, she would ask how Keith was doing.

It seemed as though all of a sudden Keith began saying not just a word or two, but began talking in sentences. Edith figured he could have put words together earlier if he had been so inclined. For the most part, he spoke clearly although he didn't seem to be able to pronounce an "r", so he substituted an "I".

Mostly, he and Helen got along well, partly because Keith seldom asserted himself, and simply let Helen have her way. He was really a very good natured little boy. His Brewbaker aunts and uncles were quick to note that he seemed to like all of them, and in turn, they showed affection for him. They thought Helen was often a little standoffish. According to the Brewbakers, Keith was much more like the Brewbakers while Helen was more like the Setteringtons.

Edith realized it would be quite some time before Blanche would visit with the baby since they were so far away. My, Edith would be glad when she could see Dale. Edith truly loved babies. She just knew Dale would be a handsome baby since she thought both Blanche and George were very good looking. Well, perhaps when spring came, she and Ralph could visit Blanche. She said nothing of her desire to Ralph, but she was determined she would find some way to visit Blanche so she could see Dale while he was still small and cuddly.

It was a Monday morning in early January. The wind was blowing strongly from the northeast. It was bitter cold.

''Edith, you don't intend to do the washing today, do you?"

"It's Monday, isn't it? Of course I'm going to do the washing. I've already got the boiler on the stove to heat the wash water."

"Have you considered that it's only about ten degrees, and with the wind blowing so hard, it seems much colder?"

"If I don't wash on Monday, it ruins my whole week. I'll have to dry some of the clothes in the house. And because the wind is so strong, I'll have to put up the rope line on the south porch. Some of the clothes will freeze dry and will have to finish drying in the house."

Ralph listened to this explanation with a skeptical expression on his face. Sometimes. he didn't understand his wife. He thought a moment, then said, "Will you give me time to take the canvases off the binder and put them up to give you some sort of shelter? (The canvases he spoke about were on the grain binder and were what pulled the stalks of grain (wheat, oats, rye) up from the cutter bar so the machine could tie the stalks into a bundle which was then ejected.) Besides, I need the engine to pump a little water for the cattle. I've broken the ice out of the tank, but there isn't enough water under that for the livestock."

"I realize the cattle need to drink. Will it take you very long? I hate to be too late getting started. Besides, how are you going to fasten these two pieces of canvases in place?"

''I'm sure I can find a way. I'll put the large one to the north and the smaller one to the east. It won't help a lot, but it will give you some protection from the wind."

"I thought I could put some pans of water on the stove so I could add hot water to the rinse water. At least that would take the chill off the water."

Ralph hurried out to get the stables cleaned while the cows were out of the barn. He knew the cows would be ready to come back into the warmth of the barn as soon as they had slaked their thirst. The horses could wait until later. He thought Edith was foolish to wash on such a day, but he would do what he could to make her work less disagreeable. He was just glad that in the winter, the amount of wash was usually smaller than in the summer. His clothes didn't get dirty as fast as when he worked in a dusty field.

Finally, all was ready for Edith to put in the batch of white clothes. Ralph shook his head as he watched the steam rise up when his wife opened the washer. Oh well, he had done what he could. If only Edith wasn't quite so set in her ways when it came to her housework and chores. She allowed nothing to interfere with her schedule. (In the years to come, Edith had pneumonia twice after she had done the washing on a particularly cold day. Ralph felt certain this was because, in spite of all his precautions, the steam rising up from the hot water had not been good for her.)

The next day, Ralph noticed that Edith's hands were so badly chapped, they had raw cracks in the skin. He felt they must be terribly sore yet she never said one word of complaint. Ralph felt that even though she used a piece of a broken shovel handle to remove the clothes from the water, her hands had to get wet when she started the clothes through the wringer. Even when she hung the wet clothes on the clothesline, she couldn't wear gloves. He knew she made her own hand lotion from rose water and glycerine. He sure hoped it promoted healing before she felt she had to do the washing next Monday.

After what seemed to be a long winter, spring finally put in an appearance.

This meant it was time to shear the sheep. Ralph was glad the farmers were no longer expected to wash the oil from the wool before shearing. Ralph supposed he would have to get hold of Harry McQuistion, the one Millie had had last year. Right now, Ralph didn't know who else to call.

McQuistion had said he'd be glad to come. He said to expect him the next day a little before one. This suited Ralph. He had 35 sheep to shear. He knew Vern would come down to help him tie the wool into bundles as it came from each sheep.

Ralph had finished his dinner and Vern had arrived to wait for McQuistion. One o'clock came, but no McQuistion. Two o'clock, then as it was almost three, here came McQuistion along with two helpers. It was apparent that the man had been hitting the bottle and was definitely half teed up. Ralph had plenty of misgivings, but it was too late to do anything about it.

Ralph was truly amazed at how fast the man could shear the sheep, and Ralph was quick to note that he did an expert job, not nicking any of them. (If cut, the blood would show up brightly against the wool which was now such a pure, clean white.) It kept the two men busy catching the sheep, and Ralph and Vern had no time to spare as they tied the bundles of wool. Much to Ralph's surprise, the work was done in plenty of time for him to be ready for supper at six.

Although the man had done an efficient job of shearing the sheep, Ralph made up his mind that next year he would certainly find someone else. Ralph had no patience with someone who showed up for work inebriated.

While Edith liked living on the Setterington farm, she wished the chicken coop was further from the house. As it was, the door to the coop opened onto the yard and a board fence between the coop and the woodshed rather discouraged the chickens from wandering in the orchard behind the buildings.

Some of the hens often came up to the steps and onto the porch or the concrete walk from the porch to the driveway. This meant they often left their droppings which Edith found annoying. She tried to chase the chickens away and keep the porch and sidewalk clean, but it seemed that some old hen would come and go without Edith realizing the hen had been there.

This morning was just such a time. The door to the coop was kept closed at night after the chickens had gone to roost. This was done partially because it was known that there were still weasels around, and they could wreak havoc in a chicken coop. They often killed several fowl, much more than they could eat. Now that it was warmer, Edith went out early to open the coop door to let the chickens out.

About midmorning, she went out the dining room door onto the porch. Keith had tagged along. Edith had just noticed the chicken droppings. One was a dark brown and shaped like the chocolate kisses Keith liked so much. Before she could stop him, Keith bent quickly, picked up the manure and popped it in his mouth. He immediately began to gag and cry.

Edith got him to spit, but he still behaved as though he was going to throw up. She took him in the house, took a wet washcloth and washed his mouth out. She even tried a tiny bit of soap figuring that would taste better than the manure.

Keith finally quit retching and crying. She asked him if he thought a cookie would make him feel better. He nodded his head solemnly, and sat at the table while Edith got him a cookie.

What a day!

When Edith related the incident to Ralph, he chuckled, then said, "Keith, I guess you learned something didn't you? And to think, one of my grandmother's home remedies for Pa when he was little was a concoction of chicken manure. Aren't you lucky you don't have to be given that?"

Keith eyed his father as though he didn't know whether his father was telling him the truth or not.

Edith felt Ralph could have been a little more sympathetic. Seemed her husband could always see the humor in situations she felt were serious.

Ralph didn't know quite when his folks would return home. He supposed if Ma had her way, she'd be there all summer. He had planted the oats early and he rather expected Pa to be around to help get the corn planted.

How right he was. However, he had not anticipated what his father proposed.

"Ralph, I've been giving a lot of thought to our farming operation. I know we have some heifers coming up, but I think we should increase the number of hogs we're raising. Hogs are a good price right now. I also think we should raise more sheep. The pasture on the forty would be ample for a larger flock. You know how much the sheep help keep down the brush, and we might want to plant some crops on the forty."

"Pa, I just don't see how I could do it. With the increase in the dairy herd, I've got all I can take care of. I just can't do it."

"Well, I guess you could if you wanted to. You'd just have to get up a little earlier and go to bed a little later."

With that admonition, Millie walked off. While Ralph watched his father leave, he felt resentment fill him. He already was milking more cows than his father had ever milked, and they were raising as many hogs as Millie had raised. They had fewer sheep, but they really didn't have room to raise many more. Besides, Pa had usually had a hired man, sometimes two. Ralph didn't feel that he could afford a hired man. Why was it that no matter what he did, he could never seem to please his father?

The pasture was not quite high enough to turn the cattle out. Another week or so, and Ralph felt the cattle could spend part of the day on the tender grass.

Then, as Ralph had feared, one day, the pump no longer provided water. He was glad his father was home from Detroit so he could see first hand the well had gone dry. Sometimes, Millie was loathe to accept an opinion from someone else.

Millie called a well driller, but the man couldn't come for at least a day or maybe two. He was busy putting down a well for someone else.

Since it was the spring of the year, the ditch that crossed the property to the west was full of water; therefore, Ralph felt the cattle and horses wouldn't suffer. The cattle and horses had to be watered twice a day, and he could haul water from Vern's for the hogs and sheep. It would be time consuming when he really wanted to be plowing for corn. Still, it couldn't be helped. He'd just have to make good in a bad situation. He figured Millie would lend him a hand.

Ralph was busy emptying water into the cast iron kettle for the sheep. Millie had said he would let the cows out. Since the pasture land on the north side of the lane was open, Fleet knew Ralph only wanted the cows to go as far as the ditch. Ralph had made her understand this the first time he had taken the cows to the ditch. He felt his father would have no trouble with the cattle.

Just as Ralph finished his job, he heard his father yelling and cussing, so he hurried to the cow stable to see what was wrong. The cows were back in the barnyard milling around, and Fleet was by the open gate that led to the lane. She was keeping the cows in the barnyard.

"Pa, what's wrong?"

"Darn dog. Makes more steps than she saves. The cows were halfway to the ditch when she brought them all back to the barn. They didn't have a chance to drink."

Rate was puzzled. Fleet had given him no problem when he let the cows out to drink. She had simply kept them from going west over the bridge.

"Pa, what did you say to her?"

"I told her to fetch. What else?"

"Well, that's just what she did. This wasn't the dog's fault. She did just what you told her to do."

Ralph then told Fleet to "take 'em to the ditch" and the dog moved to do as told. She kept them together near the bridge, and when Ralph could see the cows had drunk their fill, he hollered, "Fetch" and she brought the cows back to the barnyard where they returned to their stanchions in the barn.

"See, Pa, she simply does what she's told."

With a disgruntled "Harumph," Millie moved to fasten the cows in their stanchions.

Ralph shook his head. Pa was hopeless when it came to teaching a dog anything, partly because the man had never actually liked a dog. Ralph figured whoever had said a dog was man's best friend sure knew what he was talking about. Ralph had always liked dogs, and he had yet to see a dog he was afraid of. Besides, dogs simply liked him.

When Edith approached Ralph with the idea of them going to see Blanche and the baby, she was sadly disappointed. Ralph said there was no way he could spare the time away from the farm. They had been almost four days without water, and he felt he was behind with his field work because of the added time spent to carry water. Of course, he had been fortunate that they had ample water from the cistern to use to wash up. This meant he had only had to provide water for drinking, cooking, and doing dishes.

Edith was not a person who would travel with two children by herself. She then thought of her sister, Edna. Perhaps she would be willing to accompany her to Detroit because Edna was much more the adventuresome type.

When approached, Edna was glad Edith had asked her to go with her. After all, she had never been that far away from home. She had met Blanche and George, so it was not like they were complete strangers.

When asked, Ralph told Edith that he could get along quite well for the couple of days she would be gone. He realized how much his wife wanted to see Blanche's baby. As far as he was concerned, he'd be glad to wait until Dale was older. Somehow, holding a small baby made him uncomfortable.

Ralph took Edna, Edith, Helen, and Keith to the depot where they could take the train. They had to change trains in Durand, but Ralph figured they would manage that all right. Edith had done this before when he had taken her to Blanche's. He had checked the time for their return and promised to be at the station when their train pulled in.

Edith was pleased because Blanche had no objection to her holding Dale. She knew some first-time mothers who didn't want someone else holding their baby. She felt Dale was a very good little fellow. He had plenty of hair although it was short and silky. Edith thought him a handsome child. Both Keith and Helen seemed to be intrigued with their new little cousin. Edith was almost sorry their visit had to be short. She had always maintained babies were so nice to hold when they were content to be cuddled. She felt that all too soon, they wanted only to be held a moment, then they squirmed and wanted down.

When Edith and Edna arrived back in Elsie, Ralph was not at the depot as he had promised. After waiting a few minutes, Edna suggested they start walking to the business section of town. It was only a few blocks. She said she would carry their two suitcases, and Edith could manage Helen and Keith. Both children needed to be kept busy after what had seemed to them to be a long train ride.

They were about half way to Main Street when Ralph met them. They all had a laugh because Keith ran to his father shouting, "There's my Daddy. I've found my Daddy." One would have thought he and Ralph had been separated for weeks, not a couple of days.

Keith was just old enough now that he often felt he should be in the stables with his father. He liked being outdoors much better than being in the house. Helen enjoyed playing with her dolls; therefore, she seldom accompanied Keith when he went to the barn.

One morning, Edith looked out the window to see Keith trudging to the house. He was emphatically shaking his head. Edith wondered what had gone wrong.

Had Ralph sent the boy to the house? Keith had such a serious expression, not at all like his usual carefree countenance.

Keith came in the screened door of the kitchen, walked up to his mother, and before she could ask any questions, asked, "You tain't fatty, be you Mama?"

What had brought up that question?

"No, Mama's not fat."

Before she could ask a question, Keith turned around and left the house. Something caught his eye so he didn't immediately return to the barn.

After the children were in bed, Edith spoke to Ralph.

"Whatever did you say to Keith this morning to have him come to the house to say, 'You tain't fatty, be you Mama?' That was all he asked. I know you must have said something to start this," she accused.

Ralph laughed before he answered.

"I don't really remember the exact words. I just said something to him about his old fat mother. He didn't answer, just took off," explained Ralph as he laughed again.

"You weren't very nice. Just because I've put on a few pounds since we were married. Poor tyke. He doesn't think I'm fat. Why did you tell him I'm fat?"

"I don't know. Somehow, I felt he'd leave to go see you. It got him out of the way for a while, and no harm's done."

This was the first time Keith had come to see his mother because of what his father had said. However it was not to be the last time. The question was always the same. Sometimes, he went back to the barn, sometimes not. Ralph thought the situation was indeed humorous. Even Edith had to chuckle when she answered Keith's question. She often gave him a hug when she answered him, and she was always rewarded with a smile.

Ralph was back in the field where he was to plant corn in a few days. He looked up to see his nephew Beurmann half running across the field. He pulled in the team because he knew something must be wrong.

How right he was. Beurmann was winded, but he managed to tell Rate that something bad had happened to Wilson. His folks needed Ralph to come as quickly as possible.

Ralph unhitched the team, hurried to the barn, and put the horses in their stalls without bothering to remove their harness. He discovered Edith and the kids were not in the house, so he supposed Blanche had called Edith, and she had already gone to her brother's.

The whole place was in an uproar when Ralph arrived. The doctor had just left to take Wilson to the hospital in St. Johns. Vern, who was never level headed in a crisis, was frantic. He tried to explain to Rate what had happened.

It seems there had not been enough wind to run the windmill, so Vern had started the gasoline engine to run the pump jack. (A pump jack had a wheel, run by a belt from the gasoline engine, that turned a drive shaft. There was a large gear to which the vertical frame of the pump jack was fastened. The vertical frame had a pin that went through the shaft of the pump. As the large gear turned, it pushed the shaft of the pump up and down. This was what brought the water up from the well.) For some reason, Wilson had been standing by the pump when the belt going from the engine to the pumpjack flew off. Somehow, the belt had caught Wilson's leg and drew it into the still moving gear of the pump jack. This had badly mangled his leg. Of course, they had called the doctor immediately. The doctor had taken one look at Wilson and had said he was taking him to St. Johns to the hospital. He suggested Vern and Blanche come as soon as they could.

Ralph noticed that Vern's overalls were saturated with blood from where he had carried Wilson to the house. Ralph could see that Vern was in no condition to drive anywhere; therefore, he suggested he take both Blanche and Vern to St. Johns while Edith kept Beurmann and Wendell with her.

Wilson's leg was badly cut and some of the cuts went as deep as the bone. The doctors found it was impossible to clean all of the dirty, black, grease from the wound. They did the best they could, hoping for the best.

In what seemed like only a matter of a day or two, the doctors knew gangrene had set in. The only hope for Wilson now was to amputate the leg just below the knee. Edith was with Vern when the doctor told him what had to be done. The doctor asked Vern if Wilson had lost much blood. Edith was amazed when Vern said no. She thought of how soaked Vern's overalls were, but she said nothing. She was simply apprehensive. Could Wilson survive?"

The doctors amputated the leg, but Wilson's condition didn't seem to improve. Edith spent some time sitting by his bedside, holding his hand. She didn't think he understood that she was with him. However, he opened his eyes once and knew that she was there.

"Aunt E. I'm glad you are here." He gave a wan smile, closed his eyes and spoke no more.

Edith kissed his forehead. She hoped he knew how much she loved him.

The doctors felt Wilson had lost too much blood and it was only a matter of time before he expired. Thus on the tenth of May, Wilson's fight for life was over.

Keith was too young to understand, but Helen knew something terrible had happened. It seemed as though everyone was crying. She knew Uncle Vern was distraught because she saw him crying. It seemed that everyone was sad. Finally, Helen understood that Wilson had died.

At Wilson's funeral, the woman who had been one of his nurses came up to speak to Edith.

"I just want you to know how sorry I am. Wilson often asked if you were coming to see him. I noticed he always called you Aunt E. I was sitting with him when he died. He roused up once and said, "Aunt E?" I told him, 'Yes, I'm here with you.' I'm sure he thought I was you. That was the last he ever spoke. He simply slipped quietly away."

Edith thanked the nurse. Apparently Wilson had thought his beloved Aunt E. was with him. This gave Edith some solace.

A few days later, Blanche came to see Edith and Ralph. She was extremely upset.

"I don't know how to help Vern. He seems to be incapable of accepting Wilson's death. He says he has no reason to live. If it wasn't for Carl and Garth, I don't think he'd even do the milking let alone feed the livestock and do field work."

Ralph gave some thought to what Blanche had said, and the next morning he told Edith he was going to see Vern. Someone had to talk to him before the man did something foolish. He would see if he could get Vern to listen to reason. Apparently, no one else had had any luck, or perhaps they were hesitant to try.

When Ralph arrived at his brother-in-law's house, Blanche told him that Vern was in a rocker on the front porch. Carl and Garth had done the milking while Vern sat and rocked, speaking to no one.

Ralph went onto the porch and stood observing Vern a few moments before he spoke. Vern failed to acknowledge his presence, and stared straight ahead.

"Blanche says you didn't even go to the barn this morning. How come?"

"Why should I? Carl and Garth managed without me."

"How do you know? Blanche says you didn't even go to the barn to give them a hand. Who's going to do your field work? Need I remind you that you simply rent the farm and owe a good job to the owner. Are you being fair to Carl and Garth? They have their own lives to live."

"At least they have something to live for," came the dejected reply.

"You're saying you don't? Just because you lost Wilson doesn't mean that your life is over."

"How in the world would know? Have you ever lost a son? No! So, you have no idea how I feel after losing my son."

His tone was belligerent, as he glared at Ralph.

"You know what I see? I see a man who is so engrossed with his own feelings he is ignoring the rest of his family. You should be thankful you have two fine sons left who certainly need a father. You have a wife who is grieving, but you are too self centered to care. Don't you think Beurmann and Wendell miss Wilson? What about your sister, Edith? You know how much Wilson meant to her. But no, you are too lily-livered to accept the hand you've been dealt. Of course, it hurts like the dickens because Wilson is gone, and it's all right for you to feel sad. However, you still have a lot in this world for which to be grateful. Snap out of it, Vern. Life goes on. If you can't or won't understand that your family needs you to be a man and take charge, you are a lost cause."

With that, Ralph turned around and left. He saw both boys peeking out the door of the parlor and assumed they had heard at least some of what he had said to their dad. Well, so be it. Blanche had been in the kitchen and had heard nothing.

"Did he talk to you?"

"He managed to convey how sorry he is for himself. I have no idea whether or not I got through to him. If not, I don't know what else to do. Perhaps Father Brewbaker could talk to him."

"I haven't said anything to his folks, and I don't know what Carl and Garth have said. Believe me, those two have been a godsend. I'm at my wit's end. Thanks for trying. I hope it does some good."

A couple of days later, Vern came to see Ralph. He acted like his old self. Said he was ready to plant corn, and seemed enthused because one of his cows had just given birth to a heifer calf. Ralph avoided saying anything that would remind Vern of their previous confrontation. Perhaps all would be well after all.

Ralph wasn't certain just how long his folks would be around. He knew his mother wanted to return to Detroit to give Blanche the help she knew her daughter needed. Actually, Rate thought the situation was rather laughable. Ma just never could understand that her daughter could cope with anything. Nothing rattled Blanche's equanimity. A baby was certainly no challenge.

Ralph was in the field cultivating corn. Even though there had been less rain than usual, the corn looked good. Pa had come to rake the hay Ralph had mowed yesterday afternoon. They'd have that to haul tomorrow; therefore, Ralph wanted to get the cultivating done today. It was good haying weather--hot and sunny. This meant the hay would dry quickly.

Edith had gone into the kitchen to peel potatoes for supper. She knew Millie would be there for the meal; consequently, she had to peel about twice as many potatoes as usual. She had learned long ago that her father-in-law had a whopping big appetite. He certainly could put away more food than Ralph.

She had just finished and was taking the potato peelings to dump in a pail by the back door. They would be thrown to the hogs later. She saw Millie coming to the house carrying Keith. As they got nearer, she could see the tears running down Millie's face. What in the world? Keith looked fine, and he wasn't even crying.

"Whatever is wrong?" asked Edith as Millie reached the steps.

Keith wiggled to get down, and Millie stood him on the planks that covered the well pit. The lad scampered off.

"Edith, something terrible almost happened. I guess you know that instead of driving a team to the barn when I unhitch them, I often separate the two and let them come to the barn by themselves. With the west stable door open, they simply go in the barn to their stall to wait to be unharnessed.

"Well, today, I let the horses loose, and they came to the barn on the run. All would have been all right, but someone had left the east stable door open. Because of the open door, the horses went right on through the barn onto the lawn."

The tears started to flow again as Millie continued.

"When I got to the barn and saw what had happened, I went through to get the horses. Edith," his voice broke with emotion. "Edith, I found Keith on the cement in front of the door. (There was a concrete landing as wide as the door which projected out about four feet to the east.) My heart was in my mouth. I thought the horses had killed him. But when I knelt down, I couldn't see a mark on him. Then, when I went to pick him up, he roused up, smiled, and said, 'Hello, Grandpa.' It seems he had been asleep and both horses had simply stepped over him. Believe you me, I was never so relieved in all my life."

Edith had never seen Millie this shaken before. She was undeniably thankful that her son was all right, but she did feel sorry for her father-in-law.

"It's all right, Father. Keith is fine. I don't think he slept when I put him down for a nap. I guess he just got tired. It surprises me that the moving horses didn't rouse him. That is probably a good thing. You had better get the team before they start down the road. I'll keep Keith here with me."

Millie moved off to put the horses in the barn so he could unharness them. Edith thought how Millie often expressed the thought "What is to be, will be." She guessed the good Lord had taken good care of Keith.

Later that night, after both children were in bed, Edith related the incident to Ralph. He could tell that the episode had unnerved his wife even though she tried not to show it. To have this happen so soon after Wilson's death had simply made her realize we just never know what will happen next.

"I guess Vere Brown was right when he said they told them in the cavalry that horses would manage to step over them if they laid on the ground if they became unseated during a charge. I guess that is what happened with Keith. I'll bet that puts the kibosh on Pa turning horses loose back down the lane. I bet he'll drive them to the barn as a team from now on."

How right Ralph was. Millie had learned a lesson he was not likely to forget.

"Ralph, have you noticed that we don't see much of Carl anymore? In fact, he never drops by on a weekend. If and when he does visit, it is usually a week night."

"Guess I hadn't given it much thought. I know he's been giving Art a lot of help plus he hires out to other farmers. I guess he's just really busy."

"Gladys says Don thinks Carl has a girl friend."

"That's understandable. Did Don say who?"

"No. Only that he thinks Carl is keeping company with someone. I suppose it is to be expected. Now that Lee is married, Carl will feel he should be married too. I just hope he has found a really nice girl."

"Oh, you'd like anyone he chose. Carl has always held a special place in your heart right along with Lee."

"You know I love all of my brothers. Sometimes, they can be a pain with their teasing, but each one is special. I just wonder how long it will be before Carl brings her around to meet the family."

"Maybe Don is mistaken."

"I don't think so. Carl adores Helen and Keith. I'm sure he wants children of his own. Maybe the next time he visits, I'll say something about a girl friend just to get his reaction."

The summer was drier than usual. Crops on sandy soil suffered. Ralph's crops, while not as productive as in a better year, were sufficient for the livestock. They might not have a surplus to sell next spring, but at least they wouldn't be forced to buy feed.

Blanche and George had come to Elsie for the weekend. Edith felt Dale was growing up so fast. She guessed she noticed his growth more than she had her nephews since she didn't see him as often.

George, Blanche, Dale, Millie and Miney came to the farm on Saturday afternoon. Ralph had already finished putting up the last load of second cutting alfalfa, so he had time to spend with them until it was milking time again.

Somehow, George had learned that Keith was particularly fond of watermelon, so he had brought a large melon for them to eat. He had had the melon in a tub of cold water to give it a little chill, but now he took the melon out and dried it off. He placed it on the grass while he went to the kitchen to ask Edith for a knife to cut the melon. He decided the table to the buzz saw was the right height to hold the melon so he could slice it easily. Edith had given him a newspaper to place under the melon and a pan in which to place the slices.

"Keith," said George, "bring me the melon and I'll see that you get the first slice."

Keith went immediately to the melon which looked especially large next to the lad's rather short, stocky figure. All the adults knew the child would be unable to do as his Uncle George wanted.

Keith struggled to get his arms around the melon. Of course, the adults chuckled as the small boy tried his best to pick up the melon.

"What's taking so long?" asked George, hardly able to keep from laughing.

Finally, the lad backed off and said, "Uncle George, I just can't pick it up no matter how hard I try. Does that mean I won't get any watermelon?" He looked crestfallen, as though he would liked to have cried.

"Of course it doesn't." put in Blanche. "Uncle George will see that you get a slice or even a second one, won't you, George?"

Blanche scowled at her husband. It was evident she did not want her nephew teased any longer.

With a laugh, George got the melon and began to slice it. The family took the slices in their hands and began eating, spitting out the seeds as they went. The rinds were collected in a pail to throw in the hog pen. A few chickens came to fight over the seeds. Their antics made Dale laugh.

Everyone noticed how much Keith had enjoyed his watermelon.

Edith found it rather laughable how Miney watched Dale like a hawk. She seemed to be afraid that if the child was out of her sight, he might somehow get hurt. Miney may have wanted a granddaughter, but she certainly doted on this grandson. Since she had never given Keith much attention, nothing had changed for him, but Helen was another matter. Edith felt the little girl could not understand why her grandmother had so little time for her. Edith didn't feel that Miney even realized how much partiality she was showing.

Dale was such a good little fellow, and he and Keith played well together. Dale liked Fleet, and the dog was very good about letting him pet her. Dale seemed to enjoy being at the farm. Of course, Keith wanted to show him everything now that Dale was old enough to follow Keith around the yard and buildings. Edith thought they made a striking pair, Keith so blond and Dale with his dark hair. They were just two very nice looking little boys. She was glad they got along well since relatives were few on Ralph's side of the family.

Late in the fall, the pump in the house that drew water from the cistern began to pump dirt as well as a small amount of water. (The cistern was a concrete lined excavation to the east of the north porch. It had an opening at the top to allow access which was covered with two inch planks.) When Ralph checked, he noted that the cistern held very little water, but had a deep sludge caused by rotting leaves. When rain from the gutters spilled into the cistern, it also carried any leaves that had fallen in the gutters from the many trees around the house. Periodically, the cistern had to have this sludge cleaned out. Ralph had the suspicion that his father had put off doing this for some time since cleaning the cistern was another job Millie hated doing.

Ralph decided to get the job done while they were having a dry spell. When fall rains came, it would be next to impossible to clean the cistern at that time. Lyle Lipp, a young man from Elsie, had asked Ralph if he needed any help because Lyle was looking for work. Perhaps he could hire Lyle for the day to empty buckets of the sludge into the manure spreader while Ralph worked Inside the cistern filling them. He knew one thing for certain, he'd sure not ask Pa for any assistance.

Pasture became short a little earlier than usual. For a time, Ralph had cut numerous stalks of field corn to supplement what the cattle and horses could pick from the pasture, but that practice had to be given up after a few days. This meant the cows had to be kept in the barn where they could be fed. Of course, now stables had to be cleaned daily and fresh straw was placed under the cows to keep their body off the concrete. This was a time consuming chore, but one that had to be done.

Ralph's work increased when a couple of his heifers freshened. Milking so many took a lot of time, and there were times when Ralph's hands and arms ached from doing the milking. He began to think about buying a milking machine. There was room for a gasoline engine in the silo house. (This was the structure which joined the two silos to the barn. This was a necessary feature because the silage was thrown by the forkful down from the silo to the concrete floor of the silo house. The silos had removable doors about two and a half feet wide by just over three feet high. These doors had metal handles to keep them in place which also served as steps to get up into the silo. As the silage got lower, a door was removed. The silage could easily be transported by a wide fork to the cow's mangers. This fork was called a beet fork whose tines were much closer together than a pitchfork. The close proximity of the tines served well to carry the chopped corn which was called silage.)

Even though the second cutting of hay had been short, Ralph thought they would have a sufficient quantity for the livestock. Having silage to augment the hay for the cows would be a big help.

Ralph had been to the mill to have feed ground. Edith thought he looked a little solemn when he came to the house. She said nothing, just waited to see if he would tell her what was wrong.

"They told me at the mill that the bank building they put up where the Doty Hotel had stood is finished and open for business. I really hated to see the hotel torn down, but I guess with the coming of the automobile, it was no longer a profitable business. Mostly, the hotel had catered to salesmen that came in on the train. Wonder how well the State Savings Bank will do in its new building. That brick building must have cost a lot of money to build."

Edith felt that Ralph sometimes hated progress. It was true the hotel had more than outlived its usefulness, but it had certainly been a landmark for a good many years.

Ralph didn't seem to expect an answer. He was lost in his own thoughts and Edith hesitated to intrude.

Before it came time to till the silos, the silo pit had to be cleaned out. There was always a small remnant of spoiled silage that needed to be removed before the new corn was put in. This was another job that was not very pleasant. The silo pit, made of poured concrete, was about three feet deep, and the walls were the foundation for the wooden silo. The spoiled silage had to be thrown up onto the silo house floor, then thrown out the north door where it could be loaded onto the manure spreader and most likely spread where they intended to put corn next year.

Edith hated having Ralph do this job. Spoiled silage has a distinct smell all its own, and this smell permeated Ralph's clothes. While he changed overalls to be in the house in the evening, he wore the same pair to clean both silos, This usually took two days. Edith always hung his dirty overalls on a support of the windmill so they could air out over night.

Ralph was in a hurry to get the silos filled since there would then be a lull in field work even if he did some fall plowing. He had to cut timber from their rather sparse woodlot since wood was used to fuel both the kitchen and dining room stoves. Since two men were needed to operate the large crosscut saw to fell the trees and to cut the logs into lengths that made them easier to handle Ralph decided to hire Lyle Lipp. Lyle had worked well cleaning the cistern; therefore, Ralph reasoned he probably would be good help cutting wood. Lyle didn't expect much in the way of money. Ralph suspicioned Edith provided him with better meals than he got at home. He had talked it over with Edith, and it was decided Lyle could room there for the week or so they would be cutting wood.

Edith and Ralph were having Sunday dinner with Edith's folks. Lyle would come Sunday night to be there to work for Ralph the next week.

Ralph and Edith had been home long enough for Ralph to get his clothes changed before going to the barn to do chores. Lyle came just as Ralph was on his way to the barn. He told Ralph he'd see to letting the horses out to drink.

Ralph had let the cows back in and had fastened them in their stanchions. They were busy eating their grain allotment when Ralph heard a strange noise outside. He went to the stable door to look into the barnyard to make certain all was well.

All of the horses were back in the barn except Buster. That was odd. Usually, Buster was the first one to drink. Then, he noticed Lyle standing by the stable door, and he seemed to be somewhat unsteady. Ralph went over to him to learn what was wrong.

At first, Lyle didn't seem to understand that Ralph had asked him a question. He said a few words which came out jumbled and didn't make much sense. Lyle finally said he was all right, but Ralph wasn't so sure.

When Ralph finally got the story pieced together, it all made sense. It seems that for some reason, Lyle had jumped on Buster's back, and Buster had promptly thrown him. Lyle had struck his head on the cement foundation of the barn. Although he had not cut his head, nor had he been knocked unconscious, he had been quite dazed, and It was some period of time before he was back to normal.

Ralph figured that of the four horses, Buster had been the worst choice Lyle could have made. Ralph could just imagine how Buster had reacted when someone had the audacity to hop on his back. None of the others would have behaved in this manner. Buster simply had a mind of his own. He had never been ridden and apparently, he didn't intend to let someone he scarcely knew ride him.

CHAPTER 15

L yle seemed to be all right the next morning, so Ralph continued with his plans to get started cutting wood. He had walked through their small woodlot several days ago, and had chosen which trees they would cut. The trees he chose were partially dead, so Ralph figured he should get them cut before they blew down in a windstorm and damaged some of the younger trees. He had learned from Millie how to drop a tree where it did the least amount of damage.

Lyle was better help than Ralph had expected. Rate would notch a tree, then he and Lyle used the heavy crosscut saw to cut through the trunk. This was back– breaking work since Ralph wanted the trunk cut as close to the ground as they could manage. He knew some farmers left a stump that was over two feet high, but Ralph felt this only meant extra work when the stumps were removed. Gradually, farmers were adding land that had previously been tree covered to their cropland. Smaller stumps were easier to remove.

The limbs had to be trimmed from the trunk, and then the trunk was cut into lengths the two men could handle. The largest limbs were cut in a similar manner. These logs would be hauled to the house and cut into lengths suitable for the stoves by the motor driven saw.

Most farmers did not take the time to cut out the smaller branches, they simply burned the tree tops. Ralph felt this was wasteful. The smaller limbs made good kindling and worked well in the smaller firebox of the kitchen stove. He felt the time spent was well worth the effort.

When a log was first placed on the table which could be pushed forward and upward to bring the log in contact with the whirring saw blade run by a belt from the gasoline engine, it took two men to steady the log so it didn't pinch the saw. Most of the blocks were tossed into the north door of the woodshed. This opening was about four feet from the ground and was about four feet square. Some of the blocks were split into small pieces suitable for the kitchen stove. These were stacked in the woodshed near the south door. Ralph was meticulous about keeping the axe sharpened because the hard woods were not easy to split.

The weather turned really cold, but they had had only a slight dusting of snow. Lyle came down with a cold which then settled in his chest. His cough sounded terrible. Edith decided it was time to make him a whiskey sling. (This was a time honored remedy. Hot water and sugar was added to a small amount of whiskey for the person to drink.) Keith had been quite interested in the proceedings, and when, a couple of days later, Lyle was much improved, his mother said it was because of the whiskey sling. She impressed upon Keith that they only kept whiskey in the house for medicinal purposes.

Ralph and Lyle finished bringing the logs from the woodlot to the house where they were piled by the woodshed. Now they could cut the logs into lengths suitable for the stoves as needed. They were indeed lucky because the next day heavy snow began to fall. Winter had started late, but it certainly more than made up for lost time. The deep snow and the cold weather made Ralph's work more difficult, but this was just one of the problems farmers accepted as inevitable.

Keith had developed a slight cold. Although Edith restricted his going outside, thus far, it was nothing to be overly concerned about. Then, he began to cough. Somehow, Edith had the suspicion that the cough was somewhat contrived.

Keith had followed Edith into the kitchen coughing sporadically. "Mama, do you think my cough is bad?"

"Yes, Keith. You don't sound very good. Is your throat sore?"

"No." He shook his head. "My throat doesn't hurt. But, Mama, isn't my cough as bad as Lyle's was?"

"Nearly so, I guess."

"Then I guess you'll have to fix me a little whiskey sling." He looked at his mother with a hopeful expression.

Edith wanted to laugh because she now knew why Keith had suddenly developed such a cough. However, she could see he was completely serious, so she tried to explain to him that a whiskey sling was for adults only. Who would have thought he'd come up with such an idea? She guessed one just never knew how a child's mind worked.

The day was cold and blustery. Ralph had taken grain to the mill to have ground for the cattle. As usual, Edith had patching she was doing it sometimes seemed a never ending job. She was pleasantly surprised when her brother, Carl, came to visit.

"Hello, stranger," she said as she laid aside her sewing. "Seems you are too busy to come see your "favorite" sister any more. How are you?"

She got out of her chair to give him a hug. Carl gave her a kiss on the cheek before answering.

"I'm fine. Busy as usual," said Carl. "You know how it is."

"Yes, I'm sure paying court to some young lady does require a lot of your time." "Whatever do you mean?" asked Carl, his eyes twinkling.

"Don't give me that innocent look. Word gets around, you know. How come you haven't brought her around so we can meet her? Or do we already know her?"

"Gosh, Sis, you're absolutely right. I have been keeping company with someone. However, while I was getting serious, I didn't know for certain how she felt. Well, now I know. She feels as I do, and we are to be married."

"Her name?"

"Didn't I tell you?"

"You know you didn't, you scamp. I suppose you have told everyone else, and I'm the only one being kept in the dark."

Carl laughed, then said, "Her name is Beatrice Fisher. Her father is the Reverend L.A. Fisher. I think you probably know of him."

"Sure. Everyone hereabout knows who Rev. L.A. Fisher is. He's not only good from the pulpit, but he really cares about people. He's willing to help anyone he can even if they are a professed atheist. I don't know him personally."

"Well, you are likely to get to know him if I'm going to be his son-in-law."

"Carl, I'm really glad for you. I think you know that I simply want you to be happy. At least Lee let me know when he and Nellie started keeping company." Her tone was accusatory. "Lee wanted me kept Informed. You always wanted to be like Lee, so why were you so blamed secretive?"

"I'm sorry, Sis. I didn't intend to hurt your feelings."

"Oh sure. Well at least I know where I stand with you. It sure is nice that Lee cares more about my feelings than you do."

"Quit trying to make me feel guilty. It won't work. I don't know whether we'll have much of a wedding. I don't have a lot to offer, but Bea says she doesn't care. We might even live with her folks for a short time so I can get a little ahead. Where are the kids?"

"Keith is taking his nap although he keeps trying to tell me he doesn't need one. Helen is simply resting. She plays with her dolls, and doesn't sleep, but she is much better natured if she gets a little rest."

"You know I love those kids. I just hope Bea and I can be as fortunate."

"I hope so too. You will make a mighty fine father."

Edith thought about Carl long after he left. She wanted the best for him. Goodness, her family was growing. Art now had three and with Gladys' Gordon, and Vern's two boys, she had one niece and five nephews. She was sure Carl would have more than one child if Beatrice liked children as much as he did.

Wait until she told Ralph that Don and Gladys had been right about Carl with a girl friend. She thought Ralph would be happy for Carl too.

Earl Peterson knew Rate had worked with his father in their meat market. He also knew that Claude Conklin from Conklin's Market had often had Ralph help him butcher a cow or hog for some farmer. Therefore, Earl decided he'd ask Ralph to butcher a hog for him. Earl disliked butchering and wasn't very handy doing the job.

When asked, Ralph said he'd be glad to do Earl's butchering and they set a day and time for Rate to do the job.

The day was cold. Earl had the water heated in a large, cast iron kettle. This hot water was transferred to a wooden barrel which leaned at a slant up against a set of sleighs. It was at a convenient angle to let the hog slide into the barrel. After a few minutes, the hog could be pulled back up where they could scrape the hair from the carcass. Only then, would Ralph gut the hog, remove the heart and liver, and begin to separate the hams to be smoked and cut up the rest of the carcass for the women to make sausage, cook the chops to be layered in a crock and sealed with lard, and try lard from the pieces of fat. Often the pig's feet and ears were pickled, and head cheese was made from the rest of the meat on the head after the tongue was removed. There was plenty of work for the women.

Ralph deftly stuck the hog, and they gently lowered the hog into the barrel of hot water. However, the barrel must have been an old one because when the hog touched the bottom, half of the bottom broke away and the hot water gushed out.

Ralph laughed to himself as he saw the look of disbelief on Earl's face. Ralph explained to him that they would simply have to shave the hog which was somewhat of a pain to do, and it would take longer than scraping. Earl looked relieved. He helped Rate get the animal out of the barrel and when shown what to do, helped Ralph shave the hog. In payment, Ralph was given the heart and some loin. Actually, Ralph would have helped a neighbor with no thought of charging him, but he was glad to accept the meat.

As word got around the neighborhood that Ralph was not only good at butchering, but also willing to do the work, more of the neighbors requested his services. If he butchered a beef, the farmer usually gave Ralph the tongue, heart, and a part of the liver. Ralph always felt he was adequately paid. Edith was glad to get the extra meat because it helped on the grocery bill.

Of course, when he butchered one of their own cows, half went to his parents. This still left a lot of meat for Edith to use in short order after the beef had hung for ten days. Farmers said this hanging aged the meat, and except for the heart, tongue, and liver, they felt the meat wasn't good until after the ten days. Ralph usually left part of the hind leg hanging in the granary where no dog could get to it. In January, the weather was cold enough to keep the meat partially frozen. Ralph could cut off a slice of round steak whenever it was needed.

Edith canned much of the beef. Ralph cut the meat from the bones and into one inch by two inch by one inch pieces. Edith packed these pieces in quart jars, always putting a small piece of tallow at the top and a little salt before she put the lids on the jar. The lids were not tightened completely. The jars were placed in a water bath in a large copper boiler where the water was kept simmering. Ralph had made a lattice work from laths to fit the bottom of the boiler to keep the jars from setting directly on the metal. This allowed water to be under the jars as well as around them. When done, the lids were tightened securely, and the jars left to cool until they could be placed on shelves in the stone cellar. The cellar's stone walls were two feet thick and canned goods and produce would keep there without freezing even during the coldest winter months.

Edith cooked the scraps of meat from the bones and made a vegetable beef soup to can. While not difficult to make, the soup was time consuming and took nearly a day to make. Edith was always relieved when the task was finished.

Sometimes, Millie told them to keep the heart and tongue while he and Miney took only a good portion of the liver. Edith found that Ralph liked the way she prepared the heart. She stuffed it with dressing. Ralph was always fond of tongue with American fried potatoes, and while others might think it strange, he liked fried liver with pancakes some of the time. Otherwise, Edith used milk to make gravy after frying liver and Ralph liked the gravy on bread instead of potatoes.

Since January turned out to be exceptionally cold, Ralph was glad he had packed straw around the water pipes in the well pit. Otherwise, he felt certain the pipes would have frozen. As it was, he often had to bring a pail of hot water to the large stock tank by the barn because even with straw around it, the pipe where it curved to the tank sometimes froze. Even the pipe to provide drinking water for the house sometimes froze just enough so it wouldn't let water through. A teakettle of hot water was more than sufficient to remedy the situation. Edith could handle this herself. She was glad she didn't have to bother Ralph because she felt he had plenty to do.

She gave little thought to the fact that the water for the chickens often froze just enough so the chickens couldn't drink. She usually went to the coop twice a day with a little hot water to thaw out their fountain. (The chicken fountain was a round cylinder about eighteen inches in diameter and almost two feet high. It had a small opening which fed an area the size of a teacup with water. As the chickens drank, more water filled the receptacle.)

Ralph sat reading while Edith did the dinner dishes. As was sometimes the case, in winter he had nothing that needed doing until it was time to do the afternoon chores. He sat with his chair turned so he would get as much light from the afternoon sun as possible.

Something on the road caught his attention. He got up from his chair so he could look out the glass in the south dining room door. He gave a chuckle as he called to his wife.

"You're never going to believe this."

"Believe what? What are you talking about?"

"Come see what your nephews have dreamed up now."

Edith came into the dining room wiping her hands on the dish towel. Keith and Helen had already gone to the door to look out. Edith looked up the road, and then spoke, her amazement revealed by the tone of voice.

"Whatever possessed Beurmann to do this?"

Beurmann had hitched two of his dad's Holstein young cattle to a home-made sort of sled much as one would hitch oxen. He was driving the team while Wendell rode on the sled. A strange sight indeed.

"I've always said that Beurmann thinks differently than most kids his age. He asked me once if I had a yoke for oxen. Guess he never found a yoke because he's just made a sort of harness out of scraps of leather. He seems to be in complete control. Wonder how long it took him to break those heifers to drive?"

Beurmann stopped in the drive opposite the north porch. He stayed with his team while Wendell hopped off the sled and came into the house.

"Hello everyone. What do you think of our sled, Uncle Ralph?"

It was easy to see that Wendell was proud of their accomplishment.

"Quite some contraption, that's for certain. Guess driving those heifers is a might more challenging than driving your goat was. Do your folks know you came down here?"

"Dad said it was all right. We've been driving for a number of days now. May we give Helen and Keith a ride? We'd just go around the driveway a few times." He looked at his aunt and uncle with a hopeful expression.

Both Helen and Keith pleaded to be allowed to ride with their cousins. Edith looked at Ralph, hesitating before she voiced her opinion.

"I guess if you have time to wait for them to get their wraps on, it will be all right," said Ralph.

Wendell beamed and said they had plenty of time.

"Rate, do you really think it is wise?" asked Edith, a worried look on her face. "Keith isn't very old, you know, but if Helen goes, he'll want to go too."

"I'll look after Keith, Aunt Edith. They both can sit and I'll watch both of them," offered Wendell.

"This team isn't like a team of horses. They won't run. Besides, Vern wouldn't have let them come down here if he didn't think it was safe."

"I suppose you are right," replied Edith. She realized that her husband was far more adventuresome than she had ever been. However, she felt he would never put the children in danger.

Helen already had her outer clothing to put on, but she was in such a hurry, her fingers were all thumbs. Wendell gave her the assistance she needed while Edith saw to getting Keith dressed for the cold weather. It was a nice day with only a slight breeze, but it was still plenty cold.

Ralph had stepped out on the north porch to talk to Beurmann.

They cautioned Keith and Helen to be quiet so they wouldn't startle the heifers.

When Wendell had both of them sitting on the sled with him slightly behind them, Beurmann spoke to his team and they moved off toward the barn.

When Edith saw how quiet the heifers were, she felt some better.

"Rate, I think I have some film in the camera, so I'm going to see if I can get a picture or two. I'm not sure Keith is old enough to remember this. Helen will, but it would be nice to have a picture."

Ralph agreed. He chuckled to himself because Edith was no longer worried since her thoughts had turned to getting a couple of pictures.

After a severe winter, the warm days of spring were welcome, and it was time to shear sheep again. Ralph liked to have the lambs come in April. Since the farmer was no longer expected to wash the sheep before shearing, this meant the sheep could be sheared just before the lambs were due. Last year he had made up his mind he would find someone other than Harry McQuistion to shear the sheep. After checking around, he learned that Martin Van Deusen would not only shear the sheep, but he would also buy the wool. Ralph thought this was a good deal since it would save him the time required to take the wool into Elsie. If Millie approved, he said nothing, nor did he offer any objections.

With the warm weather came more rain than usual. This put Ralph's field work behind schedule. He chafed at the forced inactivity on the days that it rained. He hated being late to plant since this usually meant a smaller harvest.

In this respect, Millie was very understanding. He knew soil should not be worked if it was too wet, and even though he failed to say anything to his son, he was glad Ralph was in no hurry to plow a wet field.

Because of all the rain and warm weather, the pasture had grown better than usual for this time of year. Ralph was glad he had been able to turn the cows out to pasture sooner than expected. Since he was behind with his field work, he had hired Lyle Lipp to help. However, Lyle had only worked a couple of days when he came to work drunk and Ralph fired him.

Ralph was somewhat discouraged, but then he was pleasantly surprised when Millie told him he'd come each morning to help with the milking thus enabling Ralph to get in the field sooner.

The first morning when Millie arrived, Fleet was just going back down the lane to bring up the cows. Millie assumed Ralph had sent her to do the work. However, the next day, the cows were just coming into the barnyard when Millie and Ralph went to the barn. Millie tried varying the time a few minutes each day, but no matter when he came, Fleet had the cows either in the barnyard or just coming through the gate. Ralph thought the situation was extremely funny. Although his father said nothing, Ralph knew Millie was trying his best to outwit the dog. Never would Millie have admitted that the dog saved them time.

Earl Peterson had been a little slower to turn his cattle out on pasture. About the second day, he came to see Ralph just before noon. He had a worried expression on his face.

Ralph asked, "What's wrong?"

"I've got a cow that's bloated bad. Can't get Dr. Russell (he was the local veterinarian) as he's not in. Am afraid I'm going to lose her. I've never stuck a cow. Have you?"

(When a cow bloated, it was a very serious matter. Without help, she would die. The bloat was usually caused by a cow being left too long on pasture after eating only hay for the winter months. Most farmers began putting them on pasture for a couple of hours at first, then lengthening the time a little each day. Alfalfa was more likely to bother than clover. The remedy was to insert the slender blade of a knife at the proper point so the knife would puncture a section of the stomach. This procedure released the gas, and the cow lived.)

"I've done it before," admitted Ralph. "Do you want me to come try to save her?"

"By golly, that would be just dandy. She's in the barn."

"I'll tell Edith I'm leaving. I've got a knife I can use, so I'll get that and be right down."

Earl looked relieved as he left the yard. Ralph hurried, knowing time was important if the cow was as bad as Earl said. He arrived at Petersons only a few minutes after Earl.

Earl took him to the barn where the cow laid on her side. Ralph noted she was indeed in bad shape, her belly was greatly distended. He felt for the proper spot to insert the knife. Earl was holding her head to keep her from twisting about. There was no way she could have staggered to her feet, so that was not a problem.

"Did you know that the gas that comes out will burn?"

"Naw. You've got to be jokin'. Ain't it just air?"

Ralph stuck the knife through the animal's tough hide and pushed it further. All of a sudden, the gas came hissing out. Ralph struck a match and held it to the flow. To Earl's amazement, it burned. Ralph hadn't thought the pressure would push the gas quite so high. He was glad the cow was where there was no hay or straw hanging from above.

"Don't that beat all? Learned something today. All of us thought it was just plain old air," said Earl, a bemused look on his face.

Ralph felt relief that all was going well. Although he had done this before, he was always a bit apprehensive. He was glad that in short order, the cow was back to normal, and when Earl released her head, she promptly stood. Only a little blood oozed from the puncture and that was quickly drying. She would be all right now.

Earl was thankful all had gone so well. He rather matter of factly told Ralph he appreciated that Ralph had been able to handle the situation. Ralph had no way of knowing how well off the Petersons were financially, but he knew they lived rather frugally. They had four children, three boys and a girl. The second boy was about a year older than Keith, and the last one was nearly two years younger than Keith. No matter how one looked at it, the loss of a cow was a substantial loss monetarily. Ralph was just glad he had been able to help a neighbor.

A few days later, Ralph and Millie took the young cattle and sheep to the forty for the summer. Ralph wondered if his father noticed how well Fleet worked the livestock because the dog knew exactly where they were going. Ralph felt she had certainly been worth buying since she definitely saved him a lot of extra steps.

Ralph began to think more and more of getting a milking machine. When he had mentioned this to Millie, his father had been quick to voice his opinion that only a lazy person wanted a milking machine. This really rankled because Ralph was already milking more cows than his father ever had, and when the heifers freshened this fall, they would have the stanchions full.

Helen had asked Edith if she and Keith could go up the road to visit their Uncle Vern. Edith had said that now was not a good time for them to go visiting. Helen seemed to accept this explanation, and she went back outside where Keith was playing with his pet rabbit.

The rabbit was a doe and she followed Keith around like a puppy. She usually came in the house with him. Edith didn't mind because the rabbit was house broken and would ask to go outside to relieve herself. Edith had known rabbits make good house pets because her brother, Garth, had had a rabbit when he was about the age Keith was now. Garth's rabbit had been particularly fond of crackers, and Edith often thought about how her "baby" brother had looked lying on the floor eating a cracker. He'd take a bite, then he'd hold the cracker so the rabbit could take a bite. At least Keith hadn't wanted to share his food with his rabbit.

Edith knew the children had moved from the north porch to the front of the house, but she paid no further attention as she did the dinner dishes.

Just as she was hanging up the dish pans, the phone rang. This was a little unusual during the day. While many of their friends and neighbors had phones, very few used them simply to chat. For the most part, they were used for business only.

When Edith answered, she learned it was her sister-in-law, Blanche Brewbaker.

"Edith, I just wanted to let you know that Helen and Keith are up here. Now, Vern says you told them not to come, but he could see them in the ditch by the line fence, so, of course, he called out to them and told them to come see him. He says he will bring them home in a little while."

"In other words, they forgot what I had said just because Vern coaxed them to come see him. Guess I'll have to have a little chat with them when they get home. Thanks for letting me know where they are. I hadn't missed them yet."

Edith fumed. Both kids knew they were not to go that far away by themselves. There wasn't much traffic on the road as yet except for a team and wagon, but Edith worried anyhow. She'd give Vern a piece of her mind since she felt he was mostly to blame. She knew Helen liked being with Wendell. In fact, she felt Wendell was Helen's favorite cousin. She and Rita, brother Art's daughter, played nicely together, but Helen seemed to look up to Wendell. Maybe that was because he was two years older and he always treated her well.

When Vern brought the kids home, he left them outside while he came into the house to speak to Edith.

"Now, don't you dare spank those kids. I told them I'd not let their mother spank them if they came to see me. Edith, they weren't in the road, they were in the ditch by the line fence just looking my way. I couldn't ignore them. If I hadn't coaxed them, I don't think they'd have come any farther."

"You know I had told them they couldn't go to your place? They defied me and should be punished," Edith replied stubbornly.

"Oh come on, Edith, they just wanted to visit. No harm's been done. Now, I gave my word, so don't you lay a hand on either of them and make me out a liar."

Vern was usually not this dictatorial. Goodness, he really did look serious. Well, she guessed no harm was done. She'd just tell both Helen and Keith they were not to do this again.

Vern looked relieved when Edith laughed and said, "I guess you are the one that should be punished, but you are too big and too old for me to spank."

"Honest, Edith, I love those kids. I'm glad they like me enough to want to come see me. Beurmann is kind of old for them, but they both like Wendell, and he is always glad to see them. Really, no harm was done."

"I guess you are right. I just don't like having them disobey me. I'll just talk with them, and no, I won't even bawl them out. Are you satisfied?"

"Just don't forget." Vern put an arm around Edith's shoulders, then said, "I know you'll keep your word. They're good kids, Edith, and you know they are not ones to disobey, but this was a different situation."

Edith called both Helen and Keith to her after Vern left. She asked for an explanation. Neither had much to say. They merely stated they had gone for a walk and Uncle Vern had asked them to come see him. Helen said they didn't want to be rude, so they did as he suggested. Edith told them that they were not to do this again. Both kids nodded as though they completely understood and agreed not to go visit Uncle Vern again unless Mama or Daddy was with them. Edith felt the matter was settled.

For the next few days, Edith watched the kids more closely. Even though they had more or less agreed not to go see their Uncle Vern, she felt a little skeptical. Vern had a way with kids, and most kids really liked him; therefore, she thought Helen and Keith might give in to temptation once again. However, they seemed to be content to be in their own yard, so Edith became less vigilant.

A couple of weeks after the first episode, she missed the kids. She called to them, but received no answer. She went to the phone to call Blanche.

When Blanche knew who it was, she said, "I was just going to call you. Helen and Keith are both here, and, of course, Vern is making a big fuss over them. He'll bring them home shortly."

Edith fumed once again. Although she had not really bawled the kids out, she had certainly made it known that going to visit Uncle Vern by themselves was not acceptable behavior. She'd not let Vern sweet talk her out of disciplining them this time.

Vern brought them home as promised with the admonition she was not to lay a hand on them. Vern was as incorrigible as the kids, and, as an adult, she reasoned that he should know better.

After Vern left, Edith had both Helen and Keith standing in front of her. Neither looked one bit contrite which further irritated Edith.

"After all I said to you before, why did you run away?"

Before Helen could say a word, Keith gave his indignant reply. "I didn't run. I walked."

This was too much for Edith. She burst out laughing. Helen and Keith looked puzzled, as though they wondered why their mother was laughing when she had looked so stern just moments before.

"All right. So you walked, but when young children don't mind their mother and leave to go where they know they are not to go, we call that running away. Does Uncle Vern ask you to come see him?"

They both nodded.

Then Helen said, "We don't walk in the road. We walk by the fence like Uncle Vern said we should."

Keith nodded his head in agreement.

The shallow ditch by the side of the road only had water in it early in the spring. There was room enough for the kids to walk between the ditch and the fence line, so they really weren't in any danger. Edith simply did not like the idea of them disobeying her. She guessed she would talk it over with Ralph and get his opinion on how to handle the situation.

When she told Ralph of her concerns, instead of giving her the support she wanted, he merely laughed.

"It's not like Vern lived two or three miles away. Helen says they walk by the fence line, so I don't see that any harm, is done. You know how Vern is with kids. He'll make a fool of himself just so some kid will really like him. However,

I'm sure if he felt there was any danger, he'd not entice the kids up there. You worry too much."

Guess that settled the matter. Ralph was just as bad as Vern. Edith did wonder if Keith and Helen ever went up to the line fence but came back home because they had not seen their uncle. This was certainly a possibility.

Ralph had noticed several times of late that when Fleet was bringing the cows up from the pasture, they would be rather strung out until they neared the bridge. Then, suddenly, they all seemed in a rush and crowded each other to get across the bridge. Once across, they ambled toward the barn at their usual pace with Fleet some distance behind.

Ralph was puzzled by this. Something had to be spooking the cows by the bridge. He had gone to the bridge and looked around, but could see nothing out of the ordinary. When the cows went back down the lane, none of them seemed unduly concerned when they reached the bridge. The crowding only occurred when Fleet was bringing them to be milked.

This had gone on for several days, and Ralph was still puzzled. Then a couple of days in a row, he noticed that two of the cows had been bitten just above the hind foot. Ralph then began to put two and two together. Apparently, the last cow to cross over the bridge got bit by Fleet. No wonder none of them wanted to be last.

If he couldn't catch the dog doing this, how was he supposed to correct the situation? A couple of times, he had gone back down the lane, but as the cows went by him, Fleet was far back, seemingly paying little attention as the cows moved toward the barnyard.

One day when the wind was gusting from the west, Ralph had the idea that if he hid under the edge of the bridge, he could catch Fleet in the act. With the wind blowing his scent away from her, he thought she would not realize he was there.

Ralph never knew how the dog knew he was there. She hung far back as any good cattle dog would, and then after all the cows were headed on toward the barn, she came over to Ralph's hiding place.

As Ralph always maintained "in order to teach a dog anything, you had to know more than the dog." He guessed in this situation, the dog won out. However, whether Fleet tired of the game as she was playing it, or whether she really did understand she was doing something of which her master disapproved, she quit the biting, and once more the cattle were not afraid to cross the bridge.

Edith was always glad to have George, Blanche, and Dale visit. My Dale was getting so tall. He was a quiet little boy, and Edith liked having him around.

Of course, Miney made Edith laugh to herself since Miney was almost paranoid for fear Dale would get hurt. Miney had never been that concerned about Keith or even Helen. Even when all three of her grandchildren were around, most of her attention was directed toward Dale.

Helen still received Miney's attention when Dale was not visiting, but Miney still failed to have much of an interest in Keith. There were times when Edith really resented the partiality shown. Because of this, when Miney was there to shower Helen with affection, Edith gave Keith more attention than she normally would. While Miney spoiled Helen, Edith still expected proper behavior from Keith. Edith didn't even realize she was showing partiality to offset Miney's preference for Helen.

In midsummer, when Blanche, George, and Dale were there for a visit, Rate managed to have some time alone with his sister. Somehow, they seemed always to enjoy talking to each other without others present.

Ralph explained to Blanche that he would be milking seventeen cows later in the fall. She was truly impressed.

"Blanche, I want to buy a milking machine, but Pa says only a lazy person would want a milking machine. Do you know why Pa thinks I'm lazy?"

"I have no idea. You are raising more cattle than Pa did. Mostly, I think Pa just hates anything new. Progress is not something that appeals to Pa."

"I'll admit I don't understand him. How often have you heard him complain because he never could please his father? It's the same with me. Pa is never satisfied. Yet Ed Clark told me that Pa was telling him that I was a better cattle man than he had ever been, and Dave Watson told me the same thing. If Pa thinks I'm doing such a good job, why can't he tell me?"

"Ralph, I've read where people behave as they were treated when they were growing up. Although Pa resented the fact that he could never please Grandfather, he is treating you as he was treated. It doesn't make much sense, if you ask me."

"Do you think I'm lazy because I want a milking machine?"

"Heavens, no. Ralph, you just get anything you can to make your work easier. Pa can just learn to like it or lump it. I doubt if he'll be too upset as long as he continues to get good milk checks."

Well, that settled the matter. With his sister on his side, Rate felt he could do as he pleased. Of course, he'd have to come up with the money on his own for a milking machine, but he'd start pricing them so that by the time the stanchions were full, he'd have the milking machine he wanted installed. Sure would make the chore of milking a lot easier.

The family knew Edna had started keeping company with Clayton Carroll. He had bought the Dave Watson farm where Rate and Edith had begun their married life. Clayton had been to a couple of family gatherings with Edna, but there was something about him that made Edith uneasy to be in his presence. Still, she readily agreed that he treated everyone with respect and seemed very thoughtful of Edna.

Edith discovered that Gladys felt the same about Clayt as she did. Gladys told Edith that Don had been helping a neighbor with something and Clayt had been there too. He worked well, but Don said that at times his words didn't make much sense. Both Edith and Gladys worried about their younger sister. They both felt that since Carl had been married in July, Edna felt she had to rush into marriage. After all, she certainly didn't want to be an old maid, and she was almost twenty-five.

One night, Edith spoke to Ralph about something to which she had been giving a lot of thought. Both Helen and Keith were asleep, so there would be no little ears listening to the conversation.

"Rate, you once promised me that you'd quit smoking before Keith was old enough to remember he had ever seen his father smoke. Don't you think that time has come?"

Ralph looked up from his reading, but was slow to answer his wife's question.

"Guess I don't really remember making that promise." He looked straight at his wife with that wide-eyed innocent look that always made her suspicious.

"Oh, you know you did. Right after Keith was born." Edith was a little exasperated with his answer.

"If you say so. You think he is old enough to remember what goes on when he's only three and a half? How much do you remember of what happened when you were that age?"

"Probably not much. But in another few months, he will be likely to remember."

"You might be right."

Rate returned to his reading and Edith knew the conversation was over. She felt as though she had definitely lost the battle. (Edith was to state many times that Ralph's promise to quit smoking was the only promise he ever broke throughout their marriage.)

Ralph had been to Elsie, and as usual he had stopped by the pool parlor. He usually did this if he had the time to spare. He liked seeing some of the old timers, and he found talking with them was often extremely interesting.

'When he came home, he sought out Edith.

"Thought you might be interested in what I heard at the pool hall today. I didn't know the man who was doing most of the talking, but I've seen him around. Some of the others seemed to know him quite well. Anyway, I wasn't really paying any attention to what he was saying until I heard the name Clayton Carroll. I had missed most of his conversation, so I asked Cash Waldron what had been said. It seems that Clayt had been keeping steady company with Win Moore's oldest daughter. Everyone expected them to marry. Then, all of a sudden, they broke up. Now, it is being said that Win's daughter is dying of syphilis. Of course, the Moores say she got the disease from Clayt, but his mother maintains there is nothing wrong with her son, and she surely hopes he doesn't get the disease from that horrible woman.

"All of this just set me to thinking. Do you suppose Clayt has syphilis and that is why he behaves like he does? We all know that many people who have syphilis end up in an insane asylum."

"Oh, Rate, what is Edna getting herself into? Do you suppose Ma and Pa know of Clayt's background? Or does Edna?"

"I have no way of knowing. You can do as you see fit, but I think you should speak to your parents and perhaps say something to Edna. You know we don't see Edna very often any more. Maybe this is why."

"You might be right. I just thought she avoided us because she didn't want to put up with your teasing her that she had finally found a beau. And you know you'd have teased," Edith accused.

"True. But Edna has coped with my teasing before and good-naturedly too. We've always gotten along."

"I've never felt at ease around Clayt, but I never had any real reason for feeling that way. I think I'll try to find a time when I can speak to Ma when Edna isn't around. I don't want Ma to worry, but they should know what others are saying about Clayt ."

"Maybe the man knew what he was talking about and maybe he didn't. Still, it doesn't seem as though anyone would make up a story like that. Will you talk to Edna?"

"Not until after I've spoken with Ma and Pa. Edna can be awfully stubborn, so I don't know if she'd even discuss the matter with me."

Vern had planted a sizable plot of sweet corn south of the house. It was about noon when a desperate Vern called Ralph. It seems his cattle had got out and they were having a good time eating his sweet corn. He had not been able to get the cows out, so he was calling to ask Ralph for his help. Since Ralph had just come in for dinner, he told Vern he'd be right up, and he'd bring Fleet with him.

When he saw what the situation was, Rate told Vern, "I'll have Fleet bring them through here, so you be sure and have the gate to the barnyard open. Those cows will be in a rush because Fleet will bite any stragglers. She doesn't bite often, but when she does, she draws blood. Your cows aren't used to a dog so they will be scared."

"Right now, I don't care if she half skins them. I just want them out of my corn. It was coming along so nice, and I was sure I could sell what we didn't need to the stores in town."

"Well, let's not waste time."

Rate moved off with Fleet so the dog would understand what she was to do. Vern headed for the barn.

In a matter of moments, Fleet had the terrified cattle headed for the barnyard gate. Vern had just reached the gate when the cows literally came crashing through.

"Look at my gate. Just look at this mess," cried Vern.

"I warned you to get the gate open in a hurry. I can't help it if you didn't move fast enough," said Ralph.

He was tempted to laugh, but with a word to Fleet to keep the cows in the barnyard, he helped Vern do enough repair work to last until a new gate could be built.

When Ralph related the incident to Edith, he laughed. He told her the look on Vern's face was priceless.

"He probably didn't realize you meant exactly what you said. After all, you and Vern are quick to tease."

"Well, he knows now," said Ralph with a chuckle.

Edith just shook her head. She felt sorry for her brother. It just seemed that bad luck sort of followed him around.

Edna came to visit because she wanted Edith to know that she had set a date for her marriage to Clayton Carroll. It was to be the 18th of December. Edith said nothing of her misgivings, and wished her sister well. She really didn't want to dampen Edna's spirits.

Not long after this, Edith, Helen, and Keith went to spend some time with her parents. Edith hoped Edna wouldn't be home because she wanted to tell her parents about Clayt's background just in case they had heard nothing.

As luck would have it, Edna was home. However, she asked if she could take Helen and Keith to visit Rita, Arlington, and Lionel. Art and his family lived in the tenant house which was only a short distance east of the main house. Edith could hardly believe her good fortune. Since this would get Edna out of the way for a time, she, naturally, gave her approval.

Besides, Helen always liked to play with Rita, and she truly liked her Uncle Art. Part of this was because Art had made Rita a small table, and because Helen had liked the table so much, he had made one for her. Art was exceptionally skillful working with wood. He was now making Rita a doll's chest of drawers, and Edith thought he would probably make one for Helen. (He did, and that small chest was greatly treasured.)

Edith explained to her mother what Ralph had heard. Before she finished, her father came into the house, so he was told what they had learned. While her mother didn't say much, her father said he knew something was wrong with Clayt, that he wasn't normal some of the time. Besides, others had expressed their feeling to Wilson that Clayt was not always in his right mind. Wilson said he would speak with Dr. Hart to get his opinion, then he would speak with Edna.

As it turned out, almost everyone, including Dr. Hart, thought there was something wrong with Clayt. Wilson and Dr. Hart both asked Edna to wait just one year before she married. Edna informed them she had set the date, and there was no way she was going to postpone her marriage. She accused them of not liking Clayt because he was a little different than the average person. However, she could see nothing wrong with him being different. She reminded them she was old enough to do as she pleased.

No one in the entire family felt optimistic about Edna's coming marriage. Edith tried to tell her that a year was not an unreasonable time to wait, but that only served to make Edna angry. She actually felt that her family had abandoned her.

With the fall, came the last of Ralph's cows to freshen. He now had all seventeen stanchions filled. Millie was in Detroit to visit Blanche when Ralph had the milking machine installed. The gasoline engine to power the machine fit quite nicely in the southwest corner of the silo house as did the large compressor.

It took some of the cows a period of time to get used to the machine. At first, they tried their best not to let their milk down. A few of the older cows tried to kick the teat cups off their udder. Ralph had to put the hobbles on them so they could not kick. Ralph never left the cups on too long and he always stripped each cow by hand. (This meant getting the last bits of milk by hand instead of with the machine.) At least his arms and hands no longer hurt when he did the milking. Of course, Edith had more work because she was the one who washed the milking machine bucket. Ralph kept the teat cups rinsed with clear water after each milking, so Edith only had to wash them once a week. There were special brushes to facilitate the cleaning.

Ralph was in the barn finishing the milking when his father came into the barn. Millie had come in from the large barn doors by the barn floor, down the passageway to the stable. This brought him to the back of the cattle in the south row of stanchions.

Ralph was just removing the teat cups from a cow when he noticed his father standing there with a completely disgruntled look on his face.

"You've gone and done it," said Millie. "Dollars to doughnuts their milk production will fall off. You know we always work quietly around the cows, and now they've got to contend with the infernal noise of that machine."

"Pa, the cows are doing fine. In fact, since we now have more of the stock I've been breeding, we have cows that are producing more than any you ever had."

Millie ignored that explanation, then said, "It just isn't natural to have that thing hanging on their bag. It just isn't natural."

"Well, for that matter milking by hand isn't natural either. Think our hand feels like a calf's mouth?"

Ralph was losing his patience. Once more his father showed that he was against anything that would make his son's work easier.

Ralph sat down on the stool to strip the cow from whom he had just removed the milker. He ignored his father's presence.

Millie watched him a moment, then turned to leave the way he had come. Ralph heard him mutter, "It's just a lazy man's toy."

Ralph would have been delighted to tell his father that Blanche thought the milking machine was a terrific idea. However, he didn't want to put his sister in the middle of any disagreement with their father.

For the rest of his life, Millie avoided coming to the stable when he knew it was near milking time. Never did he acknowledge the milking machine had been a prudent purchase.

EPILOGUE

Since Edna Brewbaker refused to listen to the advice of her parents and Dr. Hart, she married Clayton Carroll December rs, 1922.

Their first child, a son named Gerald, was born December 22, 1923.

Clayt's mind continued to deteriorate, and it was generally accepted that he suffered from syphilis.

Alice Brewbaker died April 26, 1924. Not long after this, Clayton was no longer able to do his farming, so Edna, Clayt, and Gerald moved in with Wilson. Edna was pregnant again.

Wilson told Edith that there were times when he could not stay at the table to eat because Clayt no longer used silverware, and often dipped into a serving dish with his fingers. Dr. Hart had told Edna that she was to scald any dishes etc. that Clayt used. At that time, doctors were not certain how syphilis was spread.

Wilson was afraid Clayt would become violent, so he tried to talk Edna into having him committed to an Insane asylum. Edna was too stubborn to agree with her father.

Sons, daughters, and grandchildren were at Wilson's, and the children were amusing themselves by sliding down the bannister of the open stairway. Apparently, their noise aggravated Clayt. When Keith slid down the bannister, Clayt grabbed him and was going to throw him out the front door. Of course, the men present stopped him and rescued Keith from his grasp.

This was the last straw for Wilson. The very next day they made arrangements for Clayt to be admitted to the insane asylum at Traverse City. Since Clayt was particularly fond of Art, he was willing to take a train ride with Art. At the asylum, as instructed, Art made an excuse to Clayt to leave him in the room where they had been taken, and Art simply never went back. Art always maintained that Clayt would have remembered nothing about how he got to the institution.

Edna went to see Clayt once. He scarcely knew her, and he remembered absolutely nothing about Gerald or that she was expecting another child. She never went back. Clayt died at the institution.

On February 27, 1929, Edna married Louis Hehrer.

On October 23, 1928, Mrs. Bashore, the neighbor just north of Petersons on the northwest corner of the road, asked for help. It seemed that her husband, Howard (better known as Hod), had gone to the back of the farm to bring up the cows, but had not returned.

Ralph and some other neighbors went in search of the missing man. They found him near a fence where the Bashore property joined the farm owned by John Olhansk. He had been badly beaten, but he was still alive.

Ralph hated what he saw. He thought not only had the man been struck several blows to the head, but his face had been stepped on by someone who wore hobnailed boots. Ralph also thought Hod looked as though someone had tried to gouge his eyes out judging by the marks there. (These two facts were not related in the Clinton County Republican News.)

The men got Hod back to the house and a doctor was called. However, Hod had been too badly beaten to survive. He died October 24, 1928, which was Edith's birthday. He left a wife, who was deaf and dumb, and two daughters.

The sheriff was called and Olhansk was arrested. There was plenty of evidence that was truly damaging.

Ralph was served a subpoena to appear in court at the trial on December 3, 1928 since he had been a member of the party that found Hod.

Olhansk never really gave a reason for the killing. Most of the neighbors felt he had murdered Hod because he was afraid Hod had discovered he was operating an illegal still in his barn and was making moonshine. He feared Hod would go to the authorities.

Olhansk was found guilty and sentenced to life imprisonment.

When Consumers Power Company began to make electricity available for the rural community, Edith and Ralph were pleased. However, they had not reckoned with Millie's adversity to change. Consumers would not set their poles along the roadside, but placed them in the farmers' fields. Millie refused to have those poles cluttering up his fields where they would have to be worked around. It mattered not that he would not have to be the one to work around them.

Even though the neighbors beseeched Millie to change his mind, his stubbornness prevailed. Therefore, the farms to the south got electricity, but the farms to the north had to do without all because of Millie.

In a couple of years, another electric company came through for the neighbors to the north. Thus, the only one without electricity was the Setterington farm.

Millie died January 9, 1942, but this was during WWII; therefore, the amount of wiring allowed for private use was very limited. Ralph was unable to have as many outlets in the house or lights in the buildings as he would have liked. We finally had electric lights in 1944. Still, even the limited amount of lighting was far better than the kerosene or gas lamps or lanterns. (Also, there were no more lamp chimneys for Edith to wash each morning.)

Uncle George took me ice skating and hunting numerous times. He bought a .410 shotgun for Dale, and he let me use it when we hunted pheasants. The gun was a nice size and I could handle it even though I was only twelve. He taught me to bowl and play golf. He also taught me to read a micrometer. We often played catch. He liked it because I threw like a boy--a result of Keith's teaching.

Both Aunt Blanche and Uncle George took many places when I would spend a week or two with them in the summer. As a result, I was much better prepared to live in Lansing than I would have been otherwise. When they went on vacations, they sent me cards and always brought me a souvenir.

When I was saving money to buy a bicycle, Helen was teaching school at Westphalia, and she gave me a dollar for eight of the nine months she taught. The rest of the money for my $22.00 bike came from Uncle George and selling a dozen eggs each week. (Grandpa Brewbaker had given me guinea eggs to hatch, but one turned out to be a Plymouth Rock chick. She laid brown eggs, one each day, and Mother would give me enough white eggs to make a dozen. A dozen eggs brought anywhere from 12 cents to 20 cents a dozen.) Grandma sometimes gave me a dime for doing some work for her. However, each time Aunt Blanche and Uncle George visited, some time before he left, Uncle George would press money into my hand. No one else could see what he did, and I never knew until after they left how much I had. It was usually anywhere from 50 cents to a dollar.

Uncle George knew how much I liked ring bologna. I preferred the meat to candy, so he often brought a ring for me when they came to visit. He got it at a particular meat market, and it was better than average. This had to stop during rationing in World War II.

When it was time for my Junior-Senior prom, Aunt Blanche sent me money to buy a formal. Then, before I graduated, she told me that she would loan me the money for me to continue my education. She had done this for

Helen and Keith. Helen and her husband had already convinced me that I lacked the intestinal fortitude to become a nurse; therefore, I decided to be like Aunt Blanche and go to business school. I went to Lansing Business University and borrowed $375 from Aunt Blanche for the nine months I studied there. (My room at the YWCA residence cost me $2.75 a week, and I sometimes worked at the reception desk at the Y for 50 cents an hour.) When I procured a job at the office of Oldsmobile, (My pay was $28.00 a week.) I made regular payments to Aunt Blanche. She would not take any interest.

Aunt Blanche was always concerned about my health. She explained to me why I should see a dentist regularly. After she became a diabetic, she warned me to have regular checkups. She said I was built so much like her, she wondered if I might become a diabetic. I have been a diabetic for about five years, but medication is controlling it.

Ralph had assumed that when his father died, his mother inherited everything; therefore, he continued to pay her 50% of the profit. The only difference was that now he could purchase commercial fertilizer as he had been doing for many years, but Miney paid half the cost. Millie had never acknowledged that commercial fertilizer had helped them raise better crops, and he had steadfastly refused to pay what should have been his share. Of course, he was well pleased with the increased yields. Miney did not interfere with the way Ralph farmed feeling he was much more knowledgeable than she. Miney was simply glad when each month Ralph brought her share of the milk check and whatever else had been sold.

I went to Lansing to business school in the fall of 1943. Dad had been asked to come into the bank to see Walter S. Lusk, known to everyone as Pat. Pat explained to him that his father had left a will. In the will, Millie had left everything to Blanche. Millie had disinherited Ralph the same way Horatio had disinherited him. Pat told Ralph that Millie had had him make out the will a short time before he died. He said he had asked Millie three times if this was what he truly wanted to do, and each time Millie had said yes.

Ralph was hurt and angry. He wanted nothing more than to rent some other farm. Edith had no luck talking to him. She suggested they could buy the farm from Blanche. Ralph rejected that idea immediately. All he could think about was that his father had not wanted him to have this land. He thought of the virgin fields, and that he had been the first person to put some of this land into cultivation. No. His father had made it impossible for him to remain on the Setterington farm.

When I came home for the weekend, Mother was terribly distraut. She did not want to leave the place where she had spent so many years. I don't know if she wrote of this to Keith since he was in the Army. Helen, of course, was married, but she had never been one to share much of anything with Mom so I doubt if any of this was mentioned to her.

I was pretty upset too. After all, this was the only home I had ever had. I knew Dad would not listen to anything I had to say. I'm quite certain he would not even have discussed the matter with me. Right at that time, I truly resented my grandfather.

Once again, it was Blanche who talked to him and made him listen to reason.

She told him that she had deeded the 80 acres where he lived to him. She had kept the house in town and the forty. At first Ralph was determined not to accept what he termed her "charity." By the time Blanche was through talking to him, he agreed to her terms. Somehow, Blanche had more influence with Ralph than anyone else.

In later years, he wanted all of us to know just how honest and fair his sister had been. He made us realize that his sister had no control over their father's actions, but she had wanted to do what she felt was right. Ralph thought Miney probably never knew that she didn't own the farm. He was certain Blanche had never told her; therefore, he still behaved as though Miney owned the farm as long as she was in her home in Elsie and her mental state was such that she understood why he was giving her money.

Aunt Blanche was extremely generous when the time came to dispose of Miney's possessions. She remembered that Grandpa had always told me the marble top table would someday be mine. It seems that as a child I used to stand by the table and rub my fingers along the cold marble. I guess that truly impressed Grandpa.

After both Mom and Uncle George had died, Aunt Blanche told me that she wished she and Dad could live together. She said she knew it was impossible because she did not want to leave Royal Oak, and she knew Dad would not be content anywhere but on the farm.

APPENDIX

Listed below are comments which accompanied shower gifts and Edith's and Ralph's wedding gifts. I have copied them exactly as written, with even the misspelled words. The women who read this will undoubtedly find these contributions more humorous than the men. Some of these comments were not signed, so I have just listed them as Anon.

> When Ralph gets nervous and sweaty,
> Give him a bath and dose him with fetty.
>
> Mattie Burk

> Cousin Edith and cousin Ralph it inen't now you see
> but it soon will be.
> If you except this gift you see
> You'l half to name your first boy after me.
>
> Lawrence Burk (age 13)

> This ironing board you will surely find
> Will keep you good natured and ease your mind
> It will last you a life time and longer no doubt
> And will always stand ready to help you out.
>
> Anon.

When Ralph gets cross as cross can be
Just make him a nice little cup of tea
And maybe it would be good for you
If you would drink a cup or two.

Anon.

In this vase you may put your Flowers
Flowers that bloom in April Showers
May your lives be bright and gay
Like the flowers that bloom in May.

Anon.

Nothing looney
Just a spooney

Anon.

This dish is large enough for two
But when it comes to Paul, Mary, John, and Soo
Tell Ralph to hunt the dough For this will no longer do.

Ethel Randolph

Wash and wipe together
Live in peace for ever.

Helen Smith

Put this scarf upon your dresser
In your bedroom neat and nice
Where you can use it every day
Now please take my advice.

Best Wishes from Bessie E. Cahocn

I present to you a pan
So do the best you can
And cook to please your man.

Mrs. Gregory

Use these irons every week On
your washing coarse & fine Put
on plenty of elbow grease
And my! how the clothes will shine.

Anon.

When folks get married, its always the style,
To have something to eat, about twice in a while,
So I brought this cooker to Ralph and you,
And I hope it will hold enough for you two.

With best wishes Mabel Gower

These scales are always in the weigh
But never in the way
Sixteen ounces to the pound
Is the way they always weigh
And when that happy day arrives
With a baby here to weigh
Just put him on these little scales
And they will weigh him any way.

Coverdale

"At last" the time has come
For you "Miss Edith"
to change your name.
So brace up "Dear"
and don't forget, You
have a friend in Greenbush yet.

Lottie

When Ralph gets kinda cranky
And nothing else will do
Just spread your dining table
with a dainty lunch for two.
Then pass him up some biscuit
With a plate of cold boiled ham
With this pretty fork to serve it
He will smile to beat the band.

With Best wishes, From Lottie

I promised I would send you, This little
        granite bowl
And I hope it will last a life time, Untill
        you both get old.
If it proves to be as useful, As I have found
        such things to be
Just keep it In a handy place, And sometimes
        think of me.

Best Wishes From Alice Gower

Well Edith I have set here for and hour thinking about
that Granet shower. let see there was granet kittles basions
and pans and a granet pot. I understand its a granet
wash dish to wash your hands. I all most for got after handling
that granet pot so here is your wash dish so wash your hands
often wash your kittles pot and pans.

Carrie Burk

This little dish in friendship take
And keep it for the gineas sake
Tis from one whose love for you
Will ever prove sincere and true.

Mr. & Mrs. Milton Burk

If you are bound to have a man,
Of course you'll need a frying pan,
To fry your eggs and cook your meat
And every thing else for Ralph to eat.
And if he says you cannot bake
Good things "like Mother used to make"
Just bang him over the head with this
Then he'll take it all back,
And give you a kiss.

Best Wishes From Alice Gower

Use this dish when baking
To stir your pumpkin pies
When Ralph begins to criticize
Just bang him one between the eyes.

Carrie Burk

I send this basin with my best wishes
Twill do for one of Ralphs bread and milk dishes.

Mrs. Edith Smith

When you are in a hurry
Use this dish to make your apple sauce
When Ralph gets in a flurry
Tell him that your his boss.

Mrs. Kirby

You'll soon have a man,
So we bring you a pan.
In it, cook all the good things you can.
If you will always do this
You will ever live in bliss
And Ralph will be ready with a kiss.

With best wishes Bertha and Estella

This little dish cost but a dime
And in your kitchen it will shine
You can cook potatoes and stew your sauce
But remember Ralph will be your boss.

Anon.

Ring the bells in every steeple,
Call together all the people.
Holy Moses, shout for joy,
Edith's found a full grown boy.

Days of old will be forgotten,
Unexpected things will happen,
After years of wedded bliss,
Prehaps "their boys" will read of this.

If these words don't all come true,
I'll buy peanuts for us two,
For I'll bet most half a nation,
There'll be more Setteringtons the next generation.

Nira Silvernail

Mr. and Mrs. Ralph Setterington March 11, 1915
The bells have rung; the wedding march been played.
She's now a matron--never more a maid.
'Tis gone--the hour, the magic hour is past
You stand together man and wife at last
Your feet within the portal of the door,
Of the new life, dreamed of by both before;
And stretched far before your joyous eye
The years to come look bright as sunlight skies.
May life remain for you as fair and sweet
The pathway just as pleasant to your feet,
As full of love, and joy and peace we pray
And just as rosy as it looks today.
And should there ever come, for either one,
The slightest cloud to shadow o'er the sun,
May love give grace to each to understand,
And to the other reach a helping hand.

Is the wish of your friends Mr. and Mrs. Earl Post

This is Ralph's graduation picture.
Ralph is in the middle row, second from the right.

Millie and Ralph getting a wagon ready to go
pick up rocks from the fields.

George and Blanche Ryan

Blanche and Ralph

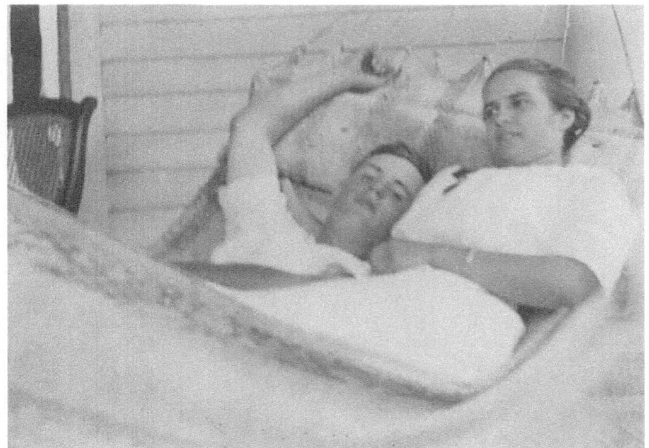

Ralph and Edith